35⁰⁰

INDUSTRIAL INFORMATION SYSTEMS

 **PUBLICATIONS IN
THE INFORMATION SCIENCES**

Rita G. Lerner, Consulting Editor

TWO CENTURIES OF FEDERAL INFORMATION/*Burton W. Adkinson*
INDUSTRIAL INFORMATION SYSTEMS: A Manual for Higher Managements
    and Their Information Officer/Librarian Associates/*Eugene B. Jackson and
    Ruth L. Jackson*
LIBRARY CONSERVATION: Preservation in Perspective/*John P. Baker and
    Marguerite C. Soroka*

INDUSTRIAL INFORMATION SYSTEMS

A Manual for Higher Managements and Their
Information Officer/Librarian Associates

Eugene B. Jackson
University of Texas at Austin

and

Ruth L. Jackson

with a Chapter by
Robert A. Kennedy

Dowden, Hutchinson & Ross, Inc.
Stroudsburg   Pennsylvania

Copyright © 1978 by Dowden, Hutchinson & Ross, Inc.
Library of Congress Catalog Card Number: 78-15890.
ISBN: 0-87933-328-6

All rights reserved. No part of this book may be reproduced or transmitted in any form or by any means—graphic, electronic, or mechanical, including photocopying, recording, taping, or information storage and retrieval systems—without written permission of the publisher.

80 79 78   1   2   3   4   5
Manufactured in the United States of America.

Library of Congress Cataloging in Publication Data

Jackson, Eugene Bernard, 1915–
   Industrial information systems.
   Bibliography: p
   Includes index.
   1. Industrial management—Information services.
I. Jackson, Ruth L., joint author. II. Kennedy, Robert A., joint author. III. Title.
HD30.35.J3   027.6'9   78-15890
ISBN 0-87933-328-6

Distributed world wide by Academic Press,
a subsidiary of Harcourt Brace Jovanovich,
Publishers.

Dedicated to the Memory of Our Parents

> A painful work it is I'll assure you, and more than difficult, wherein what toyle hath been taken, as no man thinketh, so no man believeth, but he that hath made the trial.
>
> Anthony A. Wood
> (as quoted by Karl Pearson, FRS, in *The Incomplete* Γ *Function,* 1922)

Preface

All organizations accumulate information. Some organizations underutilize it for meeting major corporation objectives and a few organizations use information to maximize profit return.

It is our purpose to provide guidance to industrial higher management and to their information officers/librarians. We wish the former to be able to identify those elements of an information service they already have on hand, what reorganization and enhancement is required and what expense in materials, facilities, and (most important of all) information service leadership is needed to achieve an optimum degree of information utilization. For the latter we wish to provide policies and procedures that are heavily based on our experience on the corporate staffs of two major industrial corporations that operate internationally.

Our justification for the bi-level approach is that higher managers typically know very little about the issues in providing a professional information service (perhaps basing their impressions on the public library of their youth, for example) and information officers/librarians are going to have to develop higher management skills in the future as they are using a scarce commodity—that is, company resources—while providing a professional service function. We are convinced that the more each "side" knows about the other's perceptions, plans and procedures, the better off both are.

Then there are the students of information science, librarianship, and management who aspire to careers in the industrial sphere. We would hope that this book could serve as a graduate text in courses in information systems/services, in industrial special librarianship, and as collateral reading in seminars on management of industrial enterprises.

We are accustomed to the industrial practice of hearing suggestions or questions of clarification as the presentation proceeds. Since that facility is not currently available to us as authors, we fall back on the device of soliciting comments, suggestions, and/or criticisms by mail to P. O. Box 7576, Austin, Texas, 78712.

Eugene B. Jackson
Ruth L. Jackson

Acknowledgments

The authors recall stimulating years at the General Motors Technical Center, Warren, Michigan, and especially appreciate the helpful discussions with John Campbell and Arthur Underwood, then of the GM Research Laboratories, and with B. J. Kelly, then of the GM Engineering Staff. Their colleagues from other staffs and divisions around the United States and Canada on the GM Committee on Technical Literature formed an excellent forum and reaction panel to ideas. Also the junior author recalls a broadening association with the late Florence Armstrong of the Ford Motor Company Central Office, Dearborn, Michigan.

The International Business Machines Corporation's headquarters at Armonk, New York, provided the locale for the IBM Engineering, Programming and Technology Staff and unparalleled communication links with other corporation facilities throughout the Free World. Both Jerrier A. Haddad and Homer Sarasohn were enlightening orientators and advisors for the senior author. The opportunities provided to visit frequently the domestic and Canadian libraries and information centers and to meet annually with the European members of the IBM library community added immeasurably to the potential of the position held as Director of Information Retrieval and Library Services.

We are indeed grateful to Robert A. Kennedy, a long time friend in the profession, for his perceptive summary look as a participant in the exemplary "Bell Laboratories Library Network" that forms Chapter 11 of this volume. We note that Dean C. G. Sparks provided certain administrative support in the preparation of this volume.

Finally, nearly a decade of association with fellow directors of Engineering Index, Inc., New York, was bound to have influenced our perception of users needs and their fulfillment. This is what information center service is all about.

Contents

Preface vii
Acknowledgments ix

Chapter 1 An Overview: The Information Explosion and Its Implications for Management   *E. B. Jackson* 1
Chapter 2 Industrial Information Systems and How to Get There 13
   What Are They? 13
   What Already Exists? 13
   What Are the Predecessor Organizational Elements? 17
   Reference 21
Chapter 3 IIS Functions: Acquisition and Processing of Information 23
   The Acquisition Functions 23
   The Processing Functions 30
   Notes and References 42
Chapter 4 IIS Functions: Generation/Production and Dissemination/Utilization of Information 43
   The Generation and Production Functions 43
   The Dissemination and Utilization Functions 50
   Reference 61
Chapter 5 IIS Administrative Functions 63
   Acquisitions 63
   Processing 64
   Generation and Production 66
   Dissemination and Utilization 67
   Special Programs 68
   Functioning within Company Goals 68
   Reference 69
Chapter 6 IIS Administrative Issues 71
   Should the Mode of Operations Be Active or Passive? 71
   Should the IIS Be Centralized or Decentralized? 72
   Should the IIS Director/Manager Be a Librarian, Information Scientist, or Subject Expert? 92
   Notes and References 103
Chapter 7 IIS Personnel and Consultants 105
   Personnel: A Closer Look 105

xii   Industrial Information Systems

Consultants: Their Care and Use	110
Notes and References	116
Chapter 8 IIS Users	119
A Closer Look at the Users	119
Who Are the Users	119
How to Study the Users	122
What User Studies Show	126
Notes and References	128
Chapter 9 IIS Budgeting: A Closer Look	129
Current Expenditures	129
Anticipated Savings	130
Expenditures Required for Additional IIS Activities	130
Determination of the Budget	130
Budgeting Systems	135
Notes and References	138
Chapter 10 Word Processing, Correspondence Control, and Records Management	141
Word Processing	141
Correspondence Control	145
Records Management	155
Notes and References	162
Chapter 11 Bell Laboratories Library Network *Robert A. Kennedy*	165
Introduction	165
The Library Network and Its Services	166
Use of Machines	168
Management of Information Programs	173
Conclusion	175
Notes and References	175
Chapter 12 Scope of IIS Operations	177
IIS Extent in *Fortune* 500 Corporations and the Implications	177
IIS International Operations	188
Predictable IIS Variations	195
Notes and References	198
Chapter 13 Considerations in Mechanizing the IIS Functions	199
Nine "Commandments" for Mechanization	199
Notes and References	208
Chapter 14 The True Worth of the IIS	209
Notes and References	211
Appendix A The General Motors Research Laboratories Library: A Case Study *Eugene B. Jackson*	219

Appendix B	Summary Data on the Industrial Library Systems of the *Fortune* 500 Corporations	229
Appendix C	Alphabetic Listing of *Fortune* 500 Corporations, with Category Number and Industrial Classification	283
Bibliography		297
Index		305
Microfiche	Summary Data on the Industrial Library Systems of the *Fortune* 500 Corporations	inside back cover

INDUSTRIAL INFORMATION SYSTEMS

Chapter 1

An Overview: The Information Explosion and Its Implication for Management

E. B. Jackson

The phrase "information explosion" is both catchy and largely accurate. Webster defines an *explosion* as "a large-scale, rapid and spectacular expansion."[1] Perhaps the first factor to consider here is the extent of the "expansion."

Some authorities say that one-half the present body of knowledge has come into existence in the last twenty years. Another statistic quoted is that five to ten times more information is available in a given subject area than thirty years ago.[2] Yet another statistic is that five million scientific and technical articles are published annually in about one hundred thousand journals, yet my former company takes around five thousand journals or less than one twentieth of those available. In August 1975, many of us received the *Harvard Business Review's* mailing in which Mitchell Reade wrote, "The world's output of new books is around 1,000 titles *per day*. The United States Government publishes over 100,000 reports a year, plus over 450,000 articles, books, and papers. The world generates new scientific and technical information at the rate of about six million pages a year."

To get even closer to home, I participated in an Ad Hoc Group meeting in Washington that developed the estimate that approximately 20,000 items are issued in the field of information science (my own specialty) during the course of a year. I try to keep up with this through the aid of colleagues in

---

Adapted from the first Lincoln lecture presented at the Arizona State University, College of Business Administration and Center for Executive Development, Tempe, March 4, 1969.

professional societies, indexing services, and a major academic library. Yet I do not feel confident that *all* important items in these 20,000 come to my attention.

If one studies the technical journals of today and those of thirty years ago, it is clear that the complicating factor is not that sheer volume alone is larger, but that the interaction with other more distant fields is greater than was true then. A trivial example of the change is that a major tobacco manufacturer now has to be concerned about marketing patterns for Chinese specialty foods, such as chop suey, while a more elegant example is the current considerations of the social implications of engineering processes that are involved in pollution and urban considerations. There are probably also areas in which *you* feel obliged to keep informed today that were foreign to your primary interests a short while ago.

It is a prime purpose of these pages to lead you to a greater awareness of the types and sources of information that could be employed in your operation and to gain a sense of the urgency in managing well your company's "information asset." One ex-Department of Defense official has pointed out: "Information is a resource whose generation consumes time and money, whose use conserves time and money, whose cost and value are not known to management."[3] We will be most concerned with this last point. A Danish colleague makes the points that "knowledge is a commodity" and that "information service is the marketing of that knowledge."[4]

I have mentioned elsewhere that operations, staff, and research formed an intertwined trinity in informational needs and that it is virtually impossible to consider any one group's informational requirements as being its own prerogative. For example, a rise in the price of one metal triggers a research group effort to find a substitute for that metal in a particular application, and the resulting project could convince the staff of the desirability of substituting this new material. This in turn could cause production problems for operations, possibly even involving toxic conditions. The matter must be referred back to research for alleviation. The result could cause a staff decision on whether the safety precautions required are so expensive as to negate the tentative decision to substitute this cheaper metal.

I summarized information needs then as:

> Staff requires information of many types: economic, legal, personnel relations, public relations, technological and others. Economic needs include prices of materials and services, rates, marketing studies, financial climate, insurance, taxation, and competitive position. Legal needs include such matters as regulatory information (codes, ordinances, statutes, decisions), extent of trade cooperation, taxation, and legislative liaison. Personnel needs include labor relations matters, management and supervision practices, industrial policies, recreation requirements, recruiting sources and tests. Public relations requires

knowledge of attitude of local or regional area toward the industry and/or its products, the responsibilities of the organization toward the local area, the regional area, the rest of the industry, the trade associations and the overall industrial complex. Procurement sources and design principles are other examples of needed information for staff.

Operations needs "how-to-do-it" information on processes, materials handling, automation, standards, material properties, scheduling, foremanship, plus detailed information in many of the fields listed above.

It might be easier to list the kinds of information that research does *not* require than to list the kinds it does. As the possession of a burning curiosity and the abhorrence of the conventional are prime requirements for a successful researcher, then the horizons of his information needs are necessarily limitless in breadth and depth . . . [For example] some years ago I had to make extensive literature searches into pipe organ literature to find information that bore on the resonance of ram jet engines — both fields concerned vibrations in pipe which phenomena were subject to the same physical laws.[5]

Information is clearly a vital asset of the firm and, if properly employed, could rank in importance with the organization's personnel resources, physical facilities, and financial resources. Other assets that have an information content are patents, franchises, and good will. A basic principle is that information must be totally exploited in support of the company's mission.

What are the sources of this information asset? They may be from within the company or outside the company. In general, information is obtained from three sources. First, there is the internal information generated within the firm. The second and third sources are external: "closed" information, such as that from military security and trade associations; and "open" information, such as that from technical societies and commercial publishers. The relative volumes of these three areas of information would not only vary from one company to another, but from one company's particular installation or division to another. For example, a defense-related division of the enterprise would have a greater volume from the second source whereas the research division would probably receive more from the third source. Marketing would use all three. (It should be noted that "outside" information that is added to existing company information can result in new company information.)

Harnessing all the information at a given location in a company is complicated by the factor called "iceberg effect," which exemplifies the relative volumes of information available at this location and in the great outside world. At the top of the iceberg, the smallest part, would be the total information immediately available at a specific company location; next larger in amount would be the additional information elsewhere in the company; at the base of the iceberg is the third and largest source, the additional information outside the company.

4   Industrial Information Systems

Each division or enterprise within a company must receive its own information flow from the three available source areas.[6]

It has been shown that the information for the company comes from a variety of sources. The *open* literature has certain characteristics, such as being a large mass; it is less obviously oriented to the company's mission and is of an uneven quality. Although the company's internal information may have great pertinence, it may not be known or available outside of the particular company unit that developed it.

As a technological lead in an industry is mainly the buying of precious time, the time should be used as effectively as possible through proper exploitation of the information upon which the lead is based. After all, competitors do have capable people and suitable facilities, and it is possible that your effective handling of proprietary information could be the edge you need.

Information can be considered as "perishable," and this contributes to the urgency of its handling. It is commonplace in technical fields that the value of information is the greatest in its first five years of existence, and falls off sharply thereafter. For example, 60 percent of the interlibrary loan requests that General Motors Research Library made on other libraries was for material up to five years old, and only 24 percent for material issued in the previous decade. One patent service in England capitalizes on this feeling of perishability by printing a special version of its service on newly issued foreign patents and airmailing it to North America at a sizable premium over that of the regular edition. Pharmaceutical firms among others are pleased to pay this premium. In nontechnical areas, nothing is so unhelpful as a superceded regulation of a regulatory body or a noncurrent labor contract.

There is a clustering of value in the "open" literature that has been repeatedly demonstrated. For example, one major industry that has a centralized photocopy service observes that 60 percent of all photocopies are requested from a list of fifty journal titles. That it would be a serious defect to ignore the other 40 percent in several hundred other journals is illustrated by the fact that Mendel's Laws of Heredity and the development of DDT were both unknown for years because of the obscure sources in which they were first published. Another illustration is that the first reporting in any detail of the Wright Brothers' Kitty Hawk flights was in a beekeeper's journal.

The "closed" literature would primarily include trade association information, draft responses to regulatory bodies, and proposed hearings statements. Company security is a consideration in the availability and utilization of this information. Individuals' access to it would vary with their work assignment. For example, being on the Corporate Headquarters Engineering Staff meant that I had far greater access to engineering information than to legal, personnel, or financial information. Of course there was some information in the latter categories I could have access to when my staff studies so required.

Formal restrictions on "closed" information may vary from one division to

The Information Explosion and Its Implication for Management 5

another. For example, in a decentralized company, it is conceivable that the financial results of each division are only known in that division and in the central financial staff, but not in the other divisions. Another example is the dichotomy between the domestic operations of a company and the foreign operations where U. S. Department of Commerce regulations would affect the "closed" information supplied to the foreign arm of the company. Still another dichotomy can be between the parent and its subsidiary organizations on matters of information. Military security regulations are imposed from the outside and their observance is an obligation of contractual relationships. Access to a very large body of "uneven" material can be secured with the possession of suitable military security "need to know."

The above is not a catalog of all the limitations that can exist on the flow of information in a firm, but they are indications that aggressive policies must be exercised to insure that all information be made available to those having a need of it to perform their assignment. The passive acceptance of unwarranted denial of access to particular classes of information has no place in a company information service.

By an understanding of the earlier quote, "Knowledge is a commodity . . . and information service is the marketing of that knowledge," we see the functions of an information service include the exploitation of the material that has been acquired by the organization. To perform its functions has entailed *acquiring* informational material by using its particular competencies and such expediting facilities as leased phone lines, leased cables, company mail service, or even company airplanes; after which the material has been *processed* (listed, analyzed, and indexed); then its existence has been made known through *dissemination* media within the company, following which it has been effectively *used*, thus completing the information cycle within the company.

In carrying out all these functions, it is important to avoid the common weakness: inertia and losses within the system can lead to the situation where all the material acquired is not effectively used. It is not represented that the development of the optimum information system that will make the needed information fully available to your firm is an easy task. However consulting and planning bodies have issued proprietary reports on information systems and see a definite trend toward active information centers succeeding the passive custodial services of the libraries of the past.

To pursue the area of dissemination or announcement of newly available information as an example, there have been listings of the "what's new in the library" type for years, but now there are many instances of "selected dissemination of information" (SDI) in existence. This is a procedure whereby individual items of information are called to the attention of persons or groups periodically on the basis of their previously declared fields of interest. In my former company, there are several hundred engineers who receive announcements on punched cards containing abstracts of articles that have been machine-selected on the basis of just such profiles of interest. Some writers in the information science field have been concerned about the cost of such service and advocate the distribution of announcements to project *groups* or subdepartment levels rather than to individuals. Such listings could be called "narrowly defined announcement bulletins."[7]

A rare attempt to express the value of such announcement services in management terms was the statement by Dr. N. B. Hannay, Chairman of the American Chemical Society's Sub-Committee on Economics of Chemical Information, that properly handled announcement services could save a firm 217 hours per week per person. At $20 an hour, a firm employing one hundred chemists would save approximately $250,000 a year, less some portion of the cost of maintaining this service.

Utilization of information can be aided by machine methods, and the legal profession has long been actively at work in this field. Under the Great Society program, efforts in the field of medical information received great impetus, and a system called MEDLARS was developed by the National Library of Medicine which employs regional information services. That library has a whole family of on-line information retrieval services now (MEDLINE, TOXLINE, and so forth) available at modest cost to medical scientists and practitioners.[8] The field of chemistry has services focusing around the Chemical Abstracts service familiar to some of you. (Note that these two pioneering "families" of services are among the 76 data bases available on-line through commercial jobbers in 1977.)

The field of engineering suffers from a fractionalization of efforts, although there was a tripartite effort going forward under the Engineers' Joint Council, United Engineering Trustees, and the Engineering Index, Inc., to study the feasibility of a national system for engineering information. One concept of what this national system for engineering might look like showed a switching and referral level. "Switching" means receiving a request that is not in your information service and sending it to a location having it for fulfillment via your center; "referral" is informing the requester of the location of the information but not securing it for him. The system envisioned by the tripartite efforts was never funded.

The next level of complexity is the even more sophisticated system to be used by the National Scientific and Technical Information System about 1978, according to a group at Battelle Memorial Institute. A significant quote from their article is, "while techniques for handling information will be gradually improved in the years to come, the basic methods have been established, and at this point no revolutionary methods appear to be emerging. The really important changes for the future appear to lie in management functions and standardization of format."[9] The very last point has to do with the facilitating of switching and interchanging among information systems when the bibliographic elements of information follow a recognizable order and are identified

The Information Explosion and Its Implication for Management 7

consistently. It is an important concept but rather detailed for us to dwell on here.

Some publications and seminars of the National Industrial Conference Board and the American Management Association are helpful in deciding on how serious the firm should be in staffing its information system function. On the subject side, the NICB Seminar on "Organizing Our Scientific Knowledge For Use" is helpful in reporting authoritative statements from NASA on its technology utilization program, from AEC on its industrial involvement program, from the Department of Commerce on its State Technical Services Acts involvement, and other services.[10]

On the management information portions of the information system, the *Conference Board Record* for October 1968 discusses the management information systems unit including key position guides for the manager/management information systems, manager/systems and procedures, manager/computer programming, manager/EDP operations, as well as a position guide for a director of the management information systems department of a second company.[11] Although a vocal minority claims that no "real" management information system exists, the following example of a pioneer operational MIS belies this view.

The Japan Broadcasting Company (NKH) has an operating sophisticated on-line management information system network where computers are used to plan and administer the production activities of two television and three radio networks, which carry one hundred hours of programs a day to some 20 million households. Schedules and budgets for 640 television and 1,200 radio shows are controlled in all stages of production. It is stated that the flow of information at NKH in a single day, which formerly involved 1,800 conversations and meetings and the exchange of some 5,000 pieces of paper, has been replaced by this information handling mechanism. *Data Management* defined MIS as "a collection of subsystems connected in such a way as to fulfill the information requirements necessary to plan, operate, and control business activity."[12]

The American Management Association has had a number of seminars and workshops in areas that impinge on this topic on such subjects as "administering the company library," which have been given several times, and repeated meetings on information retrieval, records management function, and the like. The World Trade Center is having meetings in information processing areas, too.

Employment of an effective information system can affect the manner in which the organization acts. For example, the present "layering" in our business operations does cause multiple handling and interpretations of information (so-called "red tape"). An optimum information system would eliminate this, but it would also erase certain of the dampening that intermediate layers of managers impose; and there are some who feel that this dampening prevents too violent oscillations in reactions to stimuli.

One former colleague who carefully studied what information system development *should be* saw the following effects of an information system on a business enterprise:

1. Increase in the management span of control;
2. Increase in planning and monitoring activities;
3. Increase in rapid information transmittal on management structures;
4. Increase in the removal of the present people and paper buffer between levels of management and organizations;
5. The possibility of task definition by information used by each person;
6. The possibility of using information originally gathered for some other purpose.

His down-to-earth suggestions are that management observe the following rules when reviewing information system proposals:

1. Don't abdicate responsibility to the technicians;
2. Don't get overwhelmed by details;
3. Don't expect perfection (it won't work right the first time);
4. Don't accept anything you don't understand;
5. Understand what your system is for;
6. Be involved — help the person who is trying to help you; and
7. Have a procedure to fall back on when it doesn't work initially.[13]

The channels of communication used by engineers would indicate that libraries are used directly for only 20 percent of the information the engineer needs, another 10 percent is received through national and regional information systems such as described earlier.[14] The remaining 70 percent comes from personal files, colleagues, technical sales representatives, and other informal sources.

After toiling in the library "vineyard" for thirty years, I have the feeling that the defense-related nature of the industries in the cited study affected the totals reported. An indication of firm commitment to libraries by industry and business was shown by statistical counts made in 1965 comparing *Fortune's* list of 500 U. S. industrials and 200 foreign industrials with the recognized directories of Special Libraries in North America and Europe. These counts show that 67 firms had "library pairs" operating concurrently in North America and Europe involving 552 libraries. Sample firms include: DuPont, Eastman Kodak, Ciba Pharmaceutical and Geigy Chemical. Further, 927 out of the 2,163 industrial libraries reported in the United States were in organizations listed in *Fortune's* 500. A successor study using *Fortune's* 500 for 1975 is covered in Chapter 12 and Appendix B.

As for the future, when libraries take on the active role of information centers, as foreseen by consulting firms and others mentioned earlier, they will evolve into something related to, but different from today's. As Charles H.

Stevens, associated with Project INTREX at MIT, and recently Executive Director of the government's National Commission for Library and Information Science, foresees in 1988:

> Will libraries be obsolete, too? No, but library services will change. Multiple catalogs, indexes, abstracts and bibliographies will be replaced by a finding tool that can help the user locate information that appears in any format from any source in any language. Remote access equipment will encourage the engineer to search from his desk or drawing board.
> Libraries still will have books, but films, tapes and newer data-storage elements will be pushing for space. The technical journal, burgeoning in 1968, will wane by 1988. Scientists and engineers will reach their worldwide audiences by submitting summaries of experimental or theoretical development to a computer-controlled information network. Design users of the system will have the benefits of language translation, automatic indexing, retrospective searching and an alerting service that filters and holds for use the information essential to the work at hand.
> Information communication networks must and will reach the design engineer or the field engineer wherever he is. Wireless, wallet-size teleterminals with digital keyboard and folding screen will put the individual engineer in touch with all information and data sources from anywhere on or around the earth—or the moon. Voice inquiry and responses will be supplemented by keyboard input and display response for all types of information.[15]

There has been no information emerge in the meantime to suggest the above predictions are too optimistic. However, there is abundant evidence that it is a mistake to wait for the next breakthrough in information technology to begin work on your company industrial information system. The need already exists, so how do you proceed? The steps that should be taken to develop an effective information service in your organization (and thus handle the information explosion for your purposes) are:

1. Decide to exploit the "information asset" effectively in your operation.
2. Determine *what* information will be used by source, by subject area, by management level.
3. Develop an overall information system that will have the necessary skilled staff, resources, systems and procedures to:
    insure that needed materials are acquired (obtained) expeditiously; that those materials are adequately identified (indexed and recorded) using the standard formats; that the proper and effective announcement is made of their availability; and that the

information is effectively used to support the company's primary mission.
4. Monitor and upgrade the information system on the basis of continual feedback from users so as to more effectively:
include more of the company's personnel as involved users; compact and synthesize the meaning in previously utilized information; reach "make or buy" decisions on a wider spectrum of information sources/services; develop creative methods of identifying crucial content; prepare for future direct inquiry procedures to increase effectiveness of both announcement and utilization procedures; and proceed with "deliberate haste" to accept the best of the newest procedures (perhaps you cannot always be the *first* in your industry to innovate creative uses of information, but never be the *last*).

To Summarize, I have pointed out that the potential store of information is vast, that some parts of it need to be managed for the benefit of your firm, that there are sources of information within the company and outside, that a mix of formal and informal information services needs to be employed, and that suggested steps toward the development of an effective information service need be taken.

AFTERWORD

At the end of 1975 results began appearing of the government's efforts to quantify the U. S. expenditures for R&D, the generating of scientific and technical information, and the efforts to organize it for use.

For example, the National Technical Information Service reported to the U. S. Federal Documents Workshop, January 9, 1976, that ". . . $1.4 million is spent to abstract and index the annual output of 70,000 technical reports that result from $20 billion spent on research and development."[16]

Lee Burchinal of the National Science Foundation reported somewhat earlier[17] on the efforts of an OSIS contractor to learn ". . . how much money is spent annually on scientific and technical communication in the United States? What are the trends in this expenditure? Is the country getting its money's worth from the scientific and technical communication enterprise?"

First, scientific and technical information activities in 1975 cost the United States $11.8 billion which is made up of $2.4 billion for generating and producing the information; $6.1 billion for publication, dissemination, storage, and retrieval of the information; and at least $3.3 billion for assimilation of the information by users (largely salary costs) for browsing, inquiry, and reading. Second, expenditures for scientific and technical communication were

74 percent more in 1975 than the approximate $6.8 million spent a decade earlier (or $11.9 million). However, if converted to constant dollars the increase is only 13 percent. Third, while volume of scientific and technical literature had increased in the previous decade, costs of processing and dissemination have *declined* by 4 percent in constant dollars.

What about the changes in the 1965-1975 decade for numbers of scientists, funding for R&D, and the information generated? There were 1.6 million scientists in 1975 compared to 1.3 million in 1965 (an increase of 23 percent). Those engaged in research increased by just 7 percent (from 494,000 to 528,000), which represents a much lower rate than for the preceding decade. Scientists and technologists continue to represent about 1.2 percent of the adult U. S. population. The number of scientific and technical journals has increased by $\approx$ 9 percent, which is consistent with the increase in R&D expenditures and number of scientists. By contrast technical report literature increased 16 percent. A still larger increase (40 percent, or, one book per 107 scientists) was noted in scientific books in 1974 over 1965.

Dr. Burchinal suggests these data show that scientific and technical information expenditures will increase but slightly in the near future, but that ". . . large increases in efficiency have occurred, mainly through application of improved technology to the information processing and distribution functions. Further advances can be expected as electronic publishing, networking and on-line searching become more common. But still greater efficiency may be attained at the two ends of the information transfer chain, as researchers use advanced technology, such as computer-based methods for both recording data and literature and for identifying and retrieving results reported by others. Because of the large numbers of persons and organizations involved, such advances will come slowly and only after we have the results of considerable research, demonstration, and effort."[18] Finally, he sees the U. S. in the role of "the world's first information-based society."

NOTES AND REFERENCES

1. *Webster's New Collegiate Dictionary* (Springfield, Mass.: Merriam, 1973), p. 404.
2. National Industrial Conference Board, *Organizing our Scientific Knowledge for Use*, Seminar on Science and the Humanities (New York: The Board, 1967), p. 9.
3. Walter M. Carlson, *Engineering Information for National Defense* (New York: Engineers Joint Council, 1967), pp. 41-45. (In EJC, *Engineering Societies and Their Literature Program*.)
4. K. Klinto, "Danish Technical Information Service," Presentation at FID 33rd General Assembly, Tokyo, 1968.

5. Eugene B. Jackson, "The Role of Information in Solving Business and Technological Problems," Executive Conference on Organizing and Managing Information, University of Chicago, February 1, 1957, pp. 10-19.
6. Eugene B. Jackson, "General Motors Research Laboratories Library: A Case Study," *Library Trends* **14**: 360 (January 1966).
7. Marianne Cooper, *Current Information Dissemination: Ideas and Practices* (New York: American Institute of Physics, 1968), p. A-12 (ID 68-15).
8. Stephen E. Furth, "Automated Retrieval of Legal Information: State of the Art," *Computers and Automation* December 1968: 25-27.
9. G. S. Simpson, "The Evolving U. S. National Scientific and Technical Information System," *Battelle Technical Review* May-June 1968: 21.
10. National Industrial Conference Board, *Organizing Our Scientific Knowledge for Use* (New York: The Board, 1967).
11. Harold Stieglitz, "The Management Information System Unit," *Conference-Board Record* **10**: 30-36 (October 1968).
12. Daniel T. Thomas, "A Practical Approach to Corporate-Level Computer-based MIS," *Data Management* October 1968: 22-27.
13. D. C. Burnstine, "Some Notes on the Effects of Information Systems on the Business Enterprise," Notes for a talk to textile executives, January 14, 1969.
14. Carlson, *Engineering Information.*
15. Charles H. Stevens, "Design Predictions: Information—1988 Style," *EDN* **13**(15): 47 (December 1968).
16. Marvin Wilson, Assistant Director, NTIS, Springfield, Va. Presentation at University of Houston Continuing Education Center, 1976.
17. Lee Burchinal, "Recent Trends in Communication of Scientific and Technical Information," *Notes and Comment* (Engineering Index, Inc.) **2**(4): 1-2 (December 1975).
18. Ibid., p. 3.

Chapter 2

Industrial Information Systems and How to Get There

WHAT ARE THEY?

The ideal industrial information system is composed of the totality of informational elements required by any and every officer and/or employee to accomplish his or her function and that required by every customer to effectively and properly use the company product. These elements may be generated within the company, procured from outside the company and transmitted or transformed within the company, and disseminated to all of the company's "publics."

The ideal industrial information system is so organized, staffed, and located that the information elements are inputted in an unambiguous form, in a timely fashion, in a processable format, from every conceivable source, and with conflicts resolved. The informational elements are then organized for accessibility by a number of coding means. The resulting information is then matched to the known needs and hitherto unperceived needs of the company personnel. It is then supplied in a clear, conveniently usable form to the personnel and as appropriate to the customers, to the government, to the trade association, and to the public at large.

While by definition the ideal is never achieved, the purpose of this book will have been served if more operating industrial information systems realistically assess where and how they fall short of the ideal, and at what cost in company profitability, and approach that goal.

WHAT ALREADY EXISTS?

Just because there is no box on the company's organizational chart that is labeled "information center" or "information systems manager," it does not follow that the company is hopelessly out of date or beyond help. Judicious inquiry may reveal that a *library* exists within the company but that it is not officially recognized or is too small to merit a box on the chart.

A great variety of units are labeled "libraries" that do not merit that designation. Some are merely an accumulation of books that the switchboard operator arranges in her spare time, while others are an accumulation assigned to the care of an older secretary after her executive boss has retired. One multilocation industrial firm beginning an inventory of its library resources had the firm rule that it would not include any unit that had not previously been able to convince the purchasing department to buy a rubber stamp for them that had the word "library" on it.

A step up in the hierarchy of so-called libraries are those run by veteran draftsmen or editorial writers. Typically these are based on an accumulation of engineering drawings, patents, or technical manuals with some books and periodicals (magazines) included. While some such units have had innovative leaders who established aperture card files and coded retrieval methods, the more usual situation is that the person was given the responsibility when he or she did not work out as a draftsman or editor and was not all that motivated.

Sometimes when a new attractive building was being erected for a firm, the architect or the facilities director labeled one room on the plan as "Library." Nature abhors a vacuum, we know, so in these so-called libraries bookcases or book stacks or tables may have been ordered before hiring a librarian—typically, a former schoolteacher who didn't like the discipline problems or study hall duty.

The problem with giving the reader the above examples of so-called libraries is that we know one or more examples of fine information center leaders who got their introduction to the field in one of the manners described above. Thus we hasten to reveal that our recommendations here, and throughout this book, are based on both certainties and probabilities, and the probability of a library that originates as in the above examples evolving into a showplace information center are not great. Quality library service is most likely when the unit is led by an experienced graduate librarian with a master's degree from an American Library Association accredited library school and has an adequate program of information acquisition, processing, dissemination, and utilization. Definitions of these functional terms plus the perceived differences between a library and an information center will be covered in Chapters 3 and 4.

Once whether or not a library exists within the company has been determined, next is the search for sources of information accumulation. First are units that generate *internal reports*, especially for distribution outside the originator's function or location. Some of these reports may be distributed to fulfill government contract or other subcontract obligations that may include legal requirements as to the mode of distribution, eligibility of addresses, and maintenance of distribution records and thus represent the company externally. The presumption may be made that where legal requirements do exist for distribution of such internal reports, the letter of the law of agency regulations is being met. It is frequently a different story for reports that remain truly internal or even fugitive. While in some instances the difficulty in ferreting out these reports is due to valid considerations of trade secrecy; interunit, interlocation, or interdivisional security (i.e., where "compartmentalized" security is practiced); patent priorities; personnel/personal privacy; fiscal status or marketing campaigns, more often the reason is an organizational or procedural fault. Thus, typically elaborate rules exist for the control of the minor fraction of internal reports, while the major fraction are sequestered in scattered files by persons whose prime function is not information service connected.

Consideration of patents, which were mentioned in the preceding paragraph, leads to the next probable information accumulation source: *laboratory notebooks*. These permanently bound, witnessed records of daily work performed form the basis for patent applications and are in the "permanent records" category of every company's record retention program. Frequently the only conveniently available information about these notebooks is the names of the respective investigators and the dates covered.

Company correspondence is omnipresent, as the vouchers for vertical files purchased annually attest. Where a strong policy of centralized correspondence files exists, the searcher for this source of information accumulation will have fewer locales to seek and greater rewards to find; where a decentralized or no policy exists on correspondence handling, the searcher is encouraged to strive to uncover the most likely places initially and then proceed on a lower priority basis for the remainder in parallel with other efforts. Like Gaul, correspondence is divided into three parts: that of administrative value, that of technical value, and that of trivia. Where a records retention program already exists, some presorting may have been done and material stored in an alternate location.

Vendor's catalog information may form another locatable source of information. Typically such catalogs are filed either in the procurement unit or in the technical unit concerned, or sometimes in both places. The increasing availability of microform files of current vendors' catalogs in broad subject areas makes casual accumulations less valuable information sources, especially where the company's major interests match the subject areas available for purchase.

Specifications and standards may be found together. The first could be military specifications, in which case microforms of current complete issues are far preferable to the risks of using obsolete issues. Standards may be of national, international, or trade group authority, and the importance of currency pertains here as well. Standards tend to be issued in parts with some sections superceded more frequently than others, and the files are rarely up-to-date when located.

Another possible source of information is material received as a result of *company membership* or of *unrestricted grants* the firm has made. In the first case, a given officer of a company may receive reports or membership briefings or invitations to closed seminars intended for members only that are

16   Industrial Information Systems

not of interest to him or her personally but would be to another person or unit in the company. Similarly, certain personnel may receive invitations to closed seminars held by universities for their "industrial associates"—that is, organizations that have given them unrestricted grants for research, granted them obsolete (or not currently required) equipment, or participated in extended education programs calling for "co-op" semesters spent in industry acquiring on-the-job experience.

We have thus implied that in addition to the actual informational elements that the searcher discovers, an information *potential* exists within the company that may be available for the asking: Someone just has to fill in the blank on an invitational letter to a seminar, or to request the proffered research reports, or to participate in the group inspection trip, or to forward inquiries to a distant ready-and-waiting information unit the company's membership partly pays for. There will be cases where the potentials uncovered will be more valuable in the long run than the accumulations of materials the information resources inventory locates.

What Will Be Done with the Information Inventory?

The searcher now knows more than anyone has previously known about the information elements that exist in the company. The next action includes the following possibilities:

Distribute the results of the inventory widely and suggest colleagues make use of the material where it is now (a passive approach).

Recommend that all or some critical portion of the materials be aggregated into an information unit with a person placed in charge (a more active approach).

Establish a unit if the power to do so exists a (still more active approach).

Recommend that a study be made of the information needs of the company followed by (1) a determination of how the ideal industrial information system (IIS) as described in the following chapters would meet those needs and recommend (take) appropriate action for implementation (an active approach, but politically not probable); (2) a determination of how the optimum IIS (i.e., the system that is the most sophisticated and comprehensive that can be resource-justified in the present or near-term future) would meet those needs and recommend (take) appropriate action for implementation (best option); or a determination of what portion of the optimum IIS can be implemented the soonest and with the highest probability of visible impact, thus paving the way for longer-term support

Industrial Information Systems and How to Get There 17

looking to the ideal IIS, and recommend (take) appropriate action for immediate implementation (probably the most popular option).

Establish the optimum IIS if the power to do so exists (a still more active approach).

Integrate the existing information resources into one of the above options that lead to the optimum IIS (a logical step and placed here for emphasis).

We recommend that the existing information system or the information resources in the company be assessed and the portions of the optimum IIS that can be implemented promptly with the highest impact potential and maximum use of on-hand resources be determined, and then an action program giving maximum visibility to the goals and progress toward achievement of the ideal IIS be implemented.

WHAT ARE THE PREDECESSOR ORGANIZATIONAL ELEMENTS?

In discussing information concerns with higher managements, a basic premise is that it is a waste of time to present facts prematurely. Hence, we would have been inefficient to have made a detour into the historical backgrounds of industrial information systems before pointing out that some of the system's elements may be present in a given company and need only be searched for. Then, the historical evolution of such systems as described in this section might contain some lessons or, at least, provide a broader background for proceeding toward the ideal system.

Kruzas has traced business and technical libraries back to the 1820s in his monumental history,[1] to which those interested in details should refer. Our personal contacts have included several persons whose service in industrial libraries began in the 1910s.

Legal, statistical, and handbook type materials were the earliest forms of literature that were assembled for use by a company. Published information shared attention with company-generated materials and technical and business subjects vied for preeminence. The potential contributions of technical colleagues were early recognized when special classification schemes and indexing means were being developed. The strongest unifying thread was the emphasis on *service* over considerations of form, consistency of material organization, placement on an organizational chart, or what constituted true "professionalism" in information service. These latter were luxuries that the later-day, more academically inclined special librarians/information officers could ponder.

Kruzas gives appropriate recognition to pioneer efforts at Stone & Webster and A. D. Little, along with the companies that will be repeatedly recognized

18   Industrial Information Systems

in these pages, such as General Electric, Du Pont, and General Motors, but doesn't include anecdotes such as the following:

— Caroline W. Lutz telling of Charles F. Kettering's matching the funds he made available in 1917 to the tool crib foreman at the Dayton Engineering Laboratories (later bought by GM to form its Research Laboratories) with funds for her to buy handbooks since ". . . books are as important to industrial engineers as are tools";

— Rachel M. MacDonald telling of how library funds for the embryonic Ford Motor Company Engineering Library depended in part on how good she was at teaching square dancing to the world leaders Henry Ford called to Dearborn at intervals in the 1920s and before;

— Emma C. Wedenbine telling of how eager founders of the National Cash Register Company were to accept the offer of the Dayton Public Library to establish a deposit station of the library at their factory to complement the technical holdings of the already-flourishing NCR library.

Just as there were committed individualists in company operations in the Northeast, New York, Philadelphia, and the Midwest, there were outstanding public library leaders who saw the need for "putting knowledge to work," and they were instrumental in the founding in 1909, of the Special Libraries Association, which has served as a focus for professional activity ever since. Outstanding public library subject departments in business and science/technology developed at Newark, Philadelphia, Baltimore, New York, Cleveland, and Detroit, among other cities, and "alumni" from their staffs subsequently went on to lead company libraries (much as today where most company patent operations are led by one-time U. S. Patent Office examiners).

Some persistent dichotomies the history reveals that have already been hinted at are embodied in the following questions:

Should the library be commercial or technical? Apparently the usefulness of a commercial focus was seen first. However, some companies maintained separate libraries at the same or adjacent geographic locations on both commercial and technical subjects. While Kruzas noted merging of the operations in some companies in the 1920s, not until the 1960s was it becoming clear that the distinctions between the collections of the GM Research Laboratories Library and that of the GM public relations staff were blurring because of the economic consequences of technologies and the technological consequences of economic measures.

Should the collection be of commercially published literature or of company-originated literature? The first collections were of book-trade origin (books and periodicals widely available for a price). Then it became apparent that specific and urgent reference questions were being asked that could not be answered in those sources, so "tickler files" had to be started. (These were the ancestors of the subject-approached correspondence files). Next, it became obvious that someone should keep a file of the company's own publications to help with the questions (GE was doing this as early as 1921). Then the need arose for company material not yet in published form and "the can of worms" was opened as included in the IIS acquisitions functions described in the next chapter. As recently as the 1960s, Monsanto Chemical Company had elaborate mechanization efforts going for processing and utilizing laboratory research notebooks and reports (and some company correspondence), while the "book library" went its undisturbed traditional way.

Should the library be run by librarians or subject specialists? More accurately, this dichotomy is a "multichotomy" reading: Should the library be run by clerks, librarians, technicians, subject specialists, documentalists or information officers? This issue will be considered in its current context in more detail in Chapter 6, but for the moment we should note that the first practitioners apparently were clerks with native intelligence and a few far-sighted subject persons; then came some librarian leaders with a numerically larger component of subject specialists; then a balance between librarians and subject people; then more librarians than subject people; then (with the advent of World War II and its literature consequences) the preeminence of the subject person/documentation/information officer; then the coexistence in large industrial library systems of managers and staffs with combinations of these backgrounds. (The subject specialists felt more at home in the American Documentation Institute [later the American Society for Information Science] than in the Special Libraries Association. Efforts to merge the societies have failed, so IIS leaders must follow developments in both.)

Should the library be an information center? Granting that "a rose is a rose is a rose" and that the most advanced concept of a library would include such elements as providing on-line reference inquiry service that would make it indistinguishable from an information center, we recognize that most persons think of the library as a *passive* service and the information center as an *active* service. However, at the end of World War II, a new information environment evolved due to great increases in science/technology activity, the generation of a large mass of recorded and unrecorded information/data, more sophisticated demands of users, growing dissatisfaction with existing formal services, increasing recognition of information processing as a science (and the concomitant rise of information analysis centers), and evolution of useful electronic information systems. Thus, from our present vantage point we believe that the active service is what is required in industry these days and use the phrase "information center" to describe the information service element in a function or geographic location that together with the informational elements in the company's other functions or geographic locations forms its industrial information system.

Should the information center be patron centered or company centered?

20   Industrial Information Systems

Kruzas saw the very earliest company libraries as being heavily philanthropic educational institutions having a principal object of assisting the "young gentlemen" in the company's employ find their proper place in the world (thus, patron centered). Recently there has been the effort to show indisputably that the information center "pay its way" in contributing to the company profit position (thus, company centered). Either way, the information center needs to be conscious of the way its users solve their own tasks, as diagrammed in Figure 2.1 by a leading industrial psychologist. Of course, the mid-1970s emphasis on social responsibilities of the company in addition to the always-

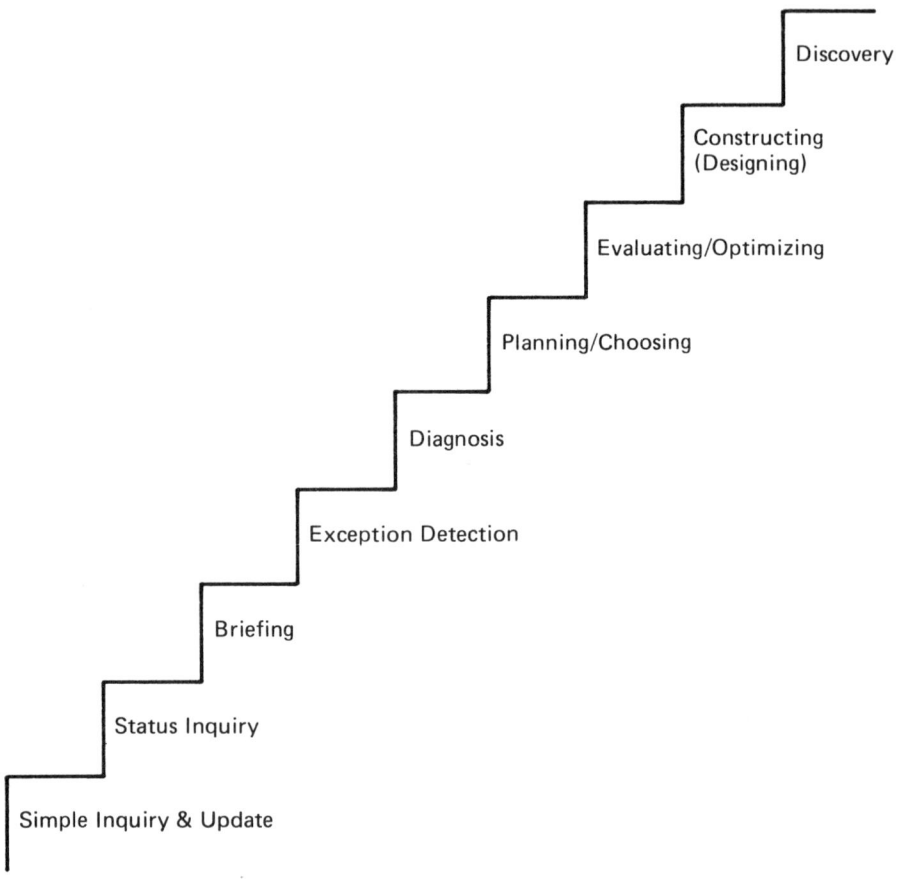

Figure 2.1   Analysis of Human Problem-Solving Tasks to be Considered by Evaluators of Information Systems (Source: R. B. Miller, Private Communication, 1969.)

recognized economic contributions will result in the need for the ideal IIS to seek an optimum balance between filling of the company's total informational needs, those of the individuals forming its personnel resource, and the several "publics" with which it interacts. Meeting this challenge forms a laudable objective, whose achievement will make our respective tasks of operating the ideal IIS as described in the following chapters worthwhile.

REFERENCE

1. Anthony Thomas Kruzas, *Business and Industrial Libraries in the United States, 1820-1940* (New York: Special Libraries Association, 1965), 133 pp.

Chapter 3

IIS Functions: Acquisition and Processing of Information

The industrial information system can be no better than its information input. The securing of that information in whatever form and from whatever source and covering whatever subject matter is termed *acquisitions*. It is one of the so-called housekeeping functions that together with *processing* consumes a large proportion of the IIS personnel and costs, but yet because of its "back room" nature is unappreciated by the typical company official.

The scale of these costs is typically equal to the purchase price of the material itself—that is, a $15.00 technical book costs another $15.00 to be fully entered into the IIS and ready for use. Incidentally, while lower costs can be found in the literature, close examination of the reports show that occupancy costs, overhead costs, or materials costs have been excluded. Of course, obtaining some significant materials free of purchase cost is possible, but no way yet has been found to input them without cost.

THE ACQUISITIONS FUNCTIONS

Establishing an acquisitions policy that states what the company wishes realistically to acquire for its IIS is necessary, and a definitive policy will be elucidated by the company's selection from the "menu" of acquisitions functions that follow.

Function Ac-1: Usual Book Trade Literature

Books may be purchased directly from the publisher, from a local book dealer, from a jobber, or from an individual member of a society. The advantages of dealing with publishers are that middlemen's profits are eliminated, a lesser delay in availability may be encountered, and certain matching of invoices with the physical items received is facilitated. In addition, partial shipments are less frequent. Where company purchase practices permit, individual purchase orders may be issued for individual books, as was done at General Motors Corporation. Disadvantages of working directly with publishers include: costs of the individual purchase orders themselves (we were unable to pin this down at either GM or IBM), variation with reliability of order fulfillment between major and minor publishers, additional delays in transshipment of order papers from New York offices to relatively new suburban metropolitan area warehouses, and refusal of some publishers to handle small orders.

Dealing with local book dealers has the advantages of utilizing personal interest and convenience, fast fulfillment when item is in stock, and possibility of petty cash or simplified purchase arrangements. The main disadvantage is the small stock of most dealers in books the typical company needs.

A jobber is an individual or firm that undertakes to supply essentially all the inventory of a group of publishers. Jobbers may specialize by subject (such as medical books) or by foreign or domestic origin. Some jobbers offer a uniform discount off the list price; others offer varying discounts depending on whether the order consists of trade books or reference books; and some offer virtually no discount but superior service. Reliability and speed of service are to be prized over discounts. Seeking the lowest bidder on books is poor operating practice.

Certain books published by professional or technical societies may only be bought through a member of that society. Others may be bought more cheaply via the member than directly from the society. In the latter situation, some companies blink at the certification requirement that the book is intended for the member's own personal use and thus benefit from the cost saving, while other corporations prefer to follow the policy of always buying at full cost and thus consider they have subsidized the program of the professional/technical society to that extent.

Recommendation: *A reliable jobber relationship be developed and an increasing proportion of books be procured in this way; further, a means of checking on the jobber's performance be instituted so that any deterioration of service could be corrected promptly.*

Periodicals (magazines, journals) represent a larger percentage of most company acquisition budgets than books do, with some larger programs including over 1,000 different titles. Because of these numbers, using one or more jobbers is the only choice open. Periodicals are one type of purchase for which a company has to permit payment in advance of receipt, although it is not a uniform practice to permit subscription for multiple years of a title. Jobbers keep track of varying expiration dates of subscriptions and accept "claims" for nonreceipt of specific issues and for indexes. Some jobbers handle foreign subscriptions only. A few jobbers have automated subscription renewal records and require only concurrence on lists from the purchaser.

Recommendation: *All domestic periodicals available through jobbers be obtained through one jobber, and all foreign periodicals be secured through a second jobber. A few periodicals are available only directly from the publisher, and*

IIS Functions: Acquisition and Processing of Information 25

since discounts are becoming shorter or nonexistent for periodicals, they should be budgeted at list price.

Function Ac-2: Government Documents (Unclassified)

U. S. government documents may be secured by purchase through the Superintendent of Documents, U. S. Government Printing Office, Washington, D. C., and the research report variety may be procured through the National Technical Information Service, U. S. Department of Commerce, Springfield, Virginia. Government documents may occasionally be obtained without charge through a member of Congress or from the authorizing agency. They are no longer available through jobbers, but some commercial locative services do exist in the Washington area that secure materials for a premium or minimum per item cost. The Superintendent of Documents and the NTIS both have deposit services that should be utilized. Some companies use their Washington liaison offices as "runners" to pick up momentarily available documents, such as congressional committee prints or hearings and the proposed texts of regulations.

Documents of foreign governments may be secured through the jobbers mentioned earlier. However, letters of inquiry to Washington or New York offices maintained by certain foreign governments for their commercial attachés may be sometimes helpful.

Recommendation: *Deposit accounts be maintained at both the Government Printing Office and NTIS to expedite document orders; also, cordial relations be maintained with local congressmen and distribution sections of the most-involved government agencies. Foreign documents, except Canadian, should be secured through agents or foreign government offices, where they exist. For Canadian documents, remittances to Ottawa should be in Canadian funds.*

Function Ac-3: Government Documents (Security Classified)

Classified U. S. government reports may only be received through a "need-to-know" certificate issued by a cognizant government contract officer (the company's government liaison officer or legal staff should have the appropriate address). If "need-to-know" is approved, material will be received on automatic distribution from the originator, via the prime contractor with which the company holds a subcontract, or by selection from lists issued by the Defense Documentation Center, Defense Supply Agency, Alexandria Virginia. After receipt, storage will be in locked facilities as per appropriate government security regulations. Items may be used only by "cleared" personnel, and a rigid system of receipting and logging must be followed. In addition, individual items must be produced upon periodic or unannounced government audit visit. The subject content of classified government documents will normally overbalance the additional personnel and facilities and compliance costs their usage requires.

Recommendation: *Maximum access be sought to listings of security classified material in the field of interest and competence of the company, and actual copies of such materials be sought when there is a reasonable basis for believing they will advance both the government's and the company's goals. Keep current on notices of declassification of such documents via listings issued periodically by the military services and/or government agency responsible for their original issuance.*

Function Ac-4: Government Specifications

Subscriptions may be entered with the Superintendent of Documents. If a broad range of categories is needed, a preferable policy is to rely on the microeditions available in complete form and to use the new paper issues for current awareness purposes only. Provision of obsolete specifications to a user is inexcusable and will result in rejection of production items.

Recommendation: *Subscriptions be entered with the Superintendent of Documents in prime categories for current awareness purposes, but the official file be in microcopy form for ease of maintenance.*

Function Ac-4a: Trade Association Specifications

There is almost invariably a company official assigned liaison duties with all the trade associations to which the company belongs. He or she is also the logical person to be involved in significant IIS contacts with trade associations.

Recommendation: *Relevant categories of trade association specifications be secured via the official company liaison officer, but scattered individual issues be secured directly to save time.*

Function Ac-4b: Company Specifications

Normally the company official named in Function Ac-4a is also in charge of the company's specification program, has established distribution policies for them, and holds the historical file of superseded issues.

Recommendation: *Appropriate files of the current company specifications be maintained by the IIS, but the specifications officer be relied on for obsolete issues.*

Function Ac-5: Government Patents

Abstracts of new patents are included in the "Official Gazette" of the U. S. Patent Office, which may be obtained by subscription from the U. S. Government Printing Office, Washington, D. C. Copies of individual, complete patents are obtainable from the U. S. Patent Office directly.

Recommendation: *File(s) of the "Official Gazette" be secured for the last* ten years, and desired complete patents be obtained from the U. S. Patent Office via the company's Washington liaison office or patent counsel; foreign patents be obtained via the patent counsel.

Function Ac-6: Reports with Limited Distribution (External Origin)

These are reports that do not fit into the preceding categories and are obtainable only when certain conditions are met. Learning of their existence might be more difficult than securing them after ordering information is known. Aggressive searching for relevant material will reveal an increasing proportion of this material.

Recommendation: *Such reports be requested directly of the originator when requirements for their access would not compromise the company's interests.*

Function Ac-7: Reports with Limited Distribution (Internal Origin)

Distribution of internal reports within the company may be limited when compartmentalized security is company policy—that is, not available between offices, departments, divisions, subsidiaries, or foreign operations for good and sufficient reasons. Caution must be exercised to make certain that limitations are not more a result of inertia or overzealousness.

Recommendation: *Such reports be requested from originators, and refusals be appealed where possibility of relevance to achievement of company's mission exists.*

Function Ac-7a: Laboratory Notebooks

These notebooks are normally bound ruled books of varying thicknesses in which are recorded in narrative and diagram form the results of project or contract work. Typically each day's entries are witnessed and the result is a legal source document in support of later contract fulfillment negotiations and/or patent applications. Usually such notebooks are maintained by an individual staff member or by a unit of three persons at the very most. These records vary widely in their thoroughness and usefulness, but they are invariably classed within the "permanent records" portion of the company's records management program.

Recommendation: *Filled laboratory notebooks be routinely turned over to the IIS for microcopying and permanent filing.*

Function Ac-8: Material on "No Cost" Basis

This type of material will vary from reference works of permanent value to pamphlets of transitory interest. They should be widely obtained by interested parties, and the best eventually included in the IIS.

Recommendation: *Materials available without charge (or "controlled circulation" basis) be widely obtained, with a procedure for screening of the more useful as candidates for input.*

Function Ac-9: Microcopy Replacement for Full Texts

Several of the preceding categories (notably periodicals and government documents) are available on roll microfilm, microfiche (sheet film), or microcard (opaque sheet or cards). Trade-in prices are available whereby reduced prices on the microcopies may be secured for return of paper copies (especially in the case of periodicals). Obvious savings in file and floor space are apparent, but user resistance to available reading devices remains.

Recommendation: *For the establishment of new service units, obtaining of back files in microform receive priority consideration, and an educational program (perhaps as a part of the records management program) be instituted on the use of microcopy since this format is clearly "the wave of the future."*

Function Ac-10: Correspondence with Substantive Content

This category is the "needles-in-the-haystack" acquisitions function. Identification of worthy material for inclusion depends heavily on a good records management program. Lacking one, some prime areas of crucial subject matter should be identified so experience with this difficult material can be obtained.

Recommendation: *File memos on travel, attendance at technical meetings, and letter reports be gathered initially as probable sources of worthy content, and then the desired subject areas within this material be gradually included in the more accustomed bibliographic records.* (See the section on records management in Chapter 10.)

Function Ac-11: Comprehensive Indexes to Materials by Subject Discipline or Format

An important financial requirement is the securing of published comprehensive indexes not only to the materials on hand but also to the near-totality of extant published information by subject discipline. Some such indexes cost several thousands of dollars per year, and they both overlap in coverage and leave voids. Ten IBM libraries each bought separately the same ten leading abstracting and indexing services in technology plus additional services to achieve the required completeness of subject coverage.

IIS Functions: Acquisition and Processing of Information

Recommendation: *The most important comprehensive published indexes in the company's areas of competence and interest be identified and secured without delay; also, a logical program of expanded purchases in this category be developed and implemented as the IIS matures.*

Function Ac-11a: On-Line Data Bases

One of the most helpful current trends is the increasing availability of the above-mentioned published indexes, plus additional bodies of nonpaper-form information, in the form of magnetic tape services with terminal access by individual users. Separate bases may be secured for mounting on the company's computers, but a more rapidly growing practice is selecting from a "menu" of such data bases that run on a "middleperson's" computer, for which the company pays access and terminal usage fees. Machine storage space considerations limit the span of year's records that are available in this mode. Availability of these files opens the possibility of a new IIS "leapfrogging" in capabilities over some longer established, staid IIS's.

Recommendation: *The influence the availability of this function has on all the preceding acquisitions functions be carefully considered in drafting the company's acquisitions strategy. (Note: More sophistication is required for optimum use of such data bases than proponents would have us believe.)*

Function Ac-12: "Make or Buy" Decisions

As the collection increases in scope and depth and as staff becomes more resourceful, custom compilation of some tools that have previously been purchased will be possible. Caution: Because these tools can be prepared within the IIS doesn't mean they should.

Recommendation: *An optimum policy/strategy be developed whereby determinations may be made on whether to buy a given information source or to custom prepare it.*

Function Ac-13: Formal Information Exchange (External)

A company is not self-sufficient and must often gain knowledge in various information exchange situations. At one extreme it will enter into patent licensing agreements with collaborator or competitor companies, and at the other, it will sit at the same Community Chest Drive table and mention "how we are good at . . . ." In the formal information exchange, there needs to be a clear idea of what is to be gained by the exchange and at what cost in terms of company lead time, prestige, or recruitment potential.

Recommendation: *Establishment of company policy/strategy on exchange of information with external sources be set at a high organization level and be appropriately monitored by the IIS as part of its acquisitions function.*

Function Ac-14: Informal Information Exchange (External)

This type of information exchange is much larger in volume than the preceding and much more difficult (or impossible) to monitor. Therefore this function is the antithesis of the formal mode and is thereby defined. Any changes in the apparent quantity or prevalence should be studied for cause.

Recommendation: *The strategy for formal information exchange should recognize the existence and influence of this informal one on the total picture of information exchange and acquisition.*

Function Ac-15: "Deacquisitions" or Weeding

It is widely accepted that technical information has a "half-life" of five years—that is, it loses half of its value after that time. Similarily, other types of information decrease in importance with the passage of time. Accordingly, there must be a specific plan for removing material no longer useful or of severely lessened interest. Subject matter is a highly relevant component in the decision process.

Recommendation: *Criteria for weeding be an inclusion in IIS policy, procedure, and operations from the beginning. Mature systems should weed up to 20 percent of some categories annually. Some of the penalties of overweeding should be accepted, as otherwise the tendency is to be too conservative.*

Summary Recommendation

We recommend that a spectrum of types, origins, format, and qualities of information resources be secured for inclusion in the IIS and that ever richer combinations be planned as experience with and acceptance of the service grows.

THE PROCESSING FUNCTIONS

The next steps after the information item has arrived at the IIS are to identify and describe it, to determine whether it duplicates an item already in the IIS, and to furnish means whereby it may be recalled from the files by an IIS staff member or potential user.

IIS Functions: Acquisition and Processing of Information 31

Collectively these functions are called *processing* functions and are another portion of the "housekeeping" segment of the IIS that absorbs considerable resources and must be clearly appreciated by the management to whom the IIS reports. The main groups comprising these functions are descriptive cataloging, subject cataloging, subject classification, and indexing. The functional descriptions that follow will separate the descriptive process from the subject analysis one, with indexing being applicable to both types.

Descriptive Cataloging

Function Pd-1: Usual Book Trade Literature

For books, the most important consideration in descriptive cataloging is determination of the *author*, which may be a personal author (John Jones) or an institutional or corporate author (Lincoln Laboratory, MIT or T. J. Watson Research Center, IBM). There are widely accepted rules for establishing the *author entry*, and first preference would be that of the Anglo-American cataloging rules issued by the American Library Association (ALA).[1] The second preference is for "ALA Rules"[2] and, since this has been the accepted standard until recent years, many of the catalogs and reference works consulted will have used this form. Therefore, familiarity with it is advised. (The short forms "Anglo-American" and "ALA" will be used for the remainder of this chapter to refer to these two standards.) Author entries may be verified in the NVC.[3]

As will be discussed more fully in the reports function, the ALA calls for the *indirect* form of author entry (MIT. Lincoln Laboratory) rather than the *direct* form (Lincoln Laboratory.) that should be used by IIS's. If a personal author has a special relationship to the contents, an indication of his or her role—for example, "editor" for editor, "trans." or "tr." for translator, or "comp." for compiler—is given following his or her name. If there is more than one personal author, the first author is given surname first, and the others are entered in normal order. Esoterics, such as titles of nobility and foreign-language usage, are very well covered in the ALA cataloging rules, but the IIS's purposes would be better served by entering Lord Kelvin and Lord Barbizon of Tara under "K" and "B," respectively, without worrying about their family names, as Anglo-American permits. Similarly, Professor Doctor Theodore von Karman would be simply entered as "Karman, Theodore von."

After the author, the next element to be entered is the *title*. (Where no author is identified for an item, the title is the most important identification entry point or "main entry.") Although the *title entry* is largely straightforward, some complications arise when the item is part of a larger work or is a translation. In these cases, an additional entry is given to indicate the title of the larger work or to show the title in the original language, respectively.

After the title entry comes the *imprint entry*: place of publication, name of publisher, and date. Short names of publishers are used (McGraw-Hill rather than McGraw-Hill Book Publishing Company). On date, the copyright date is also shown when it varies from the date on the title (main) page of the book. The *collation entry* lists the number of pages, followed by abbreviations for illustrations, maps, and other graphics. A *series notation*, if any, follows in parenthesis. This information may be found on the verso (other side) of the title page, or on a following page of the book. *Contents notes* may follow, especially in collective works, and other brief notes in paragraph form may follow when required.

Recommendation: *For descriptive cataloging of books, the Anglo-American rules be followed and gradually simplified as experience shows which elements or details are less useful. (To follow the reverse policy is to increase the possibility of having to do the work over.) The elements to be included are author, title, imprint, collation, series notes, and other notes.*

In the case of periodicals, establishment of the *title* is the most important consideration. ALA practice calls for: *American Chemical Society Journal.* Newer practice, however, and more understandable to users is: *Journal of the American Chemical Society.* Collation includes number of volumes and an indication of frequency (number of issues per year). In cases where specific articles of exceptional importance are given individual entries in the catalog, the entries are termed "analytics." The entries are patterned after those for monographs and conclude with reference to the periodical's title, volume, date, and the pages occupied by the article. If the periodicals are to be bound, the publisher's volume indication is not necessarily the sole guide for the physical binding of the volumes in the IIS. Other factors to be considered include optimum thickness for physical handling, inclusion or exclusion of advertisements (particularly those showing new instruments), and presence of special trade show or directory issues.

Recommendation: *The main approach to periodicals be by title, and the form of name used by the most important periodical indexing service to the IIS be followed; also, binding of periodical volumes be on a highly selective basis and subject to periodic review.*

For pamphlets and other materials for which no specific recommendation is made, follow the inelegant but graphic KISS principle (*K*eep *i*t simple, *S*tupid).

Summary Recommendation: In this function and all other cases where the resulting records are to be shared with others at different locations (particularly where the records will be mechanized), we recommend that the applicable standards of the American National Standards Institute (ANSI) and the appropriate international standards (ISO) be used. Table 3.1 lists the available standards developed by the ANSI Committee Z39 on Library Work, Documentation, and Related Publishing Practices for concepts, definitions, terminology, letters and signs, practices, and methods in the fields of library work; for preparation and utilization of documents; and for those aspects of publishing that affect library methods and use.

Table 3.1 Standards Available from ANSI Committee Z39 on Library Work, Documentation, and Related Publishing Practices

Z39. 1-1967	Periodicals: Format and Arrangement	$3.25
Z39. 2-1971	Bibliographic Information Interchange on Magnetic Tape	6.00
Z39. 4-1968	Basic Criteria for Indexes	3.25
Z39. 5-1969	Abbreviation of Titles of Periodicals	3.25
Z39. 6-1965	Trade Catalogs	3.00
Z39. 7-1968	Library Statistics	5.50
Z39. 8-1968	Compiling Book Publishing Statistics	2.75
Z39. 9-1971	Identification Number for Serial Publications	2.75
Z39.10-1971	Directories of Libraries and Information Centers	3.50
Z39.11-1972	System for the Romanization of Japanese	3.50
Z39.12-1972	System for the Romanization of Arabic	3.00
Z39.13-1971	Advertising Books	3.50
Z39.14-1971	Writing Abstracts	3.50
Z39.15-1971	Title Leaves of a Book	3.00
Z39.16-1972	Preparation of Scientific Papers for Written or Oral Presentation	4.25
Z39.19-1974	Guidelines for Thesaurus Structure, Construction and Use	4.50
Z39.18-1974	Guidelines for Format and Production of Scientific and Technical Reports	4.00
Z39.20-1974	Criteria for Price Indexes for Library Materials	3.00
Z39.21-1973	Book Numbering	3.00
Z39.22-1974	Proof Corrections	5.00
Z39.23-1974	Standard Technical Report Number	3.00

These standards should be ordered directly from the American National Standards Institute, 1430 Broadway, New York, NY 10018. The order may be prepaid and avoid the minimum charge of $5.00 or the handling charges for orders over $5.00. Source: <u>ANSI News about Z39</u> (New York: ANSI, July 1975).

Function Pd-2: Government Documents (Unclassified)

The main question here is whether to follow the form of the Anglo-American rules for institutional (corporate) authors or the practice of a major dissemination service such as the National Technical Information Service. Alternatives are illustrated as follows: "U. S. Department of Commerce. Bureau of Foreign and Domestic Commerce"; or "Bureau of Foreign and Domestic Commerce, U. S. Department of Commerce"; or even "Commerce, Department of. Foreign and Domestic Commerce Bureau."

Recommendation: *Where the items in the IIS files are largely those distributed by the Superintendent of Documents, the same form of entry used in the*

Superintendent's Monthly Catalog *be used by the IIS. Similarly, if the material is primarily distributed by the NTIS, the same form of entry as used in its published indexes be used by the IIS.*

Function Pd-3: Government Documents (Security Classified)

Recommendation: *The form of entry in the indexes of the Defense Documentation Center, which normally will be consistent with the NTIS form, be used by the IIS. (Note: On occasion, the entry itself will be a security classified matter.) Always show all contract numbers as notes in IIS listings.*

Function Pd-4: Government Specifications

Recommendation: *The form of entry in the indexes supplied by the Superintendent of Documents be used by the IIS.*

Function Pd-4a: Trade Association Specifications

Recommendation: *The designations assigned by the trade associations be used by the IIS. Where their usage varies from the government indexes, urge coordination of future listings.*

Function Pd-4b: Company Specifications

Recommendation: *Designations assigned by company specifications official be used in IIS entries. Inform the official of any variances in company practice from other indexes and encourage consistency.*

Function Pd-5: Government Patents

Recommendation: *Entry be made under the name of country, followed by number assigned by issuing government agency. Patentee may have designated an assignee, which also needs to be indicated in IIS listings.*

Function Pd-6: Reports with Limited Distribution (External Origin)

These reports are normally short, may be of periodic nature, and may have multiple series and/or contract number indications.

IIS Functions: Acquisition and Processing of Information

Recommendation: *The form of entry be in NTIS form or close approximation thereto. Show all contract and series indications, plus note of how distribution (use) is to be limited.*

Function Pd-7: Reports with Limited Distribution (Internal Origin)

The number of these items handled by the IIS will increase as confidence builds in the IIS.

Recommendation: *Entry be made according to the official company organizational designation. Where this practice differs from NTIS form, encourage tendency toward that form. Show all project, series, and code identifications. Show clearly any limitations on distribution (use) of the material.*

Function Pd-7a: Laboratory Notebooks

Recommendation: *Entry be made under personal author(s). Show serial number, project numbers, and organizational unit.*

Function Pd-8: Material on "No Cost" Basis

Recommendation: *The most appropriate form of entry from the preceding functions be used. KISS would pertain here, too.*

Function Pd-9: Microcopy Replacements for Full Texts

Recommendation: *A note on form and quantity of microcopies be added to the original records.*

Function Pd-10: Correspondence with Substantive Content

This material normally consists of short, numerous memos, reports, and letters, with known distribution, to external or internal addressees. The IIS files may contain original or carbon (duplicated) copies.

Recommendation: *Entry be made first by individual author, followed by company organization designation, then by serial number or other company records management indication. Indicate whether original or carbon is in the IIS files. The listing may also include distribution list.*

36   Industrial Information Systems

*Function Pd-11: Comprehensive Indexes to Materials by
Subject Discipline or Format*

   Recommendation: *Entry be made by title; also clearly show years covered and volumes held.*

Function Pd-12: "Make or Buy" Decisions

   Recommendation: *The information sources resulting from these decisions be entered as provided for in preceding relevant functions.*

Function Pd-13: Formal Information Exchange (External)

   Recommendation: *Entry be made under names of company officials and their organization designations who neogtiated the exchange. As a note, show scope of material covered and date of expiration.*

Function Pd-14: Informal Information Exchange (External)

   This area is an innovative one with ill-defined boundaries. An unanswered question is: Will attempts to "track" informal communication so interfere with the process as to destroy it?
   Recommendation: *For obvious candidate areas, scope and principle parties involved be shown in listings; also inform company participants of entries on themselves. As confidence in procedure improves, gradually extend files into murkier areas, if only for "trade secrets" protection consideration.*

Function Pd-15: "Deacquisitions" or Weeding

   Recommendation: *For some items, a note, "Discarded, month, year," be added to the original records; for most materials, the record of existence be withdrawn and discarded. The tendency should be for proportion of records simply discarded to increase.*

Function Pd-16: On-Line Data Bases

   Recommendation: *Entry be made by title; also, show years covered, and aids to their use (manual, thesaurus, and so forth).*

IIS Functions: Acquisition and Processing of Information

Summary Recommendation

Accurately describe acquired material so as to determine its presence in existing IIS files. For new material, complete the descriptive records as recommended in Functions Pd-1 through Pd-16 above. We also recommend maximum use be made of existing authoritative sources and lists.

Subject Cataloging, Subject Classification, and Indexing

Function Ps-1: Usual Book Trade Literature

For books, the important aspect of *subject cataloging* is the assignment of terms describing the discipline(s) of knowledge they include. The identifying element may be a verbal phrase, a number within a classification system, a graphical symbol, or combinations of one or a number of each of these. Subject heading lists may be comprehensive or may cover a specific discipline. An example of the first is the "Subject Heading List"[4] of the Library of Congress (LC), which shows the terms used at the bottom of the Library's widely distributed "LC Cards" and for its magnetic tape system (MARC). A penalty of using such an exhaustive listing is the difficulty of keeping current in all fields. For example, the list until 1972 used "Electronic Calculating Machines" instead of "Computers." It is an alphabetical list, with cross-references ("see" and "see also") for terms not used to the list's alternate or preferred terms.

An example of a specific discipline list, prepared by Project LEX of the Engineers Joint Council and the Defense Documentation Center, is the "Thesaurus of Engineering Terms."[5] It is more up-to-date in terminology and shows more relationships ("refer from," "refer to," "broader term," and "narrower term") between terms than does the LC list. Further, it has more direct (uninverted headings) than does LC with its traditional inverted headings that give the noun first. Another source of specific subject headings is the principal comprehensive indexes that cover the published literature in the company's main subject area(s). Typically, the headings are assigned by subject specialists and may be more up-to-date than those in the "Thesaurus of Engineering Terms."

In subject cataloging, some limitation on the number of headings assigned to a given book are normally made for economic reasons. Thus the Library of Congress might use no more than two or three subject terms to describe the content of a symposium volume, while an indexing service covering that same volume might use fifteen to twenty terms, and if it were for inclusion in an "on-line" data base, even more might be used.

The best-known comprehensive *subject classification* schemes are the Dewey Decimal System (celebrating its centennial) and the Library of Congress classification used with its "LC Cards." The Dewey scheme is almost entirely numerical, with all knowledge divided into ten spheres, which are in turn subdivided into ten, and so forth. As such numbers can get long, some organizations use the letter "C" to represent "621.38195," which is the Dewey assigned number for computers, and then add the required subdivision digits.

A variant on the Dewey Decimal System is the Universal Decimal Classification (UDC), which is used internationally (in the USSR its use is so ordered by government edict). Elaborate detailed subdivisions have been developed by committees of the International Federation for Documentation (FID) for seventy-five years, and UDC schedules are issued in several languages and from several sources. (That in English is published by the British Standards Institute as BS 1000C in separate parts.[6]) Under the UDC scheme, it is possible to assign more than one subject classification to an item and to connect the different terms by a colon. The basic UDC number for computers is 681.3. The Engineering Societies Library, New York, uses the UDC numbers as main entry points for its catalog that is available in printed book form.[7] There is unevenness in the currency and depth of coverage of UDC schedules, but if the company's subject area is currently covered, it merits serious consideration.

The Library of Congress classification scheme uses initial alphabetical characters plus numbers. For example, the basic LC classification number for computers is QA 76. Most relevant to this discussion are Schedule "Q" for Science[8] and Schedule "T" for Technology.[9] Most of the academic libraries the IIS will be relating to will either have collections fully under LC classification or are in the process of converting from Dewey to LC. The main reasons for the change are more current LC schedules in most subject disciplines and the ultimate possibility of machine searches on-line using the LC number as the first and basic approach to the on-line system.

Another option the IIS can consider is to use the special classification scheme adopted by a professional society or indexing service. One such numerical scheme is that issued by the American Institute of Physics to cover physics and astronomy.[10] The University of Toronto has a loan collection of special subject headings lists and classification schemes as developed by members of the Special Libraries Association.[11] Such classification schemes and lists are preferable to the many special lists we have seen drawn up over the years by well-intentioned colleagues in government and industry, in which a favorite device has been simply to expand a classification from a well-known encyclopedia or handbook in a particular subject discipline.

Recommendation: *Books be cataloged using the subject terms in a contemporary thesaurus covering the main subject disciplines of interest to the company; this information be supplemented by terms selected from the principal comprehensive indexing service in the company's prime field; the average number of subject entries per book be six to ten "analytics" each rather than the two to*

IIS Functions: Acquisition and Processing of Information   39

three of conventional practice; preference be given to the Library of Congress classification system over the Universal Decimal Classification; not too much reliance be placed on a classification scheme of a particular disicipline; and finally, periodicals not be classified by subject but be arranged alphabetically in one list or grouped broadly in major subject categories.

Function Ps-2: Government Documents (Unclassified)

The same terminology used for subject headings of books can be used for government documents. Alternatively, the terms used in the recompilation of indexes to the *Monthly Catalog* done by the United States Historical Institute (a nonofficial publisher with the evident "blessing" of the Superintendent of Documents) can be used. Most IISs would not have enough material in this category to use the elaborate alpha-numeric classification scheme used by the Superintendent of Documents.

Recommendation: *The same set of subject terms chosen for Function Ps-1 be used for subject cataloging and indexing of unclassified government documents; further, the same classification scheme chosen for Function Ps-1 be used as well.*

Function Ps-3: Government Documents (Security Classified)

Some subject terms, project names, and code designations will themselves be security classified and not appear in the lists recommended in Ps-1.

Recommendation: *Unless the proportion of security classified terms is more than a third of the total volume of entries, the sources recommended in Function Ps-1 be used, supplemented by the classified listings of Defense Documentation Center or that of the issuing security agency.*

Function Ps-4: Government Specifications

Recommendation: *The indexes supplied with the material be used.*

Function Ps-4a: Trade Association Specifications

Recommendation: *The subject and index terms assigned by the trade association be used. Where their usage varies from the government indexes, urge their coordination in the future.*

Function Ps-4b: Company Specifications

Recommendation: *The subject and index terms assigned by the company specifications official be used. Inform the official of any variances in company practice from other indexes and encourage consistency.*

Function Ps-5: Government Patents

Recommendation: *The subject classification and terminology of the U. S. Patent Office or other foreign patent-granting agency be used.*

Function Ps-6: Reports with Limited Distribution (External Origin)

Recommendation: *Sources of terms as for Function Ps-1 and/or Ps-2 be used; also, the same classification scheme as for the former be used.*

Function Ps-7: Reports with Limited Distribution (Internal Origin)

Recommendation: *Sources of terms as for Function Ps-1 and/or Ps-2 be used, supplemented by proprietary terms and/or classification relationships. Index in greater detail than for material of trade or external origin.*

Function Ps-7a: Laboratory Notebooks

Recommendation: *Aids should be in greater detail than for Function Ps-7 and contain more proprietary considerations. Significant, innovative indexing can be done.*

Function Ps-8: Material on "No Cost" Basis

Recommendation: *Sources of terms as for Function Ps-1 be used.*

Function Ps-9: Microcopy Replacement for Full Text

Subject cataloging and indexing is done for the original form of the material.

IIS Functions: Acquisition and Processing of Information 41

Function Ps-10: Correspondence with Substantive Content

Recommendation: *Aids as for Laboratory Notebooks (Function Ps-7a) be used, plus still further nontechnical proprietary considerations.*

Function Ps-11: Comprehensive Indexes to Materials by Subject Discipline or Format

Recommendation: *These be cataloged broadly as they cover broad areas. They are indexes in themselves.*

Function Ps-12: "Make or Buy" Decisions

Recommendation: *Subject cataloging and indexing of the resulting product be provided as in preceding relevant functions.*

Function Ps-13: Formal Information Exchange (External)

Recommendation: *Terminology as in preceding functions be used.*

Function Ps-14: Informal Information Exchange (External)

Recommendation: *Terminology as in preceding functions be used.*

Function Ps-15: "Deacquisitions" or Weeding

Recommendation: *Previously used subject and index terms be cross-referenced to currently used terminology.*

Function Ps-16: On-Line Data Bases

Recommendation: *These be cataloged broadly as they cover broad areas. They are indexes in themselves.*

Summary Recommendation

We recommend existing standard lists of subject headings, classifications, and indexes be evolved toward increasingly specific and relevant processing tools. In this way, internally useful records will be built up and will adequately serve proprietary locative purposes.

NOTES AND REFERENCES

1. C. Sumner Spalding, gen. ed., *Anglo-American Cataloging Rules*, prepared by American Library Association, Library of Congress, the Library Association, and the Canadian Library Association (Chicago: American Library Association, 1967), 400 pp.
2. Clara Beetle, ed., *ALA Cataloging Rules for Author and Title Entries,* prepared by the Division of Cataloging and Classification of the American Library Association, 2nd ed. (Chicago: American Library Association, 1949), 265 pp.
3. *The National Union Catalog, 1956 Through 1967;* a cumulative author list representing Library of Congress printed cards and titles reported by other American Libraries (Totowa, New Jersey: Rowman and Littlefield 1970), v. 1+.
4. *Library of Congress Subject Headings*, prepared by the Subject Cataloging Division—Processing Department, 8th ed. (Washington, D. C.: Library of Congress, 1975), 2v.
5. Engineers Joint Council, *Thesaurus of Engineering and Scientific Terms,* rev. ed. (New York: Engineers Joint Council, 1967), 690 pp.
6. British Standards Institution, *Guide to the Universal Decimal Classification (UDC)*, BS 1000C:1963 (FID No. 345) (London: British Standards Institution, 1963), 128 pp.
7. Engineering Societies Library (New York), *Classed Subject Catalog* (Boston: G. K. Hall, 1963), 13v.
8. U. S. Library of Congress, Subject Cataloging Division, *Classification. Class Q: Science*, 6th ed. (Washington, D. C.: Library of Congress, 1973), 415 pp.
9. U. S. Library of Congress, Subject Cataloging Division, *Technology: Library of Congress Classification: Class T*, 5th ed. (Washington, D. C.: Library of Congress, 1971), 370 pp.
10. Samuel Schiminovich, ed., *Physics and Astronomy Classification Scheme*, ICSUAB (International Classification for Physics) (New York: American Institute of Physics, 1977), 23 p.
11. Case Western Reserve University, Bibliographic Systems Center, *Selected Materials in Classification,* a bibliography compiled by Barbara Denison, (New York: Special Libraries Association, 1968), 142 p.

Chapter 4

IIS Functions: Generation/Production and Dissemination/Utilization of Information

THE GENERATION AND PRODUCTION FUNCTIONS

Acquisitions Function 12, "Make or Buy" Decisions, described in the preceding chapter, presumes a capability exists within the industrial information system so as to give its administrator a real choice on how to proceed to meet a specific need for an information tool. Yet to determine how the tool will be used, the administrator must know how that tool will meet the specific requirements of the crucial, critical users. Thus it follows that a group of functions *bridges* between acquisitions and processing of information on the one hand and *dissemination and utilization* functions on the other. We call these the *generation and production* functions and see them as providing the "leverage" to make a good IIS into a great one.

Function Gp-1: Content (Subject Matter) Development

Generating information and/or products is the reason for existence of each unit within the company. There is an omnipotential for massive outpouring of facts: Some will be significant, some will be of transitory interest, some will be of conflicting import, and some will be wrong. If the ideal IIS is to "begin at the beginning," it will be involved in alerting all units to the potential the information they generate will have on achieving the company's objectives and how their formulation of it can maximize that potential (through the operation of the IIS, of course.)
   Recommendation: *The IIS should include an active records management component that will assist all company units with forms and procedures for*

information recording, accumulation, and disposal; further, it should advise company officials on storage and protection facilities and techniques required for continued existence of the company despite natural disasters and equivalent emergencies.

Function Gp-2: Editorial

The purpose of this function is to insure that the company says what it means so that it might more surely mean what it says. A further purpose is to save the time of "front-line" people who are more interested in uncovering knowledge than in communicating it.

Recommendation: *A company editorial policy be developed with the advice of the IIS; editorial personnel be assigned to the larger units and to active collaboration with the smaller units (even by "taking in" some of their work as required or appropriate); quality standards be stratified in the following order of increasing severity: Informal (General, Internal, and External) and Formal (General, Internal, and External); and charts be supplied by IIS for ease in locating the applicable standard to a given situation.*

Function Gp-2a: Informal (General)

Recommendation: *Minimum requirements should include labeling of what the information is, who developed it, for whom it was done, what were the assumptions, what were the (tentative) conclusions, and what are the recommended next steps? (The utility of standard forms is obvious in this function.)*

Function Gp-2a1 (Internal): The principal problem is to resist "short-cutting" to save time, thereby forgetting that quality informal information undergirds quality formal information.

Function Gp-2a2 (External): This information may be generated by correspondence (preferred) or orally.

Function Gp-2b: Formal (General)

Recommendation: *More effort be given formal information development than the informal one, both in assistance rendered and in monitoring. Conclusions should be firmer and follow-up insured as to next steps to be taken.*

Function Gp-2b1 (Internal): Topics relevant to company tactics or strategy should be pointed out to all units in the company.

Function Gp-2b2 (External): This information must be generated by correspondence that is signed by appropriate company official. Additional impact is gained by hand delivery of items to addressees.

Generation/Production and Dissemination/Utilization of Information   45

Function Gp-3: Graphics

The purpose of this function is to increase the cumulative *impact* of what the company says. Graphic units are very expensive services and are subject to some abuse. They may include capabilities in machine drawing, charts and figures, lettering, photographics, slides and other visual aids, "repro" masters, and conceptualizing. Increasingly sophisticated supplies and equipment extend the capabilities of existing units and personnel. Identification of high-quality practitioners and methods of their long-term motivation are important personnel concerns. The company image begins with this function.

Recommendation: *A company policy on graphics be developed to insure that appropriate quality visualizations accompany company written and oral communications. It should be stratified as under Function Gp-2 and should have such reinforcing elements that the ultimate goal of establishing a desirable, valid, and appropriate company image—both internally and externally—is achieved.*

Function Gp-3a: Informal Graphics

Recommendation: *A limitation on processes to be used for the several strata be set, as the easiest control to monitor. Time and materials to be expended per item is another possibility.*

Function Gp-3a1 (Internal): When IIS graphics persons are detailed to work with project teams around the company, greater timeliness of response to needs is assured, but at the expense of lessened control over IIS resources and dangers of project-colleague pressures to overelaborateness in information products.

Function Gp-3a2 (External): Compliance with minimally stated corporate-wide standards on presentability is to be assured.

Function Gp-3b: Formal Graphics

The quality of graphics employed is the principal difference between formal and informal information presentations.

Recommendation: *Procedures for objective monitoring be developed.*

Function Gp-3b1 (Internal): Project "selling" within the company could result in overuse of graphics. Upgrading or reusing graphics work for external purposes assists in spreading costs.

Function Gp-3b2 (External): Strict compliance with highest standards is to be assured (do it *right*, or don't do it.) Contract for outside services if IIS services are incapable of achieving a particular objective.

Function Gp-4: Production

Given the information and the illustrations, the next step is to produce the information item, be it text, motion picture, recording, exhibit or COM (Computer-output-microform). The most usual form, text with illustrations, may vary in quantity from an original plus carbons to hundreds or thousands of copies, and from a single page to multiple signatures of pages, from black and white to multicolor, from self-cover to leather binding, and from transitory (e.g., telephone books) to stockholder presentations to permanent reference books. Where formerly it was possible to construct a direct-reading chart on when it was economical to go from a carbon process to a stencil process to an offset process to a letter-press process, those differences are "smeared" by equipment and supply improvements and the rise of the all-pervading electrostatic copy machines. Now that everyone with a photocopier key can become a producer, it is more important than ever that the company adopt the stratified quality standards mentioned earlier and recognize a rich variety of means for achieving them. Major savings in costs and in paper conservation are more generally palatable goals than the IIS objectives of consistency and appropriateness in information product.

The motion picture film or television tape can be an exceedingly expensive toy or the major difference between the achievement or failure of a major company program. Almost invariably, out-of-house capability must be secured on contract to supplement the in-house capabilities or to carry to completion concepts conceived and proved-out on in-house facilities.

Recordings are another area where outside aide is frequently required. These may bring the Christmas message from the chairman of the board, or when suitably witnessed, prove compliance with an environmental standard on noise pollution.

Exhibits may be for trade shows, for high school science fairs, or for permanent exhibits (such as an early mechanical heart machine to be included in the new halls of the Smithsonian Institution as was the case for the GM Research Laboratories). Firms exist for the sole purpose of constructing such exhibits, beginning at any stage in the process and ending at their door or with set-up on site.

Recommendation: *A stratified company policy be developed to ensure the appropriate and economic production of important information items; further, such policy include the conditions under which outside assistance will be contracted for and the means whereby procured quality of performance is to be judged. A strategy for choosing among the various items should also be included.*

Function Gp-4a: Informal Production

Recommendation: *More text and less outside help be used than for the formal information items.*

Generation/Production and Dissemination/Utilization of Information 47

Function Gp-4a1 (Internal): The information items are at the lower end of the spectrum in quantity and sophistication.

Function Gp-4a2 (External): The information items represent a considerable step upward and are nearly equivalent to the level that follows. Monitoring will ensure suitability.

Function Gp-4b: Formal Production

The information items are frequently tied to reporting of project, product, or goal achievement.

Recommendation: *Procedures be established for enforcement of standards/policies; following these is essential.*

Function Gp-4b1 (Internal): See Function Gp-4b.

Function Gp-4b2 (External): The IIS has prime responsibility to certify meeting of highest standards within realm of appropriateness and economic resources.

Function Gp-5: Public Relations Analysis

Recommendation: *In view of the totality of information produced by the company and that about the company gleaned from external sources, the appropriate company official(s) be assisted by the IIS in monitoring and affecting the company's meaning to its several "publics" and vice versa.*

Function Gp-5a: Informal PR

The information items require input from multiple sources and concentrated analysis. They are less structured than the formal items.

Recommendation: *See Function Gp-5.*

Function Gp-5a1 (Internal): See Function Gp-5a.

Function Gp-5a2 (External): See Function Gp-5a. The information items are slightly more structured than the informal-internal ones.

Function Gp-5b: Formal PR

The information items are far more structured than those in the Gp-5a functions.

Recommendation: *See Function Gp-5a; also, statements of company position and plans for action should be part of the items and appropriate company officials involved in drafting them.*

Function Gp-5b1 (Internal): See Function Gp-5b.

Function Gp-5b2 (External): See Function Gp-5b. The information items include commitments as to courses of action.

Function Gp-6: Commercial Analysis

This function calls for the creating of proprietary information from generally available external information. There is a need for circumspect procedures and discreet staff. Defensive or marketing reasons may be impetus to enter a specific area of inquiry and analysis. Care must be taken to separate this function from trade association relationships.

Recommendation: *A commercial analysis function be established to create proprietary information from generally available external information; operations emphasis be on circumspection, reliability, and search for indications of needed company response in either strategy or tactics; and recommendations be made to appropriate company officials for their action.*

Function Gp-6a: Informal CA

Recommendation: *See Function Gp-6; tactics should be emphasized.*
Function Gp-6a1 (Internal): The information items may be subject to compartmentalized security.

Function Gp-6b: Formal CA

Recommendation: *See Function Gp-6; strategy should be emphasized.*
Function Gp-6b1 (Internal): See Function Gp-6a1.

Function Gp-7: Technical Analysis

This function is similar to Function Gp-6, except that it is largely limited to scientific and technical information. It is a more widely practiced activity than Gp-6, and the results are more widely disseminated. Results may also be input into Gp-6 functions.

Recommendation: *A unit be established to consider implications and voids observed in "state-of-the-art" reports and other accumulations of hither-to unrelated phenomena; further, the results be widely disseminated within the the company and externally to the extent permitted by company policy.*

Generation/Production and Dissemination/Utilization of Information   49

Function Gp-7a: Informal TA

These information items provide a means to "showcase" the company's technical competence.
Recommendation: *See Function Gp-7.*
Function Gp-7a1 (Internal): Morale benefits are heightened when specific tasks are "farmed out" to locations and credit is given for the resultant contributions.
Function Gp-7a2 (External): See Function Gp-7a1. Peer recognition is "sweeter" when received from outside the organization. Also, some review is implied before the information items are released.

Function Gp-7b: Formal TA

Recommendation: *See Function Gp-7a; emphasis should be on broader conclusions and more widely accepted problems.*
Function Gp-7b1 (Internal): See Function Gp-7.
Function Gp-7b2 (External): See Functions Gp-7a2 and Gp-7b. The highest possible morale benefits may be realized, and the strictest possible review is required before release of the items.

Function Gp-8: Translation

Material from both company and open literature sources are received in languages other than the company's official language (usually English) and have to be translated before its significance within its field of knowledge and its impact on the achievement of the company's objectives is known. The information items may vary from an article by a Nobel Prize winner in a major periodical to an on-line information retrieval program for cathode-ray terminal access written by a foreign subsidiary staff. Maintenance manuals are an example of the need for the reverse function: *from* English to a national language for marketing reasons.
Recommendation: *A unit be established to translate relevant information from a national language to English or from English to a national language; further a portion of the effort be "farmed out" to foreign-born and -educated members of the company staff so as to insure high accuracy and to maintain their competence in their native language for morale purposes. For "overload" situations, a commercial translation agency may be used.*

Function Gp-8a: Informal Translations

The translation may be oral via tape recorder, may be only partial (introduction, summary, legends under figures, and so forth) or may be photocopy of handwritten originals.
Recommendation: *See Function Gp-8.*

Function Gp-8b: Formal Translations

The translation results in a publication, the distribution of which depends on whether the original was from open literature or of company origin. Such translations done from the open literature are normally deposited with the National Translations Center, John Crerar Library, Chicago, to prevent wasteful duplication of effort.
Recommendation: *See Function Gp-8; also, determine whether translation is already on deposit at the National Translation Center.*

Summary Recommendation

We recommend the IIS provide the capability for developing required information that cannot be procured externally or for which the company is uniquely qualified to accumulate and then present that information in a suitable medium for subsequent distribution to appropriate audiences.

THE DISSEMINATION AND UTILIZATION FUNCTIONS

Once the information has been received and processed or else generated and produced by the staff and collaborators of the IIS (and all items have been given a unique means of identification), then its existence is to be brought to the attention of appropriate patrons within and without the company so that it can be utilized productively. These functions, dissemination and utilization, are better known and more closely identified with the IIS than the ones described earlier in this chapter and in the preceding one. Company officials might be accustomed, however, to a more passive mode of operation than will be described here. (See the section in Chapter 6 on whether it should be active or passive.)

Function Du-1: Internal Announcement

Many mediums and many "publics" give almost an infinite number of

Generation/Production and Dissemination/Utilization of Information   51

possibilities of ways to announce availability of IIS-stored or -referenced information items. For example, a column on new company publications in the employee monthly letter distributed company-wide, a bulletin board near an isolated division's cafeteria entrance, or a pamphlet offered with a coupon in an institutional advertisement in *Fortune* magazine are on one side. These are to be contrasted with the telephone call to the project manager at 4:25 p.m. to come see the repro proof copy of a new translation that appears to herald a breakthrough in technology in a most troublesome area.

Potential users are now *aware* of the information elements, but the job is not done: they must be provided convenient access to a paper copy or to a microform reader or to a tape recorder or to a terminal as appropriate. Then they must be assisted in ingesting that information, even if it is necessary for the IIS to compile, for example, a glossary of proprietary code words for their special use. Information is a resource to be totally used in achieving a company's objectives and the internal announcement functions are concerned with bringing that state about.

Recommendation: *A wide assortment of means and techniques be employed by the IIS to bring the existence of each and every information element it includes to the attention of the optimal users, whether they be company officials, staff, or employees; further, the users be provided with such intellectual and equipment aids that the relevant content may be applied by them toward achievement of the company's objectives.*

Function Du-1a: Periodic List with Many Categories and Many Items

This function is the normal "shot-gun" approach whereby once a week, or semi-monthly, or the like, a listing of all information elements received and processed by the IIS is routinely sent to a standard distribution list of company names or offices. Such a list has the advantages of economy and predictability, but suffers from the faults of impersonality and lineal increase in bulk with the increase of acquisitions that always accompanies a maturing IIS. Patrons have a definite limit on their tolerance level for list-scanning, and while there are individual variances, typically the higher in the organization chart the intended audience, the shorter the list should be. No periodic announcement list thicker than one-fourth inch should ever be distributed routinely to non-IIS personnel.

Recommendation: *Such lists be inaugurated as "learning tools" by new IISs until progression to modified Selective Dissemination of Information (SDI) services are achievable (see Function Du-1d); needs of archival and marketing functions be verified before terminating such services prematurely.*

*Function Du-1b: Periodic List with Few Categories
and Many Items*

This list is an improvement over the preceding one in user acceptability. It is more costly to distribute and may be nearly the same cost to compile (and an aggregation of these, with necessary overlaps of content, would be definitely more expensive to compile and produce). The increased possibility of useful material among the contents might lead to acceptance of lessened frequency and increased thickness. Thickness is also effected by the fullness of entries included per item: from author and title only; through author and title, plus annotation or abstract; through author and title, plus conclusions and one figure from the text, and so on and so forth.
Recommendation: *See Function Du-1a.*

*Function Du-1c: Periodic List with Few Categories
and Few Items*

This type of list makes possible improvements in acceptance, frequency, and proportion of relevant information. Aggregate production costs are higher.
Recommendation: *See Function Du-1a.*

*Function Du-1d: Group "Current Awareness" or "Selective
Dissemination of Information" (SDI)*

This service is periodic notification of specific information elements that are relatively few in number and that match the interest map of the recipient. This map is called a "profile" and is subject to continual revision as the interest of the recipient changes and as the terms that define its extent yield either too few or too many notifications. Similar SDI systems have and can be handled completely manually, although the logical combinations available for computer matching of files leads to far better products and represent the usual mode. A group profile leads to a more economical service but implies less precision in results.
Recommendation: *A group SDI service be offered early in the IIS's evolution so as to advertise its existence and accumulate good will toward its future; further, a standard SDI machine program be used.*

*Function Du-1e: Individual "Current Awareness" or "Selective
Dissemination of Information" (SDI)*

This function is the next step up from the initial or group SDI's. It results

Generation/Production and Dissemination/Utilization of Information 53

in maximum good will when excellent use is made of "feedback" from the users. As this version is more expensive than Function Du-1d, most IIS's use a mixture of group and individual SDIs.

Recommendation: *Individual SDIs be offered after the group program has been proved out; emphasis be placed on proper use of "feedback"; and optimum balance be sought between expense and user satisfaction of the two modes.*

Function Du-1f: "Gatekeeper" SDI

There are certain persons within the company to whom both inside people (staff and employees) and outsiders turn to for knowledge about what's going on within the company or within a major subject field. They have been located by researchers at every organizational level and every chronological bracket. Whether they are called "gatekeepers" or "stars" is immaterial; what is crucial is that they be identified and be given every IIS aid in receiving a broad spectrum of input so that they may do well "what comes naturally."

Recommendation: *The "gatekeepers" in the company be identified and nurtured so as to perform as affiliates (formal or informal) of the IIS staff. SDI is but one of the custom aids they should receive.*

Function Du-2: External Announcement

This service has less variety in vehicles but is larger in number of copies than the preceding internal services. It needs to be carefully monitored so as to insure match of proper vehicle with proper segment of the public. Public relations and marketing objectives are crucial in dictating adjustments in this group of functions. (Note: A recent example of the formal advertising of a company's information pamphlets to the IIS community was the September 2, 1975 mailing to Special Libraries Association (SLA) members of INCO offered "more than 200 technical bulletins, catalogs, and data sheets pertaining to nickel-containing materials throughout industry" as listed in the revised *Review of Available Literature*. It was 24 pages in length with attached "bingo" reply card and was printed in 15,000 copies.[1]

Recommendation: *Appropriate announcements be made outside the company of information originated within the company when such practice would advance the public relations and marketing goals of the company; also, secondary goals include achieving better technological reputation and recruitment of staff in scarce skills and of minority origin.*

*Function Du-2a: Periodic Lists with Many Categories
and Items (External)*

Comprehensive lists are a less usual function for external distribution.
Recommendation: *Distribution of such comprehensive lists be limited to trade association colleagues and crucial university sources.*

*Function Du-2b: Periodic List with Few Categories
and Many Items (External)*

This type of list is somewhat more usual than the preceding one.
Recommendation: *Distribution should include those in the preceding function, plus relevant trade press.*

*Function Du-2c: Periodic List with Few Categories
and Few Items (External)*

Recommendation: *Distribution be as in Function Du-2b, but with wider selection of trade press.*

*Function Du-2d: Group "Current Awareness" or Selective
Dissemination of Information (SDI)*

This function could be most exceptional as an external service.
Recommendation: *Crucial public relations or marketing reasons be established for its existence.*

*Function Du-3: Response to Specific Internal Inquiry
(Retrospective Service)*

The operation of the IIS should result in a higher awareness of all to company information needs. Thus, previously ignored needs will now be recognized and fulfillment sought; some of these needs will be clarified by the periodical awareness vehicles utilized; and there will be an increasing dissatisfaction with simplistic responses and "glossing over" of details. The IIS management should continuously monitor the appropriateness of responses to inquiries in order to avoid such faults as using a ten pound sledge to crush an ant. Among other criteria, the following should be considered in rating the appropriateness of a response to a user inquiry: its relevance to a perceived company mission; its relationship to both the command and the overt response of the user to the information of the subject; its relationship to the company's competencies; its relationship to both the position within the company hierarchy and the physical location of the user; the IIS's estimate of its credibility and reliability; and its implications for IIS present functions and their necessary modifications for the future. Obviously, a mutual education process exists between the users and the IIS, whereby the users increase in their sophisticated use of information and press the IIS to more innovative and higher quality information staff, services, and products.

Recommendation: *Accurate and appropriate responses be made to all work-related informational inquiries received from company officials, staff, and employees; where answers to inquiries are not available within the IIS itself, its corps of "affiliated" staff experts from subject fields, or other internal sources, the answer be aggressively sought from appropriate external sources; a program of continuously quality monitoring IIS responses that includes solicited feedback from users be followed; and finally, as resources permit and the IIS public relations programs requires, nonwork-related informational inquiries from company officials, staff, and employees be handled but on a lower priority basis.*

Function Du-4: Response to Specific External Inquiry (Retrospective Service)

Requests for retrospective information will originate from announcement services sent "outside," contacts made by company speakers to specific groups, by liaison officers carrying out assignments, and by "gatekeepers." Inquiries will also come from the general public when the company has a reputation of being interested or capable in a given subject field (to take a 1975 issue as an example, a manufacturer of propellants for aerosol cans.) There will inevitably be a certain proportion of "crank" mail to be handled as well.

Recommendation: *Appropriate responses be made to inquiries from the outside as provided by company public relations and marketing goals and strategies; also, feedback be used both for the improvement of services and as input to possible modifications of company central policies.*

Function D-5: Full Text Distribution to Automatic List

After the operation of the generation and production functions of the IIS has resulted in an inventory of copies of an information product, the most effective mode of distributing them is to a list of persons or units that are known to be interested in the subject content and for which addressed labels are on hand. Distribution lists have to be "tuned" like a fine piano: Employment of too coarse categories as well as noncurrent addresses for recipients both waste copies, while use of too fine categories leads to some potential users not receiving copies and needing to submit individual requests for them. The latter problem delays the user and results in higher distribution costs. A potential tie-in between the information product distribution lists and categories in the company's records management program needs to be explored.

Mail volumes that result from this function can be large and can affect company mail service adversely. GE uses its own trucks to handle all company mail between Schenectady, New York, and Fort Wayne, Indiana, so information products would not be a particular problem. On the other hand, IBM "drop-ships" all its publications for European customers and company locations and laboratories to Copenhagen by SAS air freight where they are placed in the Danish mails for forwarding to addressees. A number of organizations use KLM's Schiphol facility at Amsterdam for similar purposes. Use of latest equipment for publication distribution and efficient warehousing is exemplified by IBM's facility at Mechanicsburg, Pennsylvania. An idea of its scale is provided by noting that major revision in the IBM Model 360 system required nearly nine boxcars of paper stock for printing.

Recommendation: *Maximum utilization be made of distribution of information products (especially in paper on microfiche form) to standing lists of persons and/or units having a reasonable requirement for them; such lists be under continuous review, including involvement of report authors themselves; and the most efficient equipment and procedures be utilized for physical delivery to users.*

Function Du-6: Custom "State-of-the-Art" Request Compilation on Major Internal Request

Due to high expense for the compilation of such reports, the maximum benefit should be sought, whether for precious lead time over competition or for maximum prestige impact internally or externally as company tactics or strategy dictates. A letter of transmittal should accompany the item so as to heighten the impact.

Recommendation: *Such materials be distributed on a highly custom basis and be accompanied by letter of transmittal.*

Function Du-7: Custom "State-of-the-Art" Compilation on External Request

This function would be a "rare bird" type of activity and dictated by the most important public relations or marketing goals. The advice of the authorizing company official and possibly the outside originator of the request should be sought in establishing the distribution list. It is even possible that the report might appear under the covers of or with a series number of the requestor's agency, with a credit line like "Prepared by the XYZ Company for the U. S. Office of Civil Defense as a public service." A letter of transmittal is also used in most cases.

Recommendation: *Such materials be distributed on a highly custom basis, in consultation with the authorizing official and the originator of the request, and a letter of transmittal accompany copies.*

Function Du-8: Distribution by Subject Content

This function is perhaps the most frequently used by IISs and has great advantages. However, in the usual practice, insufficient feedback from the subject cataloging functions is involved. Thus the specific proprietary subject interrelationships are not exploited. The more numerous the subject "pigeonholes" employed, the more difficult the assignment of people to the categories is, while the paper or film savings mount up.

Recommendation: *Proprietary subject interrelationships should be exploited in establishing information product distribution patterns.*

Function Du-9: Distribution by Functional Assignment

This function is the easiest to follow. It provides scope statements on what organizational units are available and is current on respective responsibilities in accomplishing the company mission.

Recommendation: *A special relationship be established with the staff that sets company structure so that "lead time" is available to aid the IIS in keeping its lists current; also, consideration be given to addressing items to a company unit, rather than to an individual (except in the case of "gatekeepers" or individual SDIs); however, a maximum of personalization as "can be afforded" should be preserved.*

Function Du-9a: Distribution to Board of Directors, Executive Office(s), Subsidiaries, Foreign Operations

This function is a very sensitive area, and top-level assistance is required in establishing distribution pattern. "Overscreen" rather than "underscreen" material sent. Care must be taken to scrupulously observe company security requirements as well as those of the U. S. government and the host foreign governments.

Recommendation: *Distribution to these groups be established by the IIS manager with advice from higher headquarters as appropriate.*

Function Du-9b: Distribution to and of Fiscal and Comptroller-Type Materials

This function is another highly sensitive area with severe "need-to-know" requirements. The IIS can operate here only after having developed an outstanding reputation for circumspection.

Recommendation: *The IIS administrator actively pursue access to these materials with concurrence of higher management.*

Function Du-9c: Distribution to and of Legal-Type Materials

This function includes information on patents, licensing, copyright, trademarks, and antitrust subjects. Some subareas are sensitive and with strong "need-to-know" requirements (especially where pending or prospective actions are concerned). Other portions require straightforward application of policy.

Recommendation: *See Function Du-9b.*

Function Du-9d: Distribution to and of Personnel-Type Materials

This function includes information on industrial relations (very sensitive indeed), comparable compensation levels as traded with other companies and government installations (sensitive), and inservice and continuing education. It is impossible to disseminate too well the latter information to suit the education staff.

Recommendation: *See Function Du-9b.*

Function Du-9e: Distribution to and of Public Relations-Type Materials

Included in this function are all the "publics" that impinge on or that the company relates to. Government and military relations are probably the most sensitive content in this area, and at the other extreme is the example of the company's public relations staff known to have refused to get involved with coverage of executive's daughters' wedding ceremonies in *The New York Times.* Adding on of local content or references to stock releases is customary, and

Generation/Production and Dissemination/Utilization of Information 59

this practice increases the cruciality of accurate distribution of the customized version to the correct "public."
Recommendation: *See Function Du-9b.*

Function Du-9f: Distribution to and of Social Concerns-Type Materials

These information items may be included partly under several of the preceding subheadings, but are separately listed for emphasis on the urgency in effective distribution. Keeping current on company goals and strategies is a "must" here.
Recommendation: *See Function Du-9b.*

Function Du-9g: Distribution to and of Technology-Type Materials

Included in this function is information that may give valuable lead time to the company. Technology itself and trade secrets might be intertwined and lead to carefully compartmentalized information dissemination. This function is an important part of the reasoning for the earlier emphasis on finding out proprietary subject interrelationships in the processing functions. Too conservative a technology release policy will lead to the competition building up a superior outside reputation for excellence and their staff getting more peer visibility. A larger proportion of research information should be freely available for wide distribution within and outside the company, unless what the company labels as "research" is really "advanced development." The latter is closer to a marketable product and hence becomes more sensitive than research. "Tipping of the hand" is frowned upon by solvent companies. Design and development may be one or two function but in any event is highly time sensitive. Maintainability creeps into this stage because of the widespread interest in consumerism.
Recommendation: *A generous policy be followed on dissemination of research information; also, a dynamic policy on technology dissemination be followed that will simultaneously protect the company's trade secrets position while enhancing the company image of excellence. Involvement of technical project personnel will be of assistance, though they would tend to make overenthusiastic recommendations. (Note: This is a "make or break" function for the IIS and the company itself.)*

Function Du-9h: Distribution to and of Facilities and Construction-Type Materials

The high costs of construction and the repetitive content of facilities planning make for "payoff" in effective information distribution. The most sensitive area here is the preliminary screening of sites of plant location. Widest possible dissemination is to be made of the plans for avoiding environmental-pollution problems in the newly announced area.

Recommendation: *Information in this function be seen as highly time-sensitive and of great community relations potential. Announcements should be by or personally approved by top company officials. Feedback from prospective occupants is to be factored in facilities documentation.*

Function Du-9i: Distribution to and of Production-Type Materials

Included in this function are production methods, techniques, controls, specifications development and application, standardization activities, and quality control. Graphic materials are also important. There will be large quantities of detailed information to distribute on short notice and with frequent revisions. Planning for updating should be precise and clear and possibility of distribution in photocopy or magnetic tape from needs to be carefully considered.

Recommendation: *Highly skilled records management staff be involved in the determination of what and how distribution of production-type information is carried out; further, the tremendous potential cost savings to the company and visibility for the IIS be recognized and exploited.*

Function Du-9j: Distribution to and of Marketing-Type Materials

The tremendous range of information items from catalogs to instruction manuals to technical reports rewritten as glossy sales promotion pieces should be recognized. Up-to-date, comprehensive, and accurate literature forms a valuable adjunct to the sales representative's presence and credibility. (For example, the pharmaceutical company representative leaves with the doctor brochures on the new drug virtually as carefully constructed and authenticated as the process for the preparation of the drug itself.) The more sophisticated the company product, the higher the probability of the information item costs in relation to it. In fact some products may require graphic media to be used on the customer's premises or a neutral conference site. Earnest attention needs to be given to the feedback from "those on the firing line" as marketing representatives.

Recommendation: *Fully appropriate informational units be provided the marketing staff so that they, the customers, and regulatory bodies may*

Generation/Production and Dissemination/Utilization of Information 61

understand precisely the variety, utility, and limitations on each company product, plus its relationship to all other company products and/or services; further, accurate distributive information be maintained so that distribution of updates may be facilitated and feedback may be relayed to production, development, research, or executive arms of the company, as appropriate.

Summary Recommendation

We recommend the IIS provide the means for informing all company officials, staff, and employees (plus, as appropriate, "outsiders") of the existence of informational IIS products and services and then extend optimum assistance for their full, effective, and active use by such patrons in achieving the company's prime objectives.

REFERENCE

1. INCO, *Review of Available Literature* (New York: INCO, 1975), 24 p. (Publication A-572; 5621.)

Chapter 5

IIS Administrative Functions

The two preceding chapters have detailed the groups of operational functions of an industrial information system: the *acquisitions* of information elements and capabilities; identification and content analysis by the *processing* functions of descriptive and subject cataloging, classification, and/or indexing; the *generation and production* of hither-to unobtainable information; and finally, the *dissemination and utilization* of the information.

There are, of course, administrative implications in all of these functions (and in the entire IIS topic), some of which have been hinted at in the functional chapters. In this chapter we intend briefly to cover the administrative implications of the interactions of the operational functions. Decisions on centralization and/or decentralization are so far-reaching that a separate section has been provided on that topic in Chapter 6.

IIS general management principles imply decisions will be made on such issues as style of management to be followed; levels for decision making to be established; degree of creativity to be encouraged; planning process to be used; delegation of authority to be practiced; type of communications, both upward and downward and internal and external, to be encouraged; and methods of motivation to be practiced. The ever present concern for financing is covered in Chapter 9.

ACQUISITIONS

Function Ad-1: Operate Acquisitions Functions

Staff: Professional librarian/technical information officer unit leader(s) with subprofessional and clerical assistance are required. Ingenuity and persistence are required from the former and accuracy in details from the latter. Not as much subject background is required as for the following functions.

Space and *facilities:* Relatively low cost semi-warehousing space with ample bins, tables, and sorting and viewing equipment for material received are required. Other requirements include determination of degree of uniqueness, transient storage means, and transportation to processing for inclusion as IIS input. If government security or company classified material is involved, additional locked areas are required. Convenient means of access to records of prior IIS input is needed.

64   Industrial Information Systems

Materials: Identification and sequence stamps, log books, jackets for transmittal and recording of subsequent processing steps and envelops for return of unneeded materials (too old, out-of-scope, superseded, and so forth) are required.

Funds: After start-up, requirements for staffing are nearly equal to or just exceed those of facilities and materials.

Function Ad-2: Conduct Acquisitions Systems Studies in Materials, Processes, and Services

Staff: Personnel are largely drawn from the IIS manager's staff.

Space: Requirements are minimal since these are "paper studies" with input and feedback from the functional activity. Not much user involvement is required.

Materials: Paper and plastic shortages and filing equipment expense are incentives for this function.

Funds: Expensive innovations are justified if resultant savings are multiplied down the line. Acquisitions are at the "mouth" of the processing pipeline and thus affect all the functions "downstream" from it.

Function Ad-3: Initiate Pilot Acquisitions Systems Operations in Parallel to Function AD-1

This function calls for a substantial amount of duplicate effort, especially at the lower end of the skill spectrum. After a fair test period, all or part of new procedure and resources would be introduced into Function Ad-1.

Staff: Staff workers in Function Ad-2 on temporary duty, plus some temporary clerical workers, are required.

Space: One-fourth to one-third more space is needed.

Materials: An increase of 25 percent is required for a limited time.

Facilities: Alternate equipment for testing is required.

Funds: About the same, or slightly higher, requirements as for the processing functions are required.

PROCESSING

Function Ad-4: Operate Processing Functions

This group of functions is labor intensive and is typically undervalued.

Staff: A higher proportion of professional personnel (management;

catalogers, preferably with some subject background; and subject people with deep interest in information problems of their discipline), but less clerical staff, is required as compared to the acquisitions functions.

Space: More desk space is needed for the professionals, but less area for gross sorting and handling operations. Probably about one-third more space than for acquisitions is required overall.

Materials: Multiple copies of authoritative corporate author lists, subject heading lists, indexing systems, or alternatively, multiple terminals to access files of them are required. Large supplies of input forms (worksheets) and cards or tape for recording the output are needed.

Funds: Nearly one-half of IIS funds are required.

Function Ad-5: Conduct Processing Systems Studies in Materials, Processes, and Services

This function has more technical/professional service content than general management, and policy considerations are time consuming.

Staff: The same number or more professionals from the line operation as from the IIS director's staff are needed. A more conservative ambience prevails in this function than in either acquisitions or dissemination/utilization.

Space and *facilities:* Some additional desk space is needed because of professional composition of team, but not nearly as much as for the acquisitions function studies.

Materials: As and if the study involves a new medium, requirements will include replacement materials; requirements for the study itself are nominal.

Funds: Requirements are more costly than acquisitions studies due to the increased professional component.

Function Ad-6: Initiate Pilot Processing Systems Operations in Parallel to AD-4

This function can be started on a more modest scale than the corresponding pilot acquisitions systems but would have to run longer because of the high stakes involved and need for greater certainty.

Staff: Professionals in Function Ad-5 on temporary duty, plus temporary clerical workers, are required. A sacrifice in quantity of production in the main line is necessary.

Space: Rearrangement of existing work stations plus additional temporary project people requires at least one-fourth more space.

Facilities: Additional book trucks or other means of storage for "in process" books or other informational items are required. Additional means for consulting the record of past holdings as well as means for keeping pilot records in suspense are needed.

Materials: Requirements are somewhat greater, depending upon the proposed new medium and its compatability with materials used under the present conditions.

Funds: Requirements are high since such projects are expensive labor-wise and have no certainty of success.

GENERATION AND PRODUCTION

Function Ad-7: Operate Generation and Production Functions

Staff: Some redeployment from existing editorial, graphic, and reproduction groups, plus supplementation of new employees with backgrounds and skills not now in the facility is required. More creative personnel is needed than for other functions.

Space: Only desk space for editorial elements is required. Graphic units and reproduction units require considerable space, both for projects in process and completed items awaiting distribution.

Materials: Expensive drafting, photographic, and reproduction equipment (some of it very noisy) is required.

Funds: Requirements for this function are expensive and conspicuous, since the activities were formerly widely distributed around the facility and through several budget lines.

Function Ad-8: Conduct Generation and Production Systems Studies in Materials, Procedures, and Services

Staff: A delegation from IIS director's staff, plus outside consultant aid, is required.

Space: Desk space only is needed.

Materials: Requirements are minor.

Funds: Requirements are variable, depending on level of sophistication sought.

Function Ad-9: Initiate Pilot Generation and Production Systems Operations in Parallel to AC-7

Staff: Additional temporary supervisor and technicians are required.

Space: About one-fourth of operational area is needed.

IIS Administrative Functions 67

Materials: Requirements include some expensive experimental units.
Funds: Requirements may be substantial.

DISSEMINATION AND UTILIZATION

*Function Ad-10: Operate Dissemination
and Utilization Functions*

This function is the heart of the rationale for IIS existence and is the function most visible to higher management.

Staff: Skilled assistance of patron personnel (reference), intense involvement of data processing personnel, and active participation of users (feedback) are required.

Space: Open desk and terminal space, book stacks and vertical files, reader tables, and lounge area are needed.

Materials: Special furniture and noninstitutional furnishings as well as data processing supplies are required.

Funds: Requirements are substantial, but readily defendable.

*Function Ad-11: Conduct Dissemination and Utilization
Systems Studies in Materials, Processes, and Services*

Staff: Leading operational professionals, plus consultant personnel, are required.

Space: Requirements are rather modest.

Materials: Mainly data processing supplies are needed.

Funds: Requirements are considerable for data processing time and taped data bases.

*Function Ad-12: Initiate Pilot Dissemination and Utilization
Systems Operations in Parallel to AD-11*

Staff: "Carry over" personnel from the system study (Ad-11) are essential.

Space: Less than for processing functions is required.

Materials: Mainly data processing and reproduction service supplies are needed.

Funds: Requirements are considerable for data processing time and taped data bases. This function requires high stakes, but the potential pay-off is large.

SPECIAL PROGRAMS

Function Ad-13: Institute Career Upgrading Program

   Staff: Minimal increment of personnel effort is required.
   Space: None is needed.
   Material: Requirements are minimal.
   Funds: Requirements are minimal to moderate.

Function Ad-14: Institute User Training and Upgrading Programs

   This function includes all present, potential, and reluctant users, plus their management.
   Staff: Involvement of all IIS professionals is required.
   Space: Effective utilization of existing general educational space and facilities is necessary.
   Materials: Effective graphics and hand-outs are needed.
   Funds: Requirements are moderate.

Function Ad-15: Establish Unequivocably the Worth of Information to the Company

   This function may be seen as an unattainable objective, yet it represents a basic challenge to IIS fulfillment.
   Staff: IIS leader, his or her higher management, and a task force from the comptroller's function are required.
   Space: Minimal desk space is needed.
   Facilities: Access to data processing facilities is required.
   Materials: Requirements are minimal.
   Funds: Requirements are moderate.

FUNCTIONING WITHIN COMPANY GOALS

It is important to recall that execution of the IIS administrative functions is carried out within the envelope of goals of the company itself. These goals have been succinctly stated by the president of Hewlett-Packard Corporation as follows:

> There are four "musts" for a corporation. Number one, of course, is profit. A recent survey of people showed that they believe business profits average about 24 percent; the actual figure is closer to four percent.

The public's mind is confused. No wonder people think there is an unlimited well. An average four percent profit must provide funds for a company to continue to operate. This is not much, especially in inflationary times.

The second "must" is making a contribution. This might be in the form of a technical breakthrough which sets your company apart from its competitors. You should have a good idea of what is needed by customers. Catalog these in your mind and match good ideas with needs.

Third is people. Supervisory training is important in this area. You should spend some time working with the first and second lines of supervisors on how to work with employees and generate ideas.

Fourth is to contribute to society more than you take out. A corporation exists simply because people believe it serves a useful function. Otherwise it is simply legislated out of existence. Corporations and employees should work with community drives and activities and employees should be encouraged to run for offices in government.[1]

REFERENCE

1. William Hewlett, "Profit, People, and Contributions," *Perspective* (Purdue University), July-August 1976:12.

Chapter 6

IIS Administrative Issues

SHOULD THE MODE OF OPERATIONS BE ACTIVE OR PASSIVE?

Industrial information systems are known to exist that cover every possibility in the administration spectrum—that is, from the most active to the most passive style of policy and operations. While elements of a given system can exhibit varying characteristics in this regard, the overall stance of a system may be called its "active-passive quotient."

Being passive may not be wholly bad, even though we mean it to imply service of the kind usually associated with museums (however, recall there is an active glass museum sharing the site of the Corning Glass Works in Corning, New York). The *passive service* exists but makes minimal or no effort to advertise its presence, its holdings, or its services. It is not held accountable for user satisfaction nor is it expected to have evaluated proposals pending for service enhancement.

The ideally *active service* fills all known information needs promptly and fully; seeks out hitherto unperceived needs and postulates ways of reaching them, accepts full accountability for user satisfaction; is in a continuous process of updating and adjusting resources (be they materials, services, products, or staff); and remains at least one budget cycle ahead in planning beyond that of its primary user units.

The value assigned to the terms in Figure 6.1 are arbitrary, but we believe distinguishing that many degrees is possible in the largest IISs with a multiplicity of service units. Most professional consultants should be able to arrive at such an assessment of the "active-passive quotient" of a given system or situation, and unless they have scales that are easily understood, they could be expected to use the one in Figure 6.1.

Our debriefings with higher managers following on-site visits to IIS units have invariably included assessment of their units' degree of activeness. In cases where extenuating circumstances existed—that is, functional assignment of the division, presence of reinforcing or conflicting IIS units, dire financial pressures, manpower freezes, or historical precedents were factors—the effect of these factors on the quotient was reviewed with the officials.

One course of action open to the higher managers would be to review the menu of functions described in Chapters 3 and 4 on acquisitions and on through to dissemination and utilization for the functions they truly saw as required by

72   Industrial Information Systems

Wholly Passive	Neutral	Wholly Active
−5	0	+5
Museums	Many Libraries	Ideal IISs

Figure 6.1 Spectrum of Degrees of Activity of an IIS

their companies. Then they would examine those same functions as charted in the next section on the issue of centralization versus decentralization and indicate those functions that should be wholly active (+5), neutral (0), wholly passive (−5), or of some intermediate value. In this way, they could make *conscious* choices as to the level of functional activity, rather than default on one or a group of functions.

What of the Cost?

There are indeed financial penalties in the short term of IISs that are more active than absolutely required, since museum-type libraries cost far less than the IIS a pharmaceutical firm, for example, finds essential. (It costs less to wait for patrons than to seek them out.) The most important element in the cost of an active program is that for personnel. Active programs require definitely higher quality personnel (better subject backgrounds, for example) and a greater quantity of supporting staff to maximize their output and effectiveness. Communications also cost more in an active service, since more computer support, as well as other equipment, is needed. Facilities and space costs increase less dramatically than personnel costs, which are the most easily "tracked" of all costs.

Summary Recommendations

Good managers should know or be advised of their active-passive quotients; they should make conscious functional choices; and they should know the costs of their programs and weigh any deviations from the norm in order to proceed in a rational manner.

SHOULD THE IIS BE CENTRALIZED OR DECENTRALIZED?

Multiunit IIS's may approach absolute centralization in functions executed on information content, in all formats of information occurance, and for all audiences. The Bell Laboratories technical libraries system is the best known example of such centralization. Its administrator sees the prime benefits of this mode as giving them competence in depth and economy of scale. A wholly decentralized IIS would be a contradiction in terms. The information units in General Electric Company, for example, appear to approach that status. An occasional breakfast together at annual conferences of the Special Libraries Association seems to be the managers' tie.

Intermediate positions on the "C-D" spectrum (see Figure 6.2) are occupied by General Motors Corporation (GM), International Business Machines Corporation (IBM) and E. I. DuPont de Nemours & Company, Inc. (DuP). In the GM case, the solid program of the Research Laboratories library dating from the mid-1920s and before led to de facto centralization of some services and functions before the emergence of the corporation-wide GM Committee on Technical Literature. IBM has had corporate staff guidance, a centralized information retrieval center and service operating in tandem in New York and in France, and exceptionally strong library units in R&D divisional locations. The IBM library managers have met annually in North America and the European managers slightly less regularly. DuPont has combined established, comprehensive libraries with a series of cost-recovered information analysis services established in units consisting of one or a few technical information analysts and administered by the office of the corporate secretary.

In Tables 6.1 through 6.5 recommendations are made *by function* on whether the IIS should follow centralization or decentralization modes. As will be apparent, the tendency is for "housekeeping" to merit the centralization mode and for service to individual users, the decentralized mode. Although the increasing availability of on-line data bases blurs this distinction somewhat in the eyes of the users, what is important is that they feel full and responsive contact with the supplier of their services.

The reader should note that when we recommend "centralization" for a particular function, we do not necessarily mean in the same geographic location or in the same organizational unit. For example, the IBM division having prime responsibility for government contracts is centered in Gaithersburg, Maryland; the information retrieval function is centered in Armonk, New York; while the patent function is centered in Washington, D. C. Yet we consider that IBM is

Wholly Decentralized	*Neutral*	*Wholly Centralized*
−5	0	+5
GE	GM IBM DuP	BTL

Figure 6.2 Spectrum of Degrees of Centralization of an IIS

Table 6.1 Recommendations for Centralization or Decentralization of IIS Functions: Acquisitions

Function No.	Name	Centralization Recommended	Decentralization Recommended
Ac-1	Usual Book Trade Literature (Books, Periodicals, Society Publications)	C	
Ac-2	Government Documents (Unclassified)	C	
Ac-3	Government Documents (Security Classified)	C	
Ac-4	Government Specifications	C	
Ac-5	Government Patents	C	
Ac-6	Reports with Limited Distribution (External Origin)	C	
Ac-7	Reports with Limited Distribution (Internal Origin)		D
Ac-7a	Laboratory Notebooks		D
Ac-8	Materials on "No Cost" Basis		D
Ac-9	Microcopy Replacement for Full Texts	C*	
Ac-10	Correspondence with Substantive Content		D*
Ac-11	Comprehensive Indexes to Materials by Subject Discipline or Format		D
Ac-12	"Make or Buy" Decisions	C	
Ac-13	Information Exchange, Formal (External)	C	
Ac-14	Information Exchange, Informal (External)		D
Ac-15	"Deacquisitions" or Weeding		D
Ac-16	On-Line Data Bases	C	

Note: Abbreviations are as follows: C = function should be/is mainly or completely centralized; C* = function should be/is centralized to a significant extent; D = function should be/is mainly or completely

IIS Administrative Issues   75

Precedents	Notes
C=BTL D=DuP, GE, GM*, IBM	Discounts for quantity buying, but delivery could be to dispersed addresses.
C=BTL D=GE, GM*, IBM	Facilitates use of deposit accounts with disseminators.
C=BTL, GM*, IBM*	Facilitates accountability procedures and negotiations on "need to know."
C=BTL, GM, IBM	Also applies to trade association specifications and company specifications.
C=BTL, GM, IBM	
C=BTL, GM, IBM	Company may have a designated official liaison officer with originator.
C=BTL* D=GM, IBM	Originator normally controls the distribution.
D=GM, IBM	
D=BTL*, GE, GM, IBM	Use liaison officer, if possibility of company obligation exists.
C=BTL D=GE, GM, IBM	Need policy statement to avoid undue variety of microcopy format purchased.
D=GM, IBM	Need for a clear records management policy.
D=GE, GM, IBM	High costs are important factor.
C=BTL D=IBM*	Numerous "make" decisions may justify information generation/publication units.
C=BTL, DuP, GM*, IBM*	Insures policy compliance.
D=GM, IBM	Clearance procedure becomes crucial.
C=BTL D=GM, IBM*	Facilitated by automated bibliographic records and procedures.
C=BTL, DuP*, IBM*	High costs are important factor.

decentralized; and D* = function should be/is decentralized to a significant extent. Where both C* and D* appear in an entry, instances of both modes would/do occur depending upon specific circumstances.

76   Industrial Information Systems

Table 6.2 Recommendations for Centralization or Decentralization of IIS Functions: Processing

Function No.*	Name	Centralization Recommended	Decentralization Recommended
Pd-1/Ps-1	Usual Book Trade Literature (Books, Periodicals, Society Publications)	C	
Pd-2/Ps-2	Government Documents (Unclassified)	C	
Pd-3/Ps-3	Government Documents (Security Classified)	C	
Pd-4/Ps-4	Government Specifications	C	
Pd-5/Ps-5	Government Patents	C	
Pd-6/Ps-6	Reports with Limited Distribution (External Origin)	C	
Pd-7/Ps-7	Reports with Limited Distribution (Internal Origin)		D
Pd-7a/Ps-7a	Laboratory Notebooks		D
Pd-8/Ps-8	Material on "No Cost" Basis		D
Pd-9/Ps-9	Microcopy Replacement for Full Texts	C*	
Pd-10/Ps-10	Correspondence with Substantive Content		D*
Pd-11/Ps-11	Comprehensive Indexes to Materials by Subject Discipline or Format	C	
Pd-12/Ps-12	"Make or Buy" Decisions	C	
Pd-13/Ps-13	Information Exchange, Formal (External)	C	
Pd-14/Ps-14	Information Exchange, Informal (External)		D

Precedents	Notes
C=BTL, IBM* D=GM, IBM	
C=BTL, IBM* D=GM, IBM*	
C=BTL, IBM* D=GM, IBM*	
C=BTL, GM, IBM	
C=BTL, GM, IBM	
C=BTL, GM, IBM	
C=BTL* D=GM, IBM	External aids and authorities would be of limited usefulness.
D=GM, IBM	External aids and authorities would be of limited usefulness.
D=BTL*, GM, IBM	
C=BTL D=GM, IBM	
D=GM, IBM	External aids and authorities would be of limited usefulness.
C=BTL, DuP*, IBM*	
C=BTL D=IBM*	External aids and authorities would be of limited usefulness.
C=BTL, GM*, IBM*	
D=GM, IBM	External aids and authorities would be of limited usefulness.

Industrial Information Systems

Table 6.2 *continued*

Function No.*	Name	Centralization Recommended	Decentralization Recommended
Pd-15/Ps-15	"Deacquisitions" or Weeding		D
Pd-16/Ps-16	On-Line Data Bases	C	

* Pd-1 - Pd-16 = Descriptive Cataloging
  Ps-1 - Ps-16 = Subject Cataloging, Subject Classification and Indexing

Note: Abbreviations are as follows: C = function should be/is mainly or completely centralized; C* = function should be/is centralized to a significant extent; D = function should be/is mainly or completely

Precedents	Notes
C=BTL D=GM, IBM	Option exists for removal with record of existence retained.
C=BTL, DuP*, IBM*	

decentralized; and D* = function should be/is decentralized to a significant extent. Where both C* and D* appear in an entry, instances of both modes would/do occur depending upon specific circumstances.

80 Industrial Information Systems

Table 6.3 Recommendations for Centralization or Decentralization of IIS Functions: Generation and Production

Function No.	Name	Centralization Recommended	Decentralization Recommended
Gp-1	Content (Subject Matter) Development		D
Gp-2	Editorial		D
Gp-2a	Informal		D
Gp-2a1	Internal		D
Gp-2a2	External		D
Gp-2b	Formal		D*
Gp-2b1	Internal		D*
Gp-2b2	External	C*	
Gp-3	Graphics		D
Gp-3a	Informal		D
Gp-3a1	Internal		D
Gp-3a2	External	C*	D*
Gp-3b	Formal	C*	D*
Gp-3b1	Internal	C*	D*
Gp-3b2	External	C*	
Gp-4	Production		D
Gp-4a	Informal		D
Gp-4a1	Internal		D
Gp-4a2	External	C*	D*
Gp-4b	Formal	C*	
Gp-4b1	Internal	C*	D*
Gp-4b2	External	C*	
Gp-5	Public Relations Analysis	C	
Gp-5a	Informal	C	D*
Gp-5a1	Internal	C*	D*
Gp-5a2	External	C	
Gp-5b	Formal	C*	
Gp-5b1	Internal	C*	D*
Gp-5b2	External	C	
Gp-6	Commercial Analysis	C	
Gp-6a	Informal	C	
Gp-6a1	Internal	C	
Gp-6b	Formal	C	
Gp-6b1	Internal	C	
Gp-7	Technical Analysis	C*	D*
Gp-7a	Informal		D*
Gp-7a1	Internal		D
Gp-7a2	External	C*	D*
Gp-7b	Formal	C*	D*
Gp-7b1	Internal		D*
Gp-7b2	External	C	D*

IIS Administrative Issues 81

Precedents	Notes
D=BTL, DuP, GE, GM	
D=GM, IBM	May be attached to subject units
D=GM, IBM	
D=GM, IBM	
D=GM, IBM	Compliance with centrally established standards
D=GM, IBM	Compliance with above standards monitored
D=GM, IBM	Compliance with above standards monitored
C=BTL; D*=GM, IBM	Strict compliance monitored
D=GM, IBM	May be attached to subject units
D=GM, IBM	Less rigorous standards
D=GM, IBM	Less rigorous standards
D*=GM, IBM	Some compliance with above standards assured
C*=GM, IBM	Compliance with above standards monitored
C*=GM, IBM; D*=GM, IBM	Compliance with above standards monitored
C*=GM, IBM; D*=GM, IBM	Strict compliance monitored
D=GM, IBM	Infrequently attached to subject units
D=GM, IBM	Moderately rigorous standards
D=GM, IBM	Moderately rigorous standards
D=GM, IBM	Strict compliance monitored
D*=GM, IBM	Rigorous standards enforced
D*=GM, IBM	Rigorous standards enforced
C*=BTL; D*=GM, IBM	Central responsibility for standards compliance
C*=GM, IBM	Dispersed input with concentrated analysis
D*=GM, IBM	Dispersed input with concentrated analysis
D*=GM, IBM	Dispersed input with concentrated analysis
C*=GM, IBM	Higher quality analysis required
C*=GM, IBM; D*=GM, IBM	Leads to company positions and actions
C*=GM, IBM; D*=GM, IBM	Leads to company positions and actions
C=GM, IBM	Leads to company commitments
C=GM, IBM	Leads to company tactics or strategy
C=GM, IBM	Leads to company tactics
C=GM, IBM	Leads to company tactics
C=GM, IBM	Leads to company strategy
C=GM, IBM	Leads to company strategy
C=BTL; D=GM, IBM	Maximum use of subject experts "in place"
C=BTL; D=GM, IBM	Maximum use of subject experts "in place"
C=BTL; D=GM, IBM	Offers peer visibility, internally
C=BTL; D=GM, IBM	Offers peer visibility, externally
C=BTL; D=GM, IBM	Use experts in special units
C=BTL; DuP, D=GM, IBM	Company strategy highly relevant
C=BTL; D=GM, IBM	Company strategy crucial consideration

Table 6.3 *continued*

Function No.	Name	Centralization Recommended	Decentralization Recommended
Gp-8	Translation	C*	D*
Gp-8a	Informal		D*
Gp-8b	Formal	C*	D*

Note: Abbreviations are as follows: C= function should be/is mainly or completely centralized; C* = function should be/is centralized to a significant extent; D = function should be/is mainly or completely

Precedents	Notes
D=GM, IBM	Use foreign-born experts "in place."
	Commercial agencies for overload
D=GM, IBM	"Quick and dirty procedures"
D=GM, IBM	Formal procedures

decentralized; and D* = function should be/is decentralized to a significant extent. Where both C* and D* appear in an entry, instances of both modes would/do occur depending upon specific circumstances.

Table 6.4 Recommendations for Centralization or Decentralization of IIS Functions: Dissemination and Utilization

Function No.	Name	Centralization Recommended	Decentralization Recommended
Du-1	Internal Announcement		D*
Du-1a	Periodic List with Many Categories and Items		D*
Du-1b	Periodic List with Few Categories and Many Items		D*
Du-1c	Periodic List with Few Categories and Few Items		D*
Du-1d	Group "Current Awareness" or "SDI"	C*	
Du-1e	Individual "Current Awareness" or Individual "SDI"	C*	
Du-1f	"Gatekeeper" SDI	C*	
Du-2	External Announcement	C*	D*
Du-2a	Periodic List with Many Categories and Items		D*
Du-2b	Periodic List with Few Categories and Many Items		D*
Du-2c	Periodic List with Few Categories and Few Items		D*
Du-2d	Group "Current Awareness" or "SDI"	C*	
Du-3	Response to Specific Internal Inquiry (i.e., Retrospective Service)	C*	D*
Du-4	Response to Specific External Inquiry (i.e., Retrospective Service)	C*	D*
Du-5	Full Text Distribution to Automatic List	C*	D*
Du-6	Custom "State-of-Art" Compilation on Major Internal Request	C*	D*
Du-7	Custom "State-of-Art" Compilation on Major External Request	C	
Du-8	Distribution by Subject Content		D

IIS Administrative Issues 85

Precedents	Notes
D=GM, IBM	May include variations in fullness of entries for individual items
D=GM, IBM	
D=GM, IBM	
D=GM, IBM	
C*=IBM	Use unit announcement media (punched cards,
D*=IBM	etc.) Quality monitoring essential
C*=IBM	Use unit announcement media (punched cards,
D*=IBM	etc.) Quality monitoring essential
	Identification of these individuals difficult, but a rewarding task
D*=IBM	Less variety but more copies than Internal Services. Monitor carefully
D*=IBM	Exceptional service dictated by company marketing or public relations goals
D*=IBM	
D*=IBM	
C*=GM, IBM	Monitor carefully, using feedback
D*=GM, IBM	
C*=GM, IBM	Exceptional service dictated by company
D*=GM, IBM	marketing or public relations goals
C*=BTL, GM, IBM	Need up-to-date lists. Economical of personnel costs, with some waste in materials
D*=GM, IBM	
C*=BTL	Very expensive, but relate to project decisions or defensive actions
D*=GM, IBM	
C=IBM	Very expensive and exceptional service, on top management concurrence
D=GM, IBM	Use the standard lists and subject classification, plus current thesauruses, codes, and proprietary listings

Table 6.4 continued

Function No.	Name	Centralization Recommended	Decentralization Recommended
Du-9	Distribution by Functional Assignment	C*	D
Du-9a	Board of Directors, Executive Office(s), Subsidiaries, Foreign Operations	C	
Du-9b	Fiscal and Comptroller	C	
Du-9c	Legal, Patents and Licensing, Copyright, Trademarks	C	
Du-9d	Personnel, Industrial Relations, Education	C	D*
Du-9e	Public Relations, Government/Military	C	D*
Du-9f	Social Concerns	C	
Du-9g	Technology, Research, Development, Design, Maintainability	C*	D
Du-9h	Facilities and Construction	C	
Du-9i	Production, Specifications	C*	D*
Du-9j	Marketing		D*

Note: Abbreviations are as follows: C = function should be/is mainly or completely centralized; C* = function should be/is centralized to a significant extent; D = function should be/is mainly or completely

Precedents	Notes
C*=GM, IBM D*=GM, IBM	Action related. Sensitive to company power structure
C*=GM, IBM	Screen carefully to avoid information "overload"
C=GM, IBM	Most sensitive single area; strict need-to-know
C=GM, IBM	Second or third most sensitive area with strict need-to-know
C=GM, IBM D*=GM, IBM	Third or second most sensitive area
C=GM, IBM D*=GM, IBM	Interrelates with the above subfunctions. Custom versions of content for local use
C=GM, IBM D*=GM, IBM	Wide availability; company as concerned citizen
C*=GM, IBM D*=GM, IBM	Greatest bulk of information content. Company strategy and tactics crucial in establishing limits
C*=GM, IBM	Both time and locale sensitive
C*=GM, IBM D*=GM, IBM	Large bulk but less than Function Du-9g. Wide variation in sensitivity
D*=GM, IBM	Company strategy and tactics variable factors in establishing limits

decentralized; and D* = function should be/is decentralized to a significant extent. Where both C* and D* appear in an entry, instances of both modes would/do occur depending upon specific circumstances.

Table 6.5 Recommendations for Centralization or Decentralization of IIS Functions: Administrative

Function No.		Centralization Recommended	Decentralization Recommended
Ad-1	Operate acquisitions services ("Ac" entries)	C*	D*
Ad-2	Conduct acquisitions system studies in materials and procedures and services	C	
Ad-3	Initiate acquisitions system pilot operations in parallel, then to Ad-1	C	
Ad-4	Operate processing services ("Pc" entries)	C*	D*
Ad-5	Conduct processing system studies in materials, procedures, and services	C*	D*
Ad-6	Initiate pilot procedure system operations in parallel, then to Ad-4	C	
Ad-7	Operate generation and production services ("GP" entries)	C*	D*
Ad-8	Conduct generation and production system studies in materials, procedures, and services	C*	D*
Ad-9	Initiate pilot generation and production system operations in parallel, then to Ad-7	C*	D*
Ad-10	Operate dissemination and utilization services ("Ds" entries)	C*	D*
Ad-11	Conduct dissemination and utilization system studies in materials, procedures, and services	C*	D*

Precedents	Notes
C=BTL	Mode determined by combination and criticality of acquisitions functions performed. Err in direction of decentralization
C*=IBM	Employ feedback optimally
D*=IBM C*=GM	Push technology, materials, and capabilities beyond "comfortable" stage
C=BTL	Same as Ad-1, except "descriptive and subject cataloging, classification, and indexing functions performed." More centralization tendency here
D*=IBM	Same as Ad-2. Include information flow considerations
D*=IBM	Same as Ad-3
C=BTL D*=IBM, GM	Same as Ad-1, except "generation and production functions performed." Err in direction of decentralization for generation and towards centralization for production
C=BTL D*=IBM	Same as Ad-2 and Ad-5
D*=IBM	Same as Ad-3
C=BTL D=IBM, GM	Same as Ad-1, except for "dissemination and utilization functions." Err in direction of decentralization with centrally formulated policy
C=BTL D*=IBM	Same as Ad-2 and Ad-5

Table 6.5 *continued*

Function No.	Name	Central- ization Recommended	Decentral- ization Recommended
Ad-12	Initiate pilot dissemination/ utilization system operations in parallel, then to Ad-10		D*
Ad-13	Institute career upgrading programs		D
Ad-14	Institute user training/ upgrading programs		D
Ad-15	Establish unequivocally the worth of information to the company	C	

Note: Abbreviations are as follows: C = function should be/is mainly or completely centralized; C* = function should be/is centralized to a significant extent; D = function should be/is mainly or completely

Precedents	Notes
C=BTL D-IBM	Same as Ad-3
C=BTL D=GM, IBM	Err in direction of decentralization with centrally formulated policy. Include both on-job and off-job elements of training. Opportunity for "growing" minority group members
D=GM, IBM	Begin with most populous groups, then cover most crucial groups with confidence
C=DuP	The ultimate function. Includes cost/benefit and cost/recovery considerations, and much more.

decentralized; and D* = function should be/is decentralized to a significant extent. Where both C* and D* appear in an entry, instances of both modes would/do occur depending upon specific circumstances.

following the centralized mode of operation in each case. An example of decentralized input to a centralized information product is the company newspaper distributed nationally with seven of eight pages identical and the first page being devoted to local news of the geographic/divisional area in which it is being distributed. Further, in some instances the function may be performed decentralized and reviewed for policy compliance centrally before additional dissemination, as with the editing function on internal government contract reports.

While sketches of principal IISs will be covered elsewhere, some corporation names are used in tables to show operational industrial practice. However, the instances cited are not all necessarily current practices, since "tides" flow between preeminence of central offices and divisions in the several corporations. What is important in these cases is that the particular mode was felt justified at a given point in time for a given function.

We suggest that the following tables merit extremely close attention as a unique contribution to IIS management evaluation. From the functional "menus," a complex, multilocational IIS can be constructed and/or "grown" with greater assurance than ever before.

Summary Recommendations

A multiplicity of avenues for inputting information to a company information base is inherently attractive. However, where there is a possibility in the acquisitions functions of a company commitment being made by receipt of information, such acquisitions should be either centralized or based on a strong, centrally disseminated policy. Quantity discounts is another, but less important, reason for centralization. Decentralized input should invariably be to centrally acceptable standards. In processing, the standards followed should include deviations from usual authorities for proprietary reasons of terminology, relationships to agencies, and so forth. Generation of information should typically be decentralized, with its significance being affected by company tactics and strategy. Formal informational materials should be produced centrally. Dissemination and utilization must be to the ultimate users to aid in the accomplishment of their portion of the company's objectives. The information product may be produced centrally, or according to centrally promulgated standards, but it must be accessible to the individual at a work station in a convenient, timely, and useful form. Administration should determine the ultimate mode for employment of each function within the company's IIS and work unceasingly toward establishment of or evolution to that mode.

SHOULD THE IIS DIRECTOR/MANAGER BE A LIBRARIAN, INFORMATION SCIENTIST, OR SUBJECT EXPERT?

One of the most important decisions to be made is who will run the IIS. The service will take on some of the characteristics of that person—that is, there will be a personal "overlay" over the inventory of functions that are selected to be included and the priorities assigned to them.

A first response may be that the person who instigated the study for an information service is the logical person to carry it through into full operation. Alternatively, it could develop that the study revealed the need for capabilities and/or training that person does not possess or that fall short of the prime management responsibilities central to his or her career path. A second response, then, would be some other interested person within the company. If the personnel records and program of the host organization are sophisticated enough to identify potential manager candidates among the present staff of the company, the IIS administrator can be "grown" with some outside consultant help. The morale aspects of such a process cannot be overlooked. However, if clear possibilities for candidates do not exist, then search for talent outside the company needs to be undertaken. This search might include contacts with relevant professional organization officers/staff executives, with management of exemplary IISs, or executive talent search agencies. The authors have had personal experiences with each of these channels.

At this point we provide a somewhat paraphrased version of the actual position description of an IIS director. Candidates for the equivalent position in any company should have their preparation assessed against a similar statement of duties:

Management Position Guide for Director of the Industrial
Information Service (IIS)

"DOE CORPORATION"

Position Concept

The Director of the Industrial Information Service (IIS) is responsible for providing staff guidance, and professional advice and counsel, to the "Doe" divisions with respect to libraries, library operations and services, and information retrieval services. The Director is responsible for evaluating these services with respect to adequacy and needs and for developing and seeking adoption of operational practices that will promote efficient use, throughout the company, of library information resources.

Responsibilities

The Director of the Industrial Information Service (IIS) will:

1. Discharge the basic management responsibilities described in the Corporation Management Manual.
2. Advise the "Doe" higher management on requirements for corporate policies, objectives, and programs that will increase the effectiveness of operations and improve the quality of results in

this assigned area of responsibility, and assist in the formulation of such policies, objectives, and programs.
3. Provide staff guidance and professional advice and counsel with respect to libraries throughout the company so as to improve the level of operations and services consistent with reasonable cost, substantiated needs, and efficient use of required resources.
4. Develop and encourage the adoption of uniform library practices, insofar as they are practicable, so as to achieve improved company-wide services at minimum cost.
5. Assist division management in the development and implementation of standards of performance and criteria for evaluation of library operations and services.
6. Provide staff guidance and professional advice and counsel on the establishment, operations, improvement, and justifiable expansion of a company-wide technical information retrieval service.
7. Continually assess new and developing technology and practices in this specialized field of interest to broaden application areas, systems and techniques of information retrieval services, and further appropriate mechanization of library processes, as justified by service improvement and/or cost reductions.
8. Develop and encourage adoption by the divisions of uniform procedures and practices that will provide useful and effective information retrieval services for "Doe" scientific and technical personnel.
9. Appraise library and information retrieval services, operations, and resources throughout the company, and recommend corrective management action as necessary and appropriate.
10. Provide guidance to the development and marketing divisions with respect to the further development and application of information retrieval systems and methodology.
11. Promote the understanding and use of library and information retrieval services and capabilities within the company through appropriate publications describing these services, and by assisting in the development of appropriate educational programs.
12. Keep informed of new developments within and outside "Doe" in his specialized field of interest and appraise these for their possible impact upon "Doe" activities and programs in this area. Advise division and corporate management accordingly.
13. Review and recommend concurrence with the research and engineering aspects of division and subsidiary annual and long range plans and revisions thereto with respect to library information retrieval services and programs.

The casual reader might suspect from our backgrounds and present educational connection that our preference for a librarian would be clear-cut. However, we have gotten to know very successful managers from the other two backgrounds as well. On balance, the potential is still greater for the librarian.

Advantages a Librarian Should Bring

1. More rounded training in a professionally accredited program at the graduate level. There are nearly sixty accredited library schools listed by the American Library Association, 50 East Huron Street, Chicago, Illinois, 60611, and the list is available free of charge. Most of these schools maintain placement services for their graduates and can be contacted for leads in filling out staffs.
2. Greater familiarity with national and regional resource libraries and union lists of periodical (magazine) holdings, both current titles and back files. The generally accepted ALA Interlibrary Loan Code calls for librarian-to-librarian borrowing and lending of scarce literature materials, and since the IIS can be neither self-dependent nor an undue parasite on others, considerable resourcefulness is required.
3. Broader experience with filling user needs.
4. Greater probability of the person's long-term satisfaction with the position as a permanent assignment.

Disadvantages a librarian might bring: (1) some "image" problems with the concept of executive librarian or librarian-as-executive (however, do not believe the velvet-choker and sneakers stereotype.); (2) some tendency toward conservatism in scope and operations; and (3) some weaknesses in the generation production of information functions.

Advantages an Information Scientist Should Bring

1. More specialized training based on most sophisticated techniques and equipment.
2. Less tendency to sacrifice results for long-term implications of preservation of knowledge.
3. Less "image" problem, plus ability to command higher salary.
4. More likely to have an original orientation in a subject discipline or librarianship and thus combines some solidity from those fields with the large vistas opened by information science.
5. Strength in the generation and production of information functions.

Disadvantages an information scientist might bring: (1) potential weaker position overall on functions other than generation and production; (2) may be too specifically hardware dependent; and (3) may "go stale" if rate of growth of challenges slackens.

96   Industrial Information Systems

Advantages a Subject Specialist Should Bring

1. Superior acceptability to ultimate users, particularly those in the same or related subject discipline.
2. May be bringing a long-term company association to bear on IIS problem.
3. Specialty could be renewed through continuing education efforts in both the subject field and information science.
4. Could more effectively relate to the analysis subfunctions.

Disadvantages a subject specialist might bring: (1) may not have been a top-flight subject specialist; (2) may not have greater credibility outside his subject areas than others would have; and (3) may have difficulty evaluating professional information service advice "from below."

Table 6.6 is an attempt to rate the potential for an IIS director/manager with the above three backgrounds plus a fourth, the administrative specialty. The administrative specialist would be a professional manager with the appropriate formal and/or continuing education background in management science and the confidence to manage *any* functional operation. Such persons have been developed and/or identified in every organization as part of the company's career enrichment program. Their potential is well known to the audience for whom this book is intended. The final overall rating of the four backgrounds would depend importantly on the relative priorities assigned to each function of a particular IIS.

Kind of Professional Preparation the Director/Manager Should Bring

The librarian's formal training is based on a master's degree in library science (M.S. in L. S., M.A. in L. S., or M.L.S.) and gained from an accredited library school as mentioned previously. If the institution permits specialization at the master's level, the student may follow the option for special libraries. A sixth-year program of study is offered by several schools after some years of professional experience, and a certificate may be awarded. A still smaller number of the schools offer the Ph. D., but these graduates typically enter library science education or administration of the largest academic or public libraries and normally not IIS work.

A comprehensive statement of the intent of one school's educational program is provided by the following excerpts from the "Statement of Goals and Objectives" as adopted by the Graduate School of Library Science, University of Texas at Austin, on April 10, 1975:

> The education program of the Graduate School of Library Science combines theory, knowledge of professional practice, and technological applications. The program is designed not only to prepare candidates

Table 6.6 Rating of Background Potential for IIS Director by Function

Function	Librarian	Info. Scientist	Subject Specialist	Admin. Specialist
Acquisitions	1st	2nd	3rd	4th
Processing	1st	2nd	4th	3rd
Generation/Production				
a) Generation	3rd	2nd	1st	4th
b) Production	4th	1st	2nd	3rd
Overall	4th	1st (tie)	1st (tie)	3rd
Dissemination/Utilization				
a) Dissemination	1st (tie)	1st (tie)	3rd (tie)	3rd (tie)
b) Utilization	1st	2nd (tie)	2nd (tie)	4th
Overall	1st	2nd	3rd	4th
Administration	3rd (tie)	2nd	3rd (tie)	1st

for professional careers but also to provide practitioners with the opportunity to engage in continuing education. It reflects the needs of a relatively large, heterogeneous, and geographically dispersed constituency . . . .

Throughout this statement the term "information" is to be interpreted in its broadest sense.

I. GOALS

A. Education:

To prepare students for service in professional positions at various levels in libraries and other information agencies, for creative service to the profession, for research in library and information science, and—additionally in post-master's programs—for teaching library and information science.

B. *Service:*

To promote increasingly effective library and other information services to a multicultural society through service activities of the school and its faculty.

C. *Research:*

To prepare students for independent research and for the evaluation and use of research findings by cultivating in them a scientific and critically constructive point of view toward the profession; to contribute to the advancement of library and information science through research and publication.

II. OBJECTIVES

A. *Education:*

1. To provide students with a foundation in the history and philosophy of librarianship and information science, with particular emphasis on the role of libraries and librarians in a multicultural society.

2. To emphasize the transdisciplinary nature of library and information science through the study of relevant theories and methodologies drawn from such areas as communications, computer science, education, management, philosophy, psychology, and sociology.

3. To acquaint students with the significant political, social, and

economic environmental determinants which affect library and information service.

4. To encourage in students empathy and sensitivity toward users, funders, and employers in order to enhance their effectiveness in organizations and professionally related public service.

5. To develop an understanding of the nature of the process of interpersonal communication, with special attention to the identification of information needs and to problems of communication between persons of different cultural backgrounds within our society.

6. To encourage a strong commitment to the principles of intellectual freedom and access to information, with due regard for privacy and proprietary rights.

7. To develop an understanding of the processes by which information is generated, published or otherwise made available, disseminated, modified, stored, retrieved, and used, in various forms and formats, via formal and informal networks.

8. To afford students the opportunity to specialize to a limited extent on the basis of a type of library or library function. To provide specially qualified students with in-depth knowledge of information science and systems technology or Latin American library and information resources.

9. To provide students with an understanding of the theory, principles, and skills related to the professional functions of selection, acquisition, organization, storage, retrieval, use, and evaluation of information in manual and automated systems.

10. To familiarize students with the form, structure, and content of the information sources and/or literatures of various subject fields, and to develop an understanding of the bibliographic techniques necessary for their organization and use.

11. To provide an introduction to the theory and practice of administration of libraries and other information agencies.

12. To develop the students' ability to relate theory to practice and to acquire skills for work in libraries and other information agencies by encouraging problem-oriented projects and field experience.

13. To encourage student contacts with professionals in librarianship and related fields through appropriate field work, lectures, visits, and special events.

14. To develop analytical and evaluative attitudes towards professional problems and practices. To familiarize students with research methods appropriate to libraries and other information services and their application to the solution of specific problems.

15. To prepare and motivate professional candidates for self-organized inquiry, life-long learning and continuing education.

B. *Service:*

1. To encourage faculty and student participation in activities of professional organizations at the local, state, regional, national, and international levels.

2. To promote the improvement of libraries and other information services through faculty and student involvement in consulting, research, and appropriate political and organizational effort.

3. To recruit for the profession competent candidates of varying ethnic, cultural, and educational backgrounds, to assist students and alumni in career planning, and to provide guidance in placement of recent graduates and other alumni.

4. To provide continuing education opportunities for professional practitioners to keep abreast of new developments in library and other information services.

C. *Research:*

1. To encourage students to develop the habit of continually reviewing, critically evaluating, and appropriately utilizing relevant basic and applied research.

2. To encourage students to contribute throughout their careers to professional knowledge through the timely publication of valid and useful research findings and professional concepts.

3. To encourage faculty research and publication, which contribute to the advancement of basic and applied professional knowledge and to improved teaching.

Other Programs of Library Education

Post-master's and advanced study. A program of advanced, non-degree study may be planned to meet the individual needs of experienced librarians and information specialists. Certificates may be awarded upon completion of at least thirty hours of work beyond the master's degree. The objective of this program is to prepare the student for higher level or specialized positions in such fields as library administration, work with special groups or programs, systems analysis and automation, a subject specialization (including the Latin American area) and direction of school media (learning resources) programs. Pertinent courses from other disciplines and programs are used in planning individual programs of study.

Doctor of Philosophy in Library and Information Science. The objective of the Ph.D. program is to prepare research scholars and scholarly instructors and leaders for the profession. The program provides advanced study in library and information science and other appropriate areas which support the effective intellectual and material access to available knowledge. Doctoral candidates are required to complete a dissertation that gives evidence of ability to do independent investigation in the major field and constitutes a contribution to knowledge. Graduates of the program are prepared for the advancement of fundamental professional knowledge, for teaching, and for creative leadership in the profession.[1]

It is clear in the quoted text that this school intends to prepare persons in information science as well as librarianship. By contrast, programs such as those at Ohio State University and Georgia Institute of Technology prepare persons in information science solely.

Kind of Professional Preparation the Information Scientist Director/Manager Should Bring

Formal training programs in information science, as distinguished from library science, are not accredited by any one professional association. The American Library Association's accreditation procedures provide the possibility for so-called single-option schools to seek accreditation under ALA procedures, but as of 1977 no free-standing information science program had as yet sought such accreditation.

The broadest based professional society in information science is the American Society for Information Science, (ASIS). One of its Special Interest Groups (SIGs) is Education for Information Science (ED) with the goal "To determine and develop the basic concepts of information science and to examine the implications for education and training of future information scientists." Interestingly enough, of their four officers, two are on the faculties of ALA-accredited library schools, the third is executive director of a discipline-based national library association, and the fourth is employed in industry.

There is a SIG cabinet in ASIS for common interest that shares with Arts and Humanities, Automated Language Processing, Behavioral and Social Sciences, Biological and Chemical Information Systems, Classification Research, Costs, Budgeting and Economics, Foundations of Information Science, Information Analysis Centers, Information Publishing, Information Services to Education, Law and Information Technology, Library Automation and Networks, Non-Print Media, Public-Private Interface, Reprographic Technology, Selective Dissemination of Information, Technology, Information and Society, and User On-Line Interaction.[2] This list can be taken to comprise the concerns of that society in information science. Many of the topics are relevant to IIS activities.

The senior author of this volume and R. E. Wyllys have recently published a chapter on curricula in information science and made some predictions of future directions.[3] In addition, one of our colleagues has a chapter on a similar topic in the *Annual Review* volume for 1976.[4] Schur's definitive study for OECD (Paris) sees problems existing in education and training of information specialists in subject knowledge, practical experience, "programme" organization, mathematics and statistics, computers and languages, and he makes recommendations.[5] (All this is to indicate that education for information science is still in a bit of flux.)

Kind of Preparation the Subject Specialist Director/Manager Should Bring

Care must be taken to insure that this alternate career path in information service is not used as a haven for the obsolete or under qualified subject discipline person. Accreditation for subject disciplines is well established and well known. Updating of employees is a part of aggressive company personnel programs and may take place on site (as some carried out by Syracuse University, for example), in short stays on campus, or in executive conference residence sites. No well-motivated subject discipline person may avoid obsolescence. However, if these capable people are detailed to (or do choose to follow) the information service career path, they should be exposed to as competent an upgrading in that new speciality as for their subject "retreading." Programs are available in the same variety of sites and formats as the earlier-mentioned programs.

Ideally the subject "cosmopolitans," "stars," or "gatekeepers" should be involved in the IIS in advisory, if not operational, roles. (These terms in quotation marks all mean the same and signify the person with a reputation both within the company and outside as knowing what is new in a given field, who the really significant workers are, and where the important work is appearing.)[6]

Summary Recommendation

The very best person should be selected for the post as Director/manager of the IIS whether from inside or outside the company and regardless of primary background. Advantages and disadvantages of the several backgrounds—librarianship, information science, or subject discipline—have been summarized and their relative potential for each of the main functions of the IIS has been outlined. The respective training environments for these classes of candidates have been stated so that a more knowledgeable choice may be made by the decisionmaker. The potential for advice in the selection from professional society and education sources has been pointed out. "May the best (wo)man win!"

NOTES AND REFERENCES

1. Self-Study Report, Presented to the Committee on Accreditation of the American Library Association (Austin: University of Texas at Austin, Graduate School of Library Science, 1975), pp. 8-12.
2. *ASIS Handbook and Directory*, 1975 Ed. (Washington, D. C.: American Society for Information Science, 1975), pp. vii-viii.
3. E. B. Jackson and Ronald E. Wyllys, "Professional Education in Information Science—Its Recent Past and Probable Future," in D. P. Hammer, ed., *Information Science Accomplishments and Predictions* (Metuchen, N. J.: Scarecrow Press, 1976).
4. E. Glynn Harmon, chapter in *Annual Review of Information Science and Technology*, Vol. 11 (Washington, D. C.: American Society for Information Science, 1976).
5. Herbert Schur, *Education and Training of Information Specialists for the 1970s* (Sheffield, Eng.: University of Sheffield, Postgraduate School of Librarianship and Information Science, January 1972), 114 pp. (DAS/STINFO/72:9).
6. For an interesting example of study in an industrial milieu, see Richard S. Rosenbloom, and Francis W. Wolek, *Technology, Information and Organization; Information Transfer in Industrial R&D* (Cambridge, Mass.: Harvard University Graduate School of Business Administration, June 1967), 255 pp. Wolek published later work along this line from Wharton School of Finance and Commerce, University of Pennsylvania.

Chapter 7

IIS Personnel and Consultants

PERSONNEL: A CLOSER LOOK

The most valuable ingredient in the industrial information system is the manpower component. Just to take the financial implications first, we know of no significant IIS that has less than a 50-50 split between manpower costs and all other expenses. In fact, some are known to be as high as 80 percent to 20 percent in favor of personnel expense.

The emergence of ever-increasing sophisticated information retrieval equipment demands a higher quality human interface than ever before. The trend to information networking between and among systems and geographic areas calls for still greater skill in interpersonal communications. The latter come into more prominence locally as project lead times get ever shorter and information users need the right answer the first time and in a convenient form.

The considerations raised in the preceding chapter on librarians, information scientists, subject specialists, and administrative specialists apply in some degree to all the professionals selected for IIS duties, although the weightings assigned vary. The professionals should be selected with much care and in accord with the existing Affirmative Action and Equal Opportunity Programs.[1]

Women Professionals

The preponderance of women in the pool of librarians and information scientists offers an exceptional opportunity for the company to select women candidates with present capabilities for growth potential to management positions. The financial industry has been the most responsive to date, with several women having achieved vice presidential rank.[2] Consulting situations show that management attention to companies' programs for professional women is in better focus than in the past, but is far from ideal.

Since there is much in the current management literature on qualifications and employment of women, we will summarize by giving instances involving our own graduates: (a) maturity—a student entered library school after her children had graduated from college, and since graduation, she has organized and is running a small industrial library in a metropolitan area with great success; (b) supervisory—a student entering with children in high school is now a supervisor of an industrial information service that includes other professionals; (c) relocation — a student, having a husband with lower educational degree than hers, determined the city where positions would be taken, and hers was in an industrial setting; (d) aggressiveness—a student, marrying upon graduation, organized a special library for an R&D concern and now has government contracts for information work, thus bringing revenue into the firm (meanwhile husband works in a bank).

Position Descriptions

The probability is that position classifiers will be seeking parallel series to establish information services titles and compensation levels. (One firm used their statistician series for "take-off.") There is often a tendency to underclassify IIS personnel because of unfamiliarity with the implications of the service to the company mission. In addition to watching for this phenomena, all IIS persons with professional degrees and past the probationary period for employment should insist they be certified as *exempt* under the Labor Standards Act. The actual current position of an industrial library manager (who incidentally is a woman) follows:

Position Description: Library Manager

Position Concepts

Responsible for overall administration and development of library services for optimum use by clientele. Responsible for coordination with internal libraries, contacts with external libraries, and other sources of information.

Responsibilities
1. Plans and manages library activities within the framework of company policy and library objectives to provide information resources for use in long-range planning work, for reviewing the state-of-the-art, for maintaining current awareness.
2. Selects, trains, supervises, and evaluates clerical and professional staff who provide library services. Establishes organizational structure of staff to accomplish library functions. Develops internal library operating procedures. Mechanizes operational procedures, if economically feasible.
3. Keeps abreast of new literature and developments in the company's field and in library science through printed source material and by attendance at meetings of professional library and documentation organizations.

4. Assists in establishing policies and practices among corporation libraries and in recommendations for information retrieval services throughout the corporation.
5. Maintains liaison with local and national libraries, associations, technical and scientific societies to supplement library resources and with book and periodical vendors for expeditious purchase of library materials.
6. Prepares annual financial operating plan for library and controls expenditures to adhere to approved budget.
7. Prepares progress reports and makes recommendations to immediate management. Maintains the statistics reflecting current activity and provides comparison with past performance along with analytical interpretation of differences.
8. Plans physical layout and equipment for the library for optimum use based on professional knowledge and experience.

Compensation Levels

Usual methods for establishing salary levels include cross-checks with other firms and salary surveys published by professional associations. Beware of the lag in the latter case, and in the former, be sure that the other firms have the same kinds of information services. The Special Libraries Association conducts a survey at about three year intervals, with most recent results published in the December 1976 issue of *Special Libraries*.[3] Its results show that salaries have increased about 16 percent since 1973 in the United States, with those in Canada being somewhat higher. The *mean* salary was $16,300 and the *median* was $15,000. There are regional differences and women still trail men, especially in the higher levels. Of particular interest are the tables showing compensation for those with subject matter background.

Fringe Benefits and Continuing Education

Of course, the same fringe benefits as available to all company employees are available to the IIS professionals, but the latter have a need for continuing education opportunities and travel that requires special attention. In addition to the familiar American Management Association sessions on current topics such as micrographics and records retention, there are expensive residence conference center presentations of three days to a week or more on facsimile transmission, information retrieval systems, and copyright implications. Of more than ordinary interest are the updates offered in conjunction with the annual conferences of the SLA, American Society for Information Sciences, American Federation of Information Processing Societies, and the like. Academic opportunities include offerings ranging from a few days workshop to full "sixth-year" specialist programs that are intended for the experienced practitioner and that culminate in a certificate. On travel, all professionals should have the opportunity to participate in activities of their state or regional professional organization and one out-of-state trip to a professional meeting annually.

Profession- or Company-Centered?

Tensions can arise that lead a manager to exclaim, "Why, Zilch is more interested in being an information professional than she is in being an employee of BBB Company!" The reverse situation is easy to handle: —The capable person should be channeled into the company's middle management training program and he or she will gradually be appointable to a higher position outside the IIS (and this has happened to most of the few racial minority persons beginning in IIS positions). The urge to stay a librarian or an information scientist can be great and specific attention to the company's "parallel ladder" career plan might have the seeds of the solution. (In these plans, the concept is that one can reach senior compensation and status recognition through subject matter contribution, irrespective of management assignment.) The desirability of open discussion of the matter at periodic performance reviews is clearly indicated. Also the fact that the day is past when every professional coming in the front door automatically wishes to stay thirty-five years with the company needs to be recognized.

Performance Evaluation

Many IISs operate in a company where management by objective is the mode. Certain of the lists in this book are designed to help the manager come to a better understanding with IIS professionals on suitable objectives. These objectives should be reviewed at the normal company-set intervals—typically every six months.

These objectives should contain *action* verbs (just doing today what we did yesterday does not qualify). A sample set of objectives for the IIS manager might include:

Appraise the IIS functions (i.e., discover mismatches between information needs of company missions/personnel on the one hand and available IIS services, staff, and resources on the other);

Initiate corrective actions within the IIS span of control.

Secure company management commitment to take corrective actions outside the IIS span of control;

IIS Personnel and Consultants 109

Insure involvement of users in the support for and upgrading of the IIS program;

Quantify the value of information content to the company;

Demonstrate professional excellence;

Develop a successor;

Participate in company's "good citizen" efforts within the professional community;

Grow in wisdom and understanding.

It is useful to recall that both the evaluat*or* and the evaluat*ee* will become more comfortable in the performance evaluation process with repetition.

The objectives of the remaining IIS personnel will be consistent with and normally subsets of the manager's.

Promotion and/or Separation

The company's professional personnel policy should be followed on promotion of professional IIS staff members as evaluations indicate. Sustained superior performance at the less-than-professional levels may necessitate promotion to positions *outside* the IIS, although care must be taken to avoid an undue clerical retraining time drain.

In the rare cases when it becomes clear from the evaluations that a professional must be separated from the company, it should be done "with all deliberate haste"—that is, neither be precipitate nor permit an intolerable situation to continue.

Personal "chemistry" mismatches are involved in many of the involuntary professional separations we know about. In these cases particularly, reasonable efforts need be made to assist the professional relocate: Permission to use the company telephone leased line, some assistance with travel expenses to distant interviews, continued use of the office mailing address and stationery after formal separation has occurred are among the rather usual aids in their "outplacement."

Unions

It is not usual for IIS professionals to be part of bargaining groups, although some of their colleagues in academic and government are so represented. Some IISs are known in companies where clerical staffs are unionized and rather unusual grievances have arisen. Reliance should be placed on providing appropriate information and assistance to those charged with handling such matters.

Mailroom and shipping/receiving operations are the usual sources of friction with company hourly employees under a bargaining agreement. We know of one instance where the use of the library book truck resolved jurisdictional grievances: if a *dolly* was used, the task was for hourly shipping/receiving personnel; if a *book truck* was used, the task was for salaried IIS clerical personnel.

Summary Recommendation

As the personnel segment is such a major part of an IIS budget and the IISs greatest resource is the skill of its professionals, the IIS "people problems" should be worthy of the utmost attention by its higher management. We recommend the topics raised in this discussion and in Chapter 5 on the administrative functions be used as an aid in focusing attention on these problems and the means for resolving them.

CONSULTANTS: THEIR CARE AND USE

An important way to extend the capabilities of the company's management and professional staff concerned with the IIS is through the effective use of consultants. They may be used to amplify and particularize the recommendations in this book at any stage of the IIS's development from inception through routine operation through interim audits to company information policy determination.

They may be "inside" or "outside" consultants—that is, company or non-company employees. Many of the recommendations included in the other chapters are based on our experience as an "inside" consultant to two major corporations, IBM and GM. However, during that same period, both authors served on the Special Libraries Association's Consultation Service Committee and made brief consultation visits to certain industries asking assistance from the association. Lately, the senior author has had the opportunity to serve as an "outside" consultant to other corporations in Fortune 500 and to state governmental agencies.

Statement of the Problem

It is an encouraging sign when an organization starts to feel the need to call in a consultant on an information-related situation. However, the more thought the organization has given to the matter of the problem it faces, the better it will be able to choose the proper consultant and the more valuable the resultant advice will be.

Although the following list is not an exhaustive one, and other questions will be suggested by reviewing the titles of the previous chapters, these questions may be used to define the problem:

1. What is the *scope* of our information-related problem? Company-wide? Division-wide? Function-limited? Project-limited? Geographic location-limited? Domestic only? Internally-generated or external? Format-limited? Security-limited? Equipment-limited?

2. What is the *urgency* of our information-related problem? Crisis situation? Management-level of awareness? Widely deplored? Just "keeping up with the 'Joneses'"?

3. What are the *resources* available to divert to the problem's eventual proposed solution? People? Materials? Facilities? Equipment? (Or, what can we do with the answer?)

4. What is the *company* climate? (Only insiders know.) Inevitably an interactive process will follow with the consultant selected that leads to a more precise statement of the agreed-upon problem, but the more "homework" done before initial contact, the better.

Selection of the Consultant

While there are some directories of consultants for information systems, the more usual practice is to find a suitable consultant through a business colleague or acquaintance known to have used a consultant in the general subject area of concern; a management association or professional information society in the area;[4] the faculty of an IIS staff person's alma mater or a university that the company has a close relationship to; professional information personnel in the company (for recommendation of outsiders with reputations known to them); the pertinent literature (select authors of outstanding or relevant articles to approach); or a known "all purpose" consulting firm. There are obvious pitfalls in each of these methods, but a key ingredient in the selection procedure is to check previous customers of the consultant as to level of satisfaction with the performance. They should be asked whether the conclusions did follow from the data presented and whether they were sufficiently particularized to the client's unique situation. (Beware of standardized "desk audits" that do, or are twisted so as to, apply to any conceivable situation without a real understanding of the company's particular problem.)

The Agreement or Contract

After sufficient communication with the consultants suggested by the above sources, the next step is to select the one(s) from which statements of proposed work and compensation expected will be requested. While these statements may take the form of legal documents drawn by the best lawyers, we are personally familiar with proposals as brief as a two-page letter returned with an "O.K. per C. B. Q. Please proceed 12/25/76" or as involved as a 25-page document looking for all the world like a National Science Foundation proposal. Elements are certain to be tasks, time period, and whether reports will be oral or written. After initial agreement has been reached and work begins, it is not unusual for adjustment in the project to be modified by letter: "confirming our telephone conversation. . . ."

Compensation is a little tricky to negotiate, but normally exceeds $175 per day and expenses (1977 figure). On the other hand one specialist consultant claims he charges a flat $25.00 per half hour. Some government agencies, such as the U. S. Office of Education, stipulate the maximum that may be paid consultants on their grants or contracts is currently $100.00 per day. Some consultants prefer a flat fee basis for completing a specific task. However, we suggest that this practice be reserved for a *second* or subsequent relationship with the same consultant.

The Findings or Conclusions

In every case, the quality of the findings will have a relation to the amount of staff interaction with and information provided the consultant. Our practice is to present an oral report at midpoint and to keep the client appraised of tentative conclusions as they emerge so that the final written report contains no substantial surprises to the client.

The Implementation Plan

It is small comfort to be told what is amiss without being offered a realistic plan to tend to rectify the situation. (The only exception we think of is when both the unfortunate problem and the unpopular solution were known in advance and the consultant was called in primarily to serve as a scapegoat.)

The quality consultant shows true mettle at the implement plan stage, and decisions as to possible further engagement or rapid "wrap-up" of relationships with that consultant should be made at this point. As to future involvement (and that is more common than otherwise), the economics of trading on the consultant's new-found familiarity with the situation should be weighed against the possible danger of paying twice for the same information.

"Marketing" the Findings

As the initiator of the consultant relationship, the IIS has the obligation to exploit the results secured through expenditure of company funds to the maximum advantage of the company.

Sample Consulting Case

It Happened... In contrast to the more complex sample case of task negotiation and execution outlined below, one instance is known of a consultant who was phoned long distance on a Wednesday by a "think tank" firm and asked, "Can you come Monday while our information officer is on vacation, spend two weeks with our users, and tell us verbally what we *really* need in the way of information services?"

The more typical and somewhat disguised sample consulting case of "FFF Corporation" follows:

Week 1

Start: Telephone inquiry by Mr. Jones, "FFF," as to possible interest in survey of the corporation's technical library operations. Mentioned source of consultant's name and that preliminary check had been made on suitability. Consultant agreed to consider the matter.

Week 3

Mr. Jones sent letter outlining existing technical library situation and asked for a proposal. He included latest company annual report and asked for resume.

Week 4

Consultant sent proposal for a three-week management audit of technical library-like activities at corporate headquarters and two geographically separated foci of company activity/installations. A quick inventory of resources and interviews with a variety of users were seen necessary. Work could begin six weeks hence.

Week 6

Mr. Jones accepted proposal by telephone. He asked for needed preliminary information. Consultant requested installation mission and functional statements, information service-like budgets, and characterization of technical personnel mix (education level, subject specialization, organizational assignment, and so forth).

Week 13

Mr. Jones relayed much of the requested information, noting that deviations were present in level and detail reported by the installations.

Week 17

On-site visits began with Mr. Jones at company headquarters. A rough company organization chart was constructed from the information service-like point of view. Several additional potential units were identified as being related to the information service situation. Their reporting lines led to a multiplicity of executives. A principal tool used was the internal telephone directory—typically more up-to-date than formal organizational charts. Walking tours and lunch provided some acquaintance with "free-standing" information services—that is, those having no apparent relationship to the Company technical libraries. Appointments made for the consultant for the next 10 days in as many cities were reviewed.

Week 17 (balance) and 18

Outline of a typical day: (Arrived at motel previous evening). Sign-in at location at 8:30. Conference in office of executive to whom library-like activity reported, covering visit objectives. Introduction to individual in charge of library-like activity (called here librarian). Briefing on user interview schedule set for day. Conference in the librarian's office on information supplied earlier, filling in lacks, addition of "free form" data in bound project notebook, meeting remainder of staff and viewing facilities—all this subject to interruption to meet users as their appointments required (always in their own offices). Services used, perceived lacks, and relationships to other company elements were noted. All recommendations from any source were recorded. Lunch was off-premises and included both management and the librarian. Opportunity was taken to get an idea of spatial relationship during escorted walks to interviews. Exit visit to management office at about 4 p.m. included mention of two or three principal observations and that the full report would be sent by headquarters to the company vice-president over this particular facility. Departed installation about 4:30.

Week 19

Mr. Jones and the consultant met at a mutually convenient airport conference room for oral debriefing: Tentative conclusions were given, reactions received, and relative weights assigned. Consultant was authorized to make any necessary telephone calls during preparation of the written report.

Week 20

A study report with recommendations was submitted by mail together with an expense statement (paid within ten days). The report had a four-page executive summary, about twenty-five pages of text and fifteen pages of a statistical appendix. Principal report sections in addition to those of proposed management actions were the inventory of currently committed information-related services and resources; summaries of site visits; need for a technical library focal point at company headquarters; and total personnel implications. Appendices included entries for the "FFF" information centers/libraries in standard directories, tables of personnel, financial and material resources, tables of target technical populations, tables of functions performed, and resumes of "outside" professionals suggested for employment consideration, and, finally, suitable acknowledgements.

Week 21

Presentation made to previously scheduled all-day meeting of "FFF" information officers/librarians at headquarters on *professional aspects* of the management audit (*not* anticipating any management actions) together with recommendations that the group constitute itself as a "FFF Company Technical Librarians Task Force." Mr. Jones announced that a systems study was to be undertaken for a parallel technical group that would impinge on technical information. Separately he requested the consultant be his representative on the survey instrument and interpretation committees.

Week 22

Following confirming telephone call, Mr. Jones extended consultancy agreement to cover advisory services on the survey.

Weeks 24-36+

Consultant was in frequent telephone contact with the survey staff and Mr. Jones. He also revisited a crucial company installation.

Week 30

Mr. Second, a company executive from a nontechnical staff, visited the consultant on possible applicability of survey results to his own function and their further elaboration.

Week 34

Mr. Second phoned requesting a proposal letter, extending the scope to assisting in preparation of functional statement for an information officer and its presentation to senior company management. Another responsibility would be securing a roster of potential appointees for the senior company information official post. The two-page proposal letter was sent and the schedule it included was accepted.

Week 37+

The consultant visited Mr. Second's function at company headquarters, secured necessary additional information, and instituted the advisory relationship with the new staff group. There was agreement that much of the informational requirement for the action memoranda could be filled from generalized information already on hand at the consultant's office and also based on growing company familiarity.

The consultant needed to be particularly careful during this evolving period of "Piggy-Backing" to insure that the recommendations made were first to the entire company's best interests and second to those of the two staffs equally.

Summary Recommendation

Consultants provide a means of extending the capabilities of "on-board" IIS personnel or may partially substitute for an IIS capability on a contract basis. Another possibility is that they may provide a "turn key" IIS operation after long-term involvement with the company. In the more usual limited time-period mode, key ingredients in the use of consultants should be a clear statement of the information problem; a responsible selection process for determining the consultant to be utilized; iteration of the problem statement and its proposed solution between the instigator and the consultant; drawing up an appropriate agreement or contract; appropriate facilitation of the study from the "inside" and provision of required information or means to accumulate same; receipt of clear findings or conclusions, preferably in written form; and taking necessary action to implement the findings—or recommend to higher levels that they take the appropriate action—and follow through to conclusion. A separate step is to determine whether continued use of the consultant is appropriate or desirable. Use of a consultant is as appropriate in the IIS field as for any other operational function, and the case study outlined above should be used to assist the reader on learning "how to do it" or about issues that will arise to be solved and pitfalls to be anticipated and met if a consultant is to be effectively utilized.

NOTES AND REFERENCES

1. Special Libraries Association, Special Committee on the Pilot Education Project, *Equal Pay for Equal Work: Women in Special Libraries* (New York: SLA, 1976), 24 pp.
2. It was not always thus even in the profession. As recently as the mid-1950s

we members of the Special Libraries Association Nominating Committee were advised "Run a woman against a woman, so she has a chance." Brilliant women such as Shell Development's Thelma Hoffman and American Cyanamid's Betty Joy Cole held national SLA office in those years, while National Cash Register's Emma Wedenbine and Ford Motor's Rachel MacDonald never rose above chapter level. Then in the 1960s, when we used the privilege of flying the members of the GM Committee on Technical Literature Activities in a company airplane to the meeting's company plant site to help call attention to the importance of the technical library functions, the local management was invariably impressed. However, the impression made on GM Flight Operations is summarized in the inevitable response to the telephoned reservation call, "Oh, yours is the group that has the women."

3. "SLA Salary Survey 1976," *Special Libraries* **67**:597-624 (December 1976); "Salary Survey Update," *Special Libraries* **68**:461-462 (December 1977).
4. A sample brochure is New York Metropolitan Reference and Research Library Agency (METRO), "When Two Heads are Better . . . Call Metro's Consultant Service" (New York: METRO, 1975), 2pp. (fanfold). METRO has a file of fifty different subject areas and will suggest names on request. Further negotiations are strictly between the requestor and the suggestees.

Chapter 8

IIS Users

A CLOSER LOOK AT THE USERS

There is probably more repetition and broader generalizations on *users* of industrial information systems in the literature than any other single topic we are considering in this book. Hence, in this chapter we offer a "boil down" based on personal experience gained in virtually every conceivable role in user studies.

WHO ARE THE USERS?

First and foremost are the IIS users who are technically qualified persons in technical assignments; second are the technically qualified persons in nontechnical assignments (including management); third are the nontechnically qualified persons in technical assignments; fourth are the persons in other corporation activities who are information sources for those served by the IIS; and fifth are persons outside the company to whom one or more IIS services are provided for reasons of commercial interest or public relations value. A sixth category, sometimes forgotten, is the group of nonusers included within each of the five preceding categories.

While one IIS proposal is known that was made to a geophysical prospecting firm employing no more than thirty-five professionals, numbers of probable users in the several hundreds or thousands are more common. For example, one corporation is known that has around 100,000 engineers and scientists worldwide, and another corporation has over 6,000 college graduate engineers/scientists working in a two-mile square area. As will be mentioned again the next chapter on budgeting, these users differ in subject background, educational level, organizational project, and information-seeking habits.

The most important group to the IIS is the first category of engineers/scientists: technically qualified users in technical assignments. Starting with the extremes in subject matter background, chemists are widely known as information center users, while drafting board-oriented industrial engineers tend toward light use. Generally speaking, those with Ph.D. degrees use the IIS more heavily than Master's recipients, while the latter, in turn, use it more than persons with Bachelor's degrees or nongraduates. Exceptions can be cited, including the

Ph.D. graduate in nuclear power at one of our corporations who was so apparatus focused that he didn't know how to use *Nuclear Science Abstracts* (the principle abstracting service in that field) and who asked, "Why didn't somebody tell me about *NSA* in graduate school?"

Organizational differences in this category of users are of two kinds, at least: the position on the project leader-to-engineering aide spectrum the users occupy, and the functional assignment/mission of their division. On average, the project leader needs much economic and marketing information plus a share of "packed-down" technical information, while the senior project staff associates need much more technical information, under stringent conditions of currency, reliability, and useful form. The latter may aid in indoctrinating the junior staff on the utility of information in their assignment.

The divisional functional assignment/mission "pecking order" is approximately:

Research

Advanced Development

Systems Development

Pilot Plant

Production

Distribution and Marketing

Customer Service

Public Relations

The professionals in the research laboratories are mostly heavy users of the IIS, are able to help themselves more than the others, require a broader range of subject matter and formats, and require both the most recent and the classics in their field. They personally know persons elsewhere in the corporation and on the "outside" who are working in their area and may "squirrel away" extensive personal files.

The advanced development people include some sent down from the research laboratories along with their projects, and they are a good influence on IIS use. They need some marketing and specifications information, plus much of the technical content used in the research laboratories. Systems development people need some of the information of the preceding groups but in less depth and time span. Simulation facts and computer access are very important. The pilot plant operation stage needs "troubleshooting" and industry standards information access.

Production people tend to "cut metal first," rather than read what the literature says. Geniuses such as C. F. Kettering who claimed, in essence, "... we just asked the diesel engine what it wanted, we gave it to it, and the engine worked," glossed over the fact that production personnel had really used much recorded information that more junior personnel had carefully searched out, "repackaged" in a palatable form, and unobstrusively provided to them. Production people who get "turned on" by technical information and its utility are to be greatly prized and carefully nurtured, as their word to colleagues is immeasurably more effective than a public relations campaign by the IIS staff.

Distribution and marketing people are rapidly becoming more aware of the utility of information; in fact, one corporation features the prompt supply of sales information and manuals via their on-line publications order program as a sales feature. When this company issues a manual on an important product system for wide distribution, the print order is on a scale such that the paper requirement is measured in number of boxcars full. Customer service was at one time provided by the information in the field engineer's memory, then it consisted of an automobile trunk full of informational manuals, and now it is at the stage where it incorporates wiring diagrams on microfiche filed adjacent to a film reader integrated into the piece of equipment, backed up by an on-line "trouble" inquiry system manned by a panel of six or seven "old timer" field engineers at a central company location.

The information requirements of public relations people are becoming more technical as their products grow more complex and government regulations "grow teeth."

We have gone into the most detail on users in category one, those technically qualified and in a technical assignment, both because we know more about filling their needs than those of others, and because more and more technical persons beginning in this kind of an assignment are being drawn to all the other functions of the company: personnel, marketing, long-range planning, standardization liaison, governmental relations, education and training, and administrative services. As category two users, technical persons in nontechnical assignments, this group has information needs that are self-evident, and some will be predisposed to consider using the IIS. For others, those in marketing, we are just becoming aware of the great complexity of their needs.

The nontechnically qualified in technical assignments, as category three users, are examples of the effects of new programs, such as the upward mobility thrust of minority employment programs. The challenge for the IIS is to remain in close contact with education, training, and apprentice officials and to emphasize the inclusion of information use components at appropriate stages in the endeavor.

The fourth category, the persons that themselves are information sources for others in the corporation (the so-called cosmopolitans or stars) need to be identified, nurtured, and aided to the very limits of the IIS capability. In recognition of the extreme usefulness of these personal sources of knowledge, one corporation has had a "Who Knows What in EEE Corporation" for some time and distributes it with the internal telephone directory. Another corporation is (1977) in the midst of preparing such a "yellow pages" directory. One caution: Some feeling exists that such compilations help the firms whose business is seeking talent (so-called ivory hunters) more than it does the company itself, especially if the company is part of a dynamic industry and has an imperfect security system.

The outside persons allowed access to the IIS form the fifth category of users. These may range from important customers to industry lobby groups to a doctoral student attending a university in a company's geographic location who has been awarded access to certain nonproprietary IIS files as a sort of "information scholarship."

The last category, nonusers, may be a subset of any of the first four categories. In general, they increase in percentage of total category membership as one proceeds down the progression from those in research with doctoral degrees and senior project associate status (i.e., the top of the "pecking order") down to the nontechnical, nongraduates in the routine entry-level positions. The priority and concern for nonusers of the IIS management should be all-consuming at the top of the category list and sloped downward at an angle dictated by resources. A contributing factor to management's problems in this area is the paucity of solid information in the literature on experience with unfailing means for identification of these persons.

HOW TO STUDY THE USERS

There have been several reviews of user surveys and subsequent general agreement that no startling basic truths have emerged. Lancaster's workmanlike "assessment" is easy to follow and is recommended.[1]

The Written Survey

The most difficult method of surveying users is the one most frequently used: the *written survey*. By difficult, we mean the task of insuring beyond question that the instrument is validly constructed, properly administered, completely understood by the respondents, the responses properly interpreted, and the correct conclusions drawn.

One recent survey of a multidivisional, multilocational corporation we know about had two parts: "I" for the professional users and "II" for the location librarians. The "I" instrument had about a dozen pages and had space for the responses. The questions were in the following categories: type of work done by the respondent; mission of his or her employing division; frequency of visits to the library/information center (hereafter referred to as "library"); types of information needed and relative frequency; access points used (e.g., by author's name, and so forth) and approximate annual "traffic"; and relative utility of various formats and sources of *externally* issued information (from outside the company)—such as commercial publications, those of nonprofit professional societies, those of governments and trade associations, and academic origin (with the expected heavy emphasis on periodicals and their secondary services)—and of *internally* issued information—such as company research and development reports, laboratory notebooks, technical correspondence, company specifications, patent disclosures, technical drawings, product parts lists, and SOPs (standard operating procedure manuals). Next were requests for information on the following: specific titles of greatest interest and greatest usefulness in the past, plus indication of lacking formats or titles; type of usual reference query (e.g., comprehensive, "quick and dirty," and so forth); the most recent critical incident—that is, an important need for information and how it was resolved (e.g., source, degree of satisfaction, precedent-setting nature, and so forth); type of response received (e.g., prompt, appropriate, misrouted); perceived need for better facilities (e.g., more staff, more space, longer hours, higher skills, more sophisticated equipment); what information was secured outside the library and its channels (e.g., personal contacts, sensitive information, nonrecorded information); attitude toward microcopies and microform generally; and critical lacks seen and principal recommendations for library service improvements.

The survey instrument was presented orally at a group meeting of about a dozen technical staff at each location and by the same person. After questions were answered and assurance of local management support of the survey effort had been given, the respondents were asked to mail their responses to a central point in the next two weeks. The results were analyzed for significance, and a few questions were eliminated that had received inconclusive or confused answers.[2]

The persons in charge of the respective libraries and information centers of the same multilocational, multidivisional company received the similarly formatted questionnaire "II," which was slightly longer and more detailed. The information requested included: organizational name and administrative reporting line; the location's mission; library staff composition and needs; financial support received; hours of operation; and space and equipment utilized. A major section on literature resources covered all formats mentioned in the similar section of the "I" survey of *externally* generated and *internally* produced information sources (both totals and annual rate of acquisition were requested). Information was also requested on the following: data bases and systems for information retrieval, together with indication of annual "traffic"; policy for acquiring and stocks of microform materials; relative rate of growth of the several formats of information units over a four-year time period; processing techniques and access points provided for these materials; how word of materials was disseminated; how newly available utilization services had been received and what were proposed for the future; and automated practices and sophisticated equipment requirements. Similar inquiries on types of reference questions, turn-around times, and apparent urgency were made as on "I" survey. Participation of the library in external (noncompany) networks, referral systems, union lists, and the like was asked along with a series of inquiries on relative importance of company confidential and proprietary information sources as compared to "open" sources. Finally, names were sought of higher management who were aware of the library, its services, and its needs.

After oral briefings, a written report was submitted to management for its consideration of such recommendations as the need to formalize relationships among the libraries and less formal information sources within the company, to do some pilot tests of new services, and to establish guidelines for future evolution of a corporate information system.

The Interview Method

In addition to the written survey of users, other measures may be employed to study them. The *direct interview method* enables the inquirer to make explanations as required, secure greater details where intense interest has been revealed by the user, solicit continuing interest in the activities of the IIS and put particular users in touch with other users who have expressed similar attitudes and desires. The disadvantages of "one-on-one" interviews are in the personnel expense involved, slowness of aggregation of preliminary results and trend indications, difficulty of selecting the ideal members as the sample for interviews, and the possible intrusion of the interviewer's opinions and personality into the interview occasion. (We will assume that the interviewer *does* report factually on the responses made.) Some major studies using the personal interview approach have used comprehensive interview guides as training tools to eliminate some of the weaknesses implied above.

The *group interview method* has the advantage of speeding up the process and cutting the number of interviewers needing to be trained and paid. Further, it permits group reinforcement of points made and can spark new directions of response and contribution. The disadvantages include intimidation of the more introverted of the interviewees in the group and obscuring of differences in interpretations of questions posed and significance of responses made. Most important of all, it involves a much more limited number of respondents than either the direct interview or the written survey and hence their selection is the "make or break" factor.

In both the direct group interview situations there is a difference in what people feel is the socially acceptable answer and the true answer of what they really think or do. Also they may not reveal certain informal information sources for fear of causing them to "dry up." (We have had access to authorities in our corporations to whom we could turn for subject matter assistance or for aid in getting through the company maze, but the understanding was that we would not reveal the source of our information, but rather would use the equivalent to the newspaper's "usually reliable source" phrase.)

The Observation Method

Another method for studying users is by observations. The *direct observation method* risks the well-known "Hawthorne Effect" that says the presence of the observer affects the very actions to be observed. Direct observation is very costly and has invasion-of-privacy overtones. The diary technique, the name of which is self-explanatory, may be used here or in the next category, but its problems relate to those of human nature including recording more sources than actually consulted, foreign language materials only really read by title or abstract, and items by persons in the company higher up in the management scale. The *unobstrusive observation method* does not necessarily sidestep the privacy issue, but it tends to interfere less in what actually happens.

Other Techniques

Electronic counters used in library traffic areas or adjacent to crucial sources have been effective. (Although one case of abnormally high counts was, after investigation, blamed on the leaky roof over the library: The counters had dutifully counted each rung on the workmen's ladders as they carried it in and out!) Stationing personnel at the door at random intervals to hand survey forms to all leaving in a certain half-hour period has been a repeatedly used tactic. Similarly, all requests by telephone or mail on certain days have been recorded and analyzed in detail. These approaches, however, do not cover failures or nonusers.

Rather less laborious than the diary technique mentioned earlier is the one involving a pocket alarm or cricket set to go off at random intervals and the person's recording what information-related task he or she is involved in that moment. We suggest limiting this technique to the heaviest users and for clarification of obscure points in interpretation of level of use or non-use of expensive aids.

Auditing from records of on-line searches is a heavily used technique in one corporation to learn most valuable data sources, users' departments, recency of references drawn, terminology employed, and the like.

Bibliometric studies may be handled with increasing valuable information, not only to show the relationship between sources the company is publishing *in* but also the ones it *uses*. (An early effort of this kind showed that GE was publishing *more* in the American Society of Mechanical Engineers publications than GM was, and GM was primarily thought of as a mechanical engineering-based firm.) Citation counts show more clearly the most highly regarded authors in the field. (For example, Nobel Prize winners such as Linus Pauling are cited by more junior authors in their references or bibliographies.) This information may, at the very least, be used to establish lists of possible company seminar speakers, potential consultants, or desirable candidates for IIS staff.

The panel of subject experts technique is used by broad-based studies of information needs. One pioneering example was conducted in the DuPont Company by the Secretary's Department using engineers and chemists from every conceivable technical assignment. Its success as a technique flowed along with DuPont staffers and exstaffers into efforts of the Department of Defense and by the Tripartite Committee of the Engineering Profession (a three-year project cofunded by the Engineering Foundation, the National Science Foundation, and the Boards of the Engineers Joint Council, the Engineering Societies Library, and Engineering Index, Inc.) and a few professional societies in the mid-1960s. Several such studies are known that were technically interesting but whose recommendations were never carried out, usually for reasons of timing constraints or financial requirements. The time is about ripe for another surge of interest in the panel of subject experts technique.

Other methods and techniques for studying users have been employed from time to time, but the above are the most useful.

WHAT USER STUDIES SHOW

Most study results can be boiled down into the following types of problems: the IIS is not the first nor the most important information source used; the IIS is not aggressive enough in making its wares known; using the IIS library requires effort; personal files are overrelied on; confidence in personal contacts is strong; and the existence of information dilution and pollution is evident.

It is probably not necessary to comment on such findings in depth, but we should assume they exist for a fledgling IIS unless their effect on it is minimized by careful planning and appropriate public relations efforts. For example, using theatrical skits as a device to interest higher management and project leaders in technical information's contribution to the mission dates back at least to Col. A. A. Arnhym and the Central Air Documents Office (Army-Navy-Air Force, Wright-Patterson Air Force Base, Ohio) in the late 1940s. The colonel was able to attract such attendees as Generals Charles A. Lindberg and Curtis LeMay to full-day presentations, and Orville Wright was personally briefed. Later, we also participated fully in GM Research Laboratories' annual three-day long open houses for its thirty-three divisions. A successful device there was having a monthly after-hours book review open to all technical center staffs. Ingredients included coffee served from the corporation's sterling silver coffee service (brought out under escort from the Detroit headquarter's vaults), cookies made by library staff members, and the gift of the reviewed book to the scientist or engineer who did the review.

Making the library convenient to use includes such aspects as location, limited number of regulations on use of material or requesting services, and accessibility after normal hours. Having the library near the cafeteria seems a fool-proof principle (technical people will be able to stop by before or after lunch, for example). However, in one laboratory we know the new library and the cafeteria were only separated by a decorative open-work wooden grill, and the silverware clatter was stupendous. In another instance, a laboratory library chose more roomy quarters in the basement rather than severely cramped second floor quarters, only to find too late that the dumpster trucks regularly operated adjacent to the reading room window. To provide accessibility after normal hours, at least one corporation has a uniform policy that any company library may be accessed by any badged employee of that location at any hour day or night (admittance to and egress from the library is by the security officer on duty). Security classified materials are excluded from after-hours use, and inventories have shown losses of library material to be minimal.

Some of the more forward IISs have addressed the matter of the personal files problem directly by offering technical staff assistance in setting up minimachine locational systems to make their files more useful to themselves and possibly their colleagues. This practice is expensive but more constructive than the fairly usual edict "We're not going to buy another vertical file for this department and that's that."

As for the "cosmopolitans" or other personal information contacts within the corporation, we have earlier recommended they be located and assisted in every way. In fact, one laboratory had our recommendation to recognize "cosmopolitan-ship" by a step increase in pay. The management thought the idea was interesting and agreed with us on several of the nominees, but did not proceed as the payment for information usefulness would be precedent setting and interfere with current compensation schedules.

The roster of distinguished scientists who have deplored the volume of technical information and seen its need for evaluation and reduction to "state-of-the-art" form is long and includes such names as Theodore von Karman (inventor of NATO's AGARDographs) and Conyers Herring (Bell Laboratories). However, an appropriate reward system has not yet been devised to popularize the expenditure of the required writing effort by those with appropriate immersion in the detail of the past efforts and knowledge of the "leading-edge" results of today.

Summary Recommendation

The users are the reason for existence of the IIS. All of their information needs related to the company mission and their own professional development must be met. The IIS management should involve the users in a council or via task groups so as to insure a maximum of coidentification and involvement with the IIS, while insuring a minimum of operational interference. We recommend that a consultant with known experience in IIS user studies be engaged to carry out a cooperative study with an internal task force including the senior company official committed to the establishment of a new or improved IIS; that the consultant be paid a flat fee for his services and be charged to construct a study plan that would identify the potential uniquenesses of the company's user population and include a minimum of time of reproving known findings such as covered in this chapter. (Particularization to the company, not undue generalization, is the objective); and that both an oral and written reports be submitted that include specific recommendations for management action. One recommendation must be on how the users are to be effectively involved in the operational IIS.

NOTES AND REFERENCES

1. F. W. Lancaster, "Assessment of the Technical Information Requirements of Users," in Alan Rees, ed., *Contemporary Problems in Technical Library and Information Center Management: A State-of-the-Art* (Washington, D. C.: American Society for Information Science, 1974), pp. 59-85.
2. Two ground rules for surveyors: Don't ask the question if you don't know what you are going to do with the answers you get; and don't ascribe unwarranted significance(s) to the numerical results you accumulate.

Chapter 9

IIS Budgeting: A Closer Look

No administrative problem is more basic than the establishment of an appropriate budget for the operation of the industrial information system. After decisions have been made on the operational functions to be carried out and the issues of activity, centralization, leadership, personnel, and users, as described in preceding chapters, have been resolved, the next step is to proceed with budgeting. Logical steps to take include:

Determine current expenditures for functions now a part of the IIS;

Calculate anticipated savings from reorganization of existing functions, less transitional costs;

Cost out the required expenditures for any proposed additional functions;

Establish a justified, prioritized budget for implementing functions and operating the IIS;

Secure budget adoption by the company, including approval of the implementation timetable;

Proceed with implementation of the budget.

CURRENT EXPENDITURES

A portion of the current costs of providing IIS functions is straightforward and capable of being inventoried: personnel, materials, facilities, equipment, and users. However, usually it will be found that more resources are being expended on carrying out these functions than had been realized by the company management. Some causes of inadvertent previous costs will be: marginal employees charged to their "home department's" budget but detailed to the IIS function to "save face" for weak supervisors; equipment purchased through error or found unsatisfactory in higher priority departments; areas found too inconveniently located or inadequately served by utilities to be employed by higher priority departments. There may even have previously existed a desire to *not know* the costs, as was the case in one steel company (per the Vice President of R&D's statement to the authors).

The evidence of current higher management commitment to an effective IIS program will be of material aid in the establishment of the true level and true nature of existing resource commitment to the IIS program.

ANTICIPATED SAVINGS

Materials and supplies costs are probable candidates for savings. Such items as duplicate periodical subscriptions and excess vertical file procurement almost invariably occur and can be avoided. Some floor space savings are probable as is elimination of some supervisory "slots." On the other hand, allowances must be made if a move is to be made from one operational mode to another. Accordingly, projected savings should be figured realistically. We recommend that final calculated savings be reduced by one-fourth and the budgeting proceed on the basis of this lowered total.

EXPENDITURES REQUIRED FOR ADDITIONAL IIS ACTIVITIES

Comparative and empirical data are of great importance in this budgeting step. The Special Libraries Association has published "Profiles" of special libraries for a variety of industrial and service firms giving typical tasks carried out, resources utilized, and budget percentages. Personnel costs cited were uniformly between 60-70 percent of total costs while the percentages for types of materials and equipment varied from an advertising agency through a public utility firm to an R&D organization. Individual pamphlet reprints of these "Profiles" and "Objectives and Standards" may be secured free from the Special Libraries Association, 235 Park Avenue South, New York, N. Y. 10003.[1] Note that further elaboration of this topic appears in the next section.

DETERMINATION OF THE BUDGET

There is much greater comparability among organizations on the expenditures for what is commonly known as the special library portion of the IIS than among such functions as generation and production of information. While the ASIS (American Society for Information Sciences) has a Special Interest Group (SIG) on Costs, Budgeting, and Economics with the responsibility to "study cost analysis, cost accounting, cost effectiveness, cost benefits (what is information worth?), PPB (planning-programming-budgeting), standards and definitions of cost and effort, selling a budget, and economics of the information industry on national and international scales,"[2] its contributions must still be considered fragmentary, but do merit close following in view of the broad spectrum of functional interests. We concentrate for the remainder of this section on fairly conventional information sources and the library staff to service them—that is, "special libraries" in the sense used by the Special Libraries Association.

Industrial Special Library Budgeting

There is empirical evidence that given steady state conditions (i.e., the special library is not in its first or second year of operation and no new major function has been assumed), the industrial special library service may be provided for the cost equal to that currently expended by the company for telephone service for each of the "probable library users" in that company location.

Some terms need to be defined. First, the cost of telephone service includes the instrument, some intercom capacity, and the station's *prorata* share of local and leased long-distance line expense. Typically this expense runs from a low of $130 to about $175 per year per *most probable user* (MPU). We use this phrase MPU rather than the usual count of users that an electric eye at the door or tallies on a scrap card at a desk note because users differ in backgrounds, intensity of use, and level of satisfaction of need. When empirical weights are applied to specific groups in the location population, adjusted figures are obtained that when multiplied by the figures cited above result in budget levels corresponding to real-life situations, as was the case in one major multidivisional, multilocational company. Similarly budget levels for three other industrial organization locations were calculated from available sources as class projects by the senior author's student classes. (While the latter companies did not reveal their exact budget figures to the student groups, each observed that the student concensus achieved results "quite within the correct ball park" when applying our empirical equation. A typical set of assumptions and results will follow this section.)

For the first and most significant term in the empirical equation—(MPU_1)—take the number of professional engineers and scientists in the location, plus 1/3 the technicians plus 1/3 higher level administrative staff. Modify this total upward if there are significant numbers in such subject fields as chemistry and modify it downwards if there are significant numbers of "drafting board-type" design and industrial engineers.

A second modification of the MPU total is obtained by weighting personnel totals on the basis of educational attainment. Multiply each Ph.D. in the location by a weight of 3, each Master's possessor by 2, each Bachelor's possessor by 1, each professional nondegreed person by 3/4, and each technician by 1/3. In addition other staff persons are to be multiplied by 1/10. The resulting total is MPU_2 and would be divided by some number (here called n_2) as experience dictates.

The third and final modification of the MPU total is computed from the job classification held by these same persons, with weights of 3 to project leaders, departmental heads, or equivalents (professional managerial), 2 for senior project staff (senior professional), 1 for each project junior staff person (junior professional), 1/3 for each technician and 1/5 for administrative leaders (MPU_3). This total is divided by some number (here called n_3) as experience dictates.

Add MPU_1, some fraction of MPU_2, and some fraction of MPU_3. Multiply this sum by about $150-175 for a research-type location, or by about $140-155 for a developmental-type location, and around $130 for a production-type location.

$$(MPU_1 + \frac{MPU_2}{n_2} + \frac{MPU_3}{n_3}) \times \frac{\text{Telephone service cost for this location}}{\text{Instruments provided this population}} =$$

Adequate Industrial Special Library Budget.

To cross-check these calculations and to build confidence in the procedure, the probable budget of the industrial location can be built up in a second way from open literature sources: Bowker's *Industrial Research Laboratories of the United States* and Young, Young, and Kruzas' *Directory of Special Libraries and Information Centers*, and *American Library Directory*.[3] From these sources, we may learn the size and composition of the technical and library staffs, the library holdings, and can compute the acquisition rate using the "Useful Life Principle." This latter says that since much industrial library information has a useful life of five years, we can assume that the annual acquisition rate for books of such libraries will be one-fifth the present holdings. (A more conservative approach would be to assume a useful life of ten years for the material, which would halve that acquisition rate.) Table 9.1 contains the other basic assumptions used in the cross-check procedure.

The following are sample calculations according to our empirical equation, for what we called the "Big State Rotary Wing Company" (conducts research, design, development, testing, and evaluation of rotary wing/VTOL type aircarft and associated electronic systems):

Professional staff: Chemists 12; electrical engineers 25; mechanical engineers 12; aeronautical engineers 75; instrument engineers 9; metallurgical engineers 6; psychologists 9 (Subtotal 154); technicians 90; other Lab staff 15. Of above, 1/6 are Ph.D. possessors, 1/3 are Master's possessor's, and 1/2 Bachelor's possessors; technicians are nondegreed. Also of above 10 are project leaders, 40 are senior project staff, and 104 are junior product staff.

$MPU_1 = (154) + 1/3 \times 90 = 154 + 30 = 184.$

$MPU_2 = 3(1/6)(154) + 2(1/3)(154) + 1/2(154) + 1/3(90)$
$= 72 + 102 + 72 + 30 = 276.$

$MPU_3 = 10(3) + 40(2) + 104(1) + 1/3(90) = 30 + 80 + 104 + 30 = 244.$

Table 9.1 Assumption in the Cross-Check Procedure for Budget Calculations

LIBRARY STAFF

Average Salaries		Ratio
Professional	$12,000/year	2 clerks to 1 professional
Clerk	$ 6,500/year	

MATERIALS

Average Prices		Ratios
Periodical subscription	$30.00/year	Book budget = 1/3 of the periodical budget
Book	$15.00 ea.	
Pamphlets	$ .30 ea.	
Maps (U.S. Geological Survey)	$ 3.00 ea.	Travel, binding ⎫ = 1/6 of the Supplies ⎬ materials Photocopy, etc. ⎭ budget
Govt. and state publications	$ 1.00 ea.	
Dissertations (microfilm) (xerox copy)	$ 5.00 ea. $10.00 ea.	

Presumably in this type installation MPU_2 would be about the right number; however, to involve all three terms, assume $n_2 = 5$ and also $n_3 = 5$.

Therefore, $MPU_2 \times \$140 = (276) \times (140) = \underline{\$38,640}$.

Alternatively, $(MPU_1 + \dfrac{MPU_2}{5} + \dfrac{MPU_3}{5})(140) = (184 + \dfrac{276}{5} + \dfrac{244}{5})(140) = \underline{\$40,320}$.

The cross-check procedure for these calculations appears in Table 9.2.

The budget calculations in Table 9.3 resulted from a class project and were rated as "substantially correct" by the company.

Randall uses somewhat different assumptions in his latest *Special Libraries* article on budgeting—that is, he importantly bases certain figures on borrowers,

Table 9.2 Sample Budget Cross-Check for "Big State Rotary Wing Company"

LIBRARY STAFF

```
1 Professional x $12,000 = $12,000
1 Clerical      x $ 6,500 =   6,500
         Personnel Total = $18,500
```

MATERIALS

Book collection -- 3,000 volumes x 1/5 "useful life" x $15.00 each	= $ 9,000
Periodicals -- 145 current titles x $30.00 each	= 4,350
(Assume) 7 Abstracting services x $150.00 each	= 1,050
(Assume) 2,000 Technical reports x $1.00 each	= 2,000
(Assume) 500 Government publications x $1.00 each	= 500
(Assume) 10 Dissertations x $10.00 each	= 100
(Assume) Pamphlets, etc.	= 200
Travel, binding, supplies, photocopies = 1/6 of above	2,866
Total Materials =	$20,066
Budget =	$38,566*

* This figure seemed *close enough*, but was not verified with the company

---

rather than MPUs.[4] He points out three ways of budget making: this year's figure plus a statistically appropriate increase for next year, increasing or decreasing a percentage upon management edict, or using statistics and trade data to construct a rational, defensible budget. Randall suggests that where salaries and materials (books and periodical subscriptions) are considered together, they should total 50-70 percent of the library spending, with overhead being excluded. He suggests one staff member for 60-80 active borrowers; staff should be in the ratio of 2 in reference services for 1 in processing; further there should be 1:1 to 3:1 professionals to subprofessionals; the professional salary should average $14,000 with the library assistants averaging $9,000 (obviously he reflects a higher "cost-of-living" area).

On book costs, he feels 2 to 3 books should be bought for every user (at about $20/title in science and nearly $18/title in technology) with replacement rate at about 6 percent/year. Randall sees 1.5 to 2 periodical titles/user at about $65/title.

The more minor items he sees are binding, supplies, and travel. Costs of binding approximate $7.00/volume as bound (alternative of microfilm needs considering). Supplies call for about $.50 for monograph acquired. Travel for each professional staff member should be at least $600. Randall finds costs peculiar to a specific location as being subject more to policy than to reason. reason. New technologies such as photocopy replacement for loan from other libraries (the authors are accustomed to requests for many hundreds of pages annually) and the costs for machine-based literature services from governmental, professional society, or information "broker" sources are not yet stabilized. (One broker has stated they plan to consider adding one new data base to their service each month for 1978.)

Two cautions are offered when the IIS is subject to a budget policy of "this year's figure plus the anticipated inflation for next year . . . upon management edict": first, a percentage increase in an inappropriate figure for required services remains inappropriate for next year as well, and second, a higher budget request than what higher management instructed be submitted will always have to be defended. (Over the years the authors have consistently prepared exhibits for the anticipated budget level + 10 percent; in years when the sales were better than expected, the higher management knew who could use supplemental funds, while on other occasions expensive laboratory equipment could not be delivered before fiscal year deadlines and largish sums had to be spent quickly to avoid return to general company funds.)

BUDGETING SYSTEMS

There is a high probability that the budgeting for the IIS will be impinged upon by one of the newer management philosophies or systems pervading the firm. We refer to management by objectives (MBO), planning-programming-budgeting system (PPBS), and zero-based budgeting.

According to a leading advocate of MBO, McConkey, *management by objectives* ". . . is a systems approach to managing an organization in which the managers first determine what results they want the organization to accomplish (including [their] order . . .), they then formulate concrete plans for attaining the results, establish target dates by which the results must be achieved, and lastly, establish a control or monitoring technique by which they can measure . . . progress toward the required results—taking corrective action as necessary."[5] He sees the MBO system composed of "objectives, plans, managerial direction and action, control (monitoring), feedback."[6] A most useful part of his presentation is the case study on The Western Company (the major independent oil well service operation), which covers experiences with MBO to 1970. We have been privileged to examine The Western Company's MBO flow charts for all-level management indoctrination as of 1975 and found them clear and impressive.

PPBS has been defined by Hamburg et al. as having these basic elements: ". . . specification of objectives, derivation of performance measures to evaluate achievement of these objectives, specification of a program structure oriented toward achievement of stated objectives, specification of input and output

Table 9.3 Sample Budget Cross-Check for "Fox Petroleum Company" Laboratory

Part I

"FOX Petroleum Company," Production and Exploration Lab

Part I: Itemized Calculation of the Budget

Staff: 2 professionals, 4 clerks

Complete Material Holdings		Yearly Acquisitions
Periodical subscriptions	550	550 subscriptions
Books	11,200	1/3 of periodical budget
Govt. & state publications	4,000	1/5 x 4,000 = 800
Maps (U.S. Geological Survey)	1,000	1/5 x 1,000 = 200
Dissertations	600	1/5 x 600 = 120
Pamphlets	400	1/5 x 400 = 80

Determination of the Budget

Staff

```
Professional - 2 x $12,000 = $24,000
Clerks        - 4 x   6,500 =  26,000
Personnel Total              $50,000
```

Materials

```
Periodicals                       550 x $30.00 = $16,500
Govt. & state publications        800 x $ 1.00 =     800
Maps (U.S. Geological Survey)     200 x $ 3.00 =     600
Dissertations                     120 x $ 5.00 =     600
Pamphlets                          80 x $  .30 =      24
Books -- 1/3 of $16,500                        =   5,500
Total Materials                                  $24,024
```

Travel, supplies, binding, photocopying -- 1/6 x $24,024 = $4,004

```
Materials      $24,024
Staff           50,000
Travel, etc.     4,004
               $78,028
```

Library type: 66-33 (approximately 66% of budget for staff and 33% for materials)

Part II

Part II: Library Budget in Terms of Probable Users

<u>Employees</u>

Professional	256 (1/3 Ph.D.'s: assume the remainder are Master's)
Technicians	198
Other staff	218
Number of Ph.D.'s	1/3 x 256 = 85
Number of Master's	256 - 85 = 171

Weighted variables for measuring employee library use:
- Ph.D.   3
- Master's   2
- Technician 1/3
- Other staff 1/10

Multiply the number of employees in each classification by their respective weighted variables; and add the resulting numbers to get the *Most Probable User* (MPU) figure:

Ph.D.	85 x 3	= 255
Master's	171 x 2	= 342
Technician	198 x 1/3	= 66
Other staff	218 x 1/10	= 22
		685 (MPU)

Consider "x" is the amount of money spent by the library per probable user; multiply the (MPU) figure by "x"; set this amount equal to the estimated budget; and solve for "x":

$$685x = \$78{,}028$$
$$x = \$\ 114 \text{ (approximately)}$$

Therefore, the library spends $114 per probable user, which is in the low part of the range.

indicators for programs in the program structure, determination of relationships between performance measures and input and output indicators, and development of a multiyear plan."[7] The flow charts and decision tables they include merit close study. We have kept in touch with government colleagues learning to live with PPBS procedures and also examined PPBS results in the budgeting for a major metropolitan area library. Although not mentioned in the textbooks, a prime ingredient in the latter library's success with PPBS is the *rapport* its budget officer has established over fifteen years with the municipal comptroller—his figures and priorities are believed.

Zero-based budgeting is currently being actively utilized by a major chemical company in establishing support levels for a complex of mini-information analysis centers within their IIS. The originator of the technique, Peter A. Pyhrr, described zero-based budgeting as ". . . requiring that each organization analyze its entire budget request in detail—both current and new activities. The first step requires the preparation of a decision package for each activity or operation. This decision package includes an analysis of the cost, purpose, alternative courses of action, measures of performance, consequences of not performing the activity and the benefits. The second step requires that each decision package be ranked in order of importance against other current and new activities. A significant feature of the process is the requirement that each manager evaluate two types of alternatives: first, different ways of performing each activity . . . and second, different levels of effort for performing each activity."[8] Installations do occasionally impose this technique on top of PPBS procedures, and Pyhrr describes how this may be done (an exceptional degree of management skill and personal charm would seem to be necessary, however).

Summary Recommendation

We recommend that the IIS director submit realistic, yet fully innovative, budget requests that correctly reflect the best current budgeting practices/procedures/systems found acceptable by the company's senior management.

NOTES AND REFERENCES

1. R. S. Leonard, "Objectives and Standards for Special Libraries," *Special Libraries* 55(10):672-680 (December 1964). See also her "Profiles of Special Libraries . . . ABC Manufacturing Corporation, . . . DEF Industrial Corporation," *Special Libraries* 57(3):179-184 (March 1966); ". . . GHI Public Utilities Firm, . . . JKL Bank, *Special Libraries* 57(4):227-231 (April 1966); ". . . MNOP Advertising Agency Library, . . . Research and Development Division of the QRS Chemical Manufacturing Company," *Special Libraries* 57(5):327-331 (May/June 1966).

2. "Special Interest Groups (SIGS)" in *ASIS Handbook & Directory*, 1975 Ed., *Bulletin of the American Society for Information Science* **2**(2):vii (August 1975).
3. *Industrial Research Laboratories of the United States,* 14th ed. (New York: Bowker, 1975), 585 pp.; M. L. Young, H. C. Young, and Anthony T. Kruzas, *Directory of Special Libraries and Information Centers* (Detroit: Gale Research Co., 1974), 1435 pp. and *American Library Directory*, 30th ed. (New York: Bowker, 1976), 1389 pp.
4. Gordon E. Randall, "Budgeting for Libraries," *Special Libraries* **67**(1):8-12 (January 1976). See also his "Randall's Rationalized Ratios," *Special Libraries* **66**(1):6-11 (January 1975).
5. Dale D. McConkey, *Management by Objectives for Staff Managers* (New York: Vantage Press, 1972), p. 15. Also see pp. 145-168 for the MBO experiences of The Western Company.
6. Ibid., p. 17.
7. Morris Hamburg et al., *Library Planning and Decision-making Systems* (Cambridge, Mass.: MIT Press, 1974), p. 3.
8. Peter A. Pyhrr, *Zero-Base Budgeting, a Pratical Management Tool for Evaluating Expenses* (New York: Wiley, 1973); see pp. 154-157 for how this is accomplished.

Chapter 10

Word Processing, Correspondence Control, and Records Management

Internally generated information items require IIS management consideration of three procedures: word processing, correspondence control, and records management. The "front end" of internally generated textual matter is currently termed *word processing*. *Correspondence control* includes both filing and retrieval of internally and externally generated textual information, and *records management* of these items embraces a range of document destinations from perpetual storage underground in a "salt mine" to the shredding machine. No example is yet known of the optimum employment of this trinity of procedures, but enormous potential exists for managements with both vision and courage.

WORD PROCESSING

IBM started upgrading its office products concepts to "word processing" about 1970, following up on the pioneering work in the 1960s by IBM World Trade Corporation (Germany) on *textverableitung* (TA). A parallel development in "Office Landscaping" or the "Open Office" also occurred in Germany. It took *Business Week* nearly forty pages in June 1975 to explain what the concept of "word processing" was and what it means to "The Office of the Future."[1] *Business Week* used as the definition for its story, "Word Processing (WP) is the manipulation of words, sentences, and paragraphs by advanced hardware, while data processing (EDP) is the manipulation of numbers."[2]

One way to amplify this concept is to note that *Business Week* covers the "paperless office," cost control, productivity, alteration in concept level of the office, errors made in recent past, effect of new technology, involvement of top management, only giant manufacturers need apply, acquisitions of marginal suppliers, financial stresses and strains, and pathways toward the "paperless office." Another way to look at its scope is to examine the advertisers *Business Week* attracted and what were the offerings (some multiple listings are included):

Marketers of architectural concepts with complexes of stations = 2

Marketers of work stations = 6

Automatic editing typewriters = 4

Minicomputers = 4

Dictation equipment = 2

Stand-alone filing equipment = 2

Copiers = 1

Mailing systems = 1

Microfilm equipment = 1

Interestingly enough, IBM—the pioneer in the concept—was not an advertiser, but one of the architectural marketers showed an IBM facility using its products.

Significant quotes from the *Business Week* article include: "Where office costs used to be twenty percent to thirty percent of the total in a company, they have now grown to forty percent to fifty percent of all costs" (Allan Purchase, Stanford Research Institute),[3] and "The office information system has to be easy to use, require little training and it must be adaptable to changing requirements . . . . It will not be a mammoth system for a whole division, plant, or company, but will focus on a manager and his department. What we have to develop is the friendly machine" (Jack Goldman, XEROX, Palo Alto).[4]

IBM's unruffled approach is to define WP unaggressively as ". . . a program for improving the efficiency of business communications." This program is carried out in an "establishment" having a single "work group" or "multiwork groups." A work group is two or more employees, working in close proximity and having a unique organizational identification or function. It must have at least two "work stations" (i.e., a location at which a job is performed by a worker). Both "hardware procedures" and "work flow procedures" are studied with a view to achieving the optimum combination for maximum improvement in business communications (WP).

Personnel may be affected by a "physical personnel change" (i.e., relocated to a new location) or a "nonphysical personnel change" (i.e., the job changes but the location is retained). Examination of hardware procedures may result in recommendations for changes in input, output, and/or distribution equipment.

IBM looks at work group systems or multiwork group systems, but an integral part of the strategy is prospect/customer involvement from the study inception. Thus, the more complex the establishment is and the more complex the isolated crucial factors are, the greater the probability of heightened personnel sociological implications and the greater the customer-originated content of the final proposal/plan or "study."[5]

The building-blocks of WP are combinations of principal persons (or "principals") and secretaries. The latter in the past did both administrative (filing, mail handling, telephone communications, records maintenance, and schedule "watching") and typing/transcription duties. The traditional combination has been one principal and one secretary. This combination is the most mutually satisfying one, as we can testify: "Professional secretarial support over the years from Millie, Donna, and Peggy featured report and article deadlines met, final repro copy delivered on weekends to suburban mailboxes from the shambles of draft copy that was cut-and-paste and had handwritten cryptic emendations, airplane tickets with interline transfers that were humanly possible to achieve, persistent good will (Christmas cards are still exchanged), and their sure reinforcement that the information center was the most important and productive unit in the establishment!" Nonetheless, this combination is expensive for universal practice, particularly when the inevitable slack times appear between crises and it is neither party's advantage to "advertise" them.

We first became aware of WP in 1970 when essentially all typewriters at the IBM Lexington facility were withdrawn to a central location and *all* written communications had to be dictated by telephone (including headings to be placed on catalog cards and overdue notices). The reactions were predictably vigorous ("I worked hard to get out of the typing pool and now we're all back in one," on the one hand, and on the other, "How can I be a manager with no one outside my door?") Such drastic simplistic solutions are no longer in vogue.

The WP *systems* approach should be followed in determining alternative combinations of principals and secretaries. Criteria for rating performance are crucial and undergirded by considerations of job fulfillment (JF), which is the mutual concern of management and employee. Depending on the functional assignment of the principal(s) other criteria will vary in importance but will typically include relative excellence, reactivity, ease-of-use, and resultfulness.

The higher the principal in the organizational chart the greater the emphasis on relative excellence. Ease-of-use is assured by the operation of the ancient truism, "rank has its privileges," and resultfulness is a consideration for continued employment. Principals might reasonably be provided an ungrouped support system retaining the normal combined administrative and typing stations. Any overload would be expeditiously handled by the WP Center (i.e., the least changed from the normal situation).

Marketing principals emphasize relative excellence. They are logically supported by the first variation of the above: Introduction of grouping, but retention of administrative/typing stations, in which, typically, the group would be self-sufficient. Engineering principals' aid is primarily judged on resultfulness, with reactivity and ease-of-use ranking low. The second variation would typically have several "purely" administrative stations, with one being a part-time coordinator, and the majority of the typing would be done in the WP Center. Manufacturing principals are almost exclusively rated on job fulfillment and resultfulness. The third variation would have a full-time leader manning one administrative station, one or more additional administrative stations, and the typing would be wholly done in the WP Center.

After secretarial task analysis is completed and the supervisory hierarchy established (normally headed by a WP systems manager), assignments of tasks are made to individual work stations on a "prime" or "relief" basis. Clear understanding of reasonable assignments is facilitated by the preciseness and care given to the study underlying the WP effort.

WP Systems Case Study

A 1976 "showcase" WP installation is sketched below to bring some of the above considerations of WP systems into focus.

> Establishment Able (as we're calling it) has nine departments. The head of one department felt its principal product was paperwork and hence WP should be explored for effective deployment of sixty-nine principals and fifty-two secretaries.
>
> After executive briefing of the establishment's director and the department head at the contractor's local office, the department head and the most senior "graduate" from the secretarial ranks were sent out of town for a week's schooling. This executive schooling was taken along with equivalent personnel from other organizations, and there was ample time to exchange impressions and rationales for action. Heavy emphasis was placed on the need to bring departmental employees "on board" if a decision were made to introduce a WP study on the leaders' return.
>
> The study was made, suitable alterations in physical facilities were carried out, and some upgrading in dictating, transcribing, typing, and copying equipment was achieved. The educational program for departmental employees was stepped up, a flare-up involving an indignant petition by affected persons was capably and considerately handled, and operational status was achieved. Visitors are now well received and perceived good morale exists.
>
> Nine principals were instrumental in "rescuing" their secretaries from the WP Center on the basis of need for their shorthand skills. These secretaries are titled "Correspondence Secretaries" and are located outside the principals' doors. Interestingly enough, the

department's telephone dictation procedures have since been so "debugged" that the correspondence secretaries' shorthand skills are being used less and less.

The other sixty principals share thirty-four "Administrative Secretaries" who perform all the usual services on telephone requests. The latter have administration support from nine entrance-level secretaries who do copying, alphabetizing, miscellaneous typing, and relieve the administrative secretaries as required.

Capping the career path of secretary-administrative secretary-correspondence secretary is the "Word Processing Systems Manager." The WP system manager feels that participation in the WP study was exhilarating, the Study results were reasonable and required for the department's growth. She feels that the other eight departments are watching closely and about half of them will go into a WP study in the more-or-less near term. She emphasized the importance of the total commitment of Able's department head to the word processing (WP) concept.

There are no current plans for extending interconnections into Able's correspondence control or records management functions.

Summary Recommendation

Word processing (WP) has a place in IIS considerations, is a workable and working concept, and has been woefully neglected heretofore as an input source of company originated information. We recommend that WP be considered for vertical integration into optimum IISs.

CORRESPONDENCE CONTROL

The information generated as the result of the word processing (WP) activities just described are combined with information gleaned from incoming letters, memoranda, and other communications from higher headquarters in and outside the company, trade associations, and the several "publics." Based on these materials, decisions are made and actions are taken by the company. Hopefully, these are consistent, nonduplicative, and in accordance with stated policy and priorities.

Typically, an organization's "hold" on its correspondence is less than ideal. Evidence of that state includes bulging correspondence files, growing personal files of magazines, vendor literature, and other types of reference materials at "work stations," and the uncoordinated creation of microfilm and hard-copy files in storage areas.

"Baker Division" Case Study

A major division of an engineering organization had the above symptoms, and our review[6] of their situation seems to have considerable general applicability. Note that the discussion that follows touches on records management incidentally (although we have chosen to treat it separately in the following section) since it is so intertwined with correspondence control in real life.

Correspondence Files

In determining the extent of the problems associated with correspondence control in the Baker Division (our nomenclature for the "major division of an engineering organization"), we had to make certain assumptions in relation to correspondence activity. The primary assumption was that the activities of the division would continue to show a healthy growth with a commensurate growth in correspondence. Additional assumptions included the idea that correspondence files contain a record of all of Baker's activities, that technical capabilities for the creation of a correspondence control system already existed in the division, and that any manager over the correspondence operations would have an appropriate level of competency.

A few terms needed to be precisely defined in order to clarify the nature of correspondence operations. The definitions included the following:

> *Correspondence:* formal letters and letters of transmittal received or written by the Baker Division. It includes Baker Division-to-other divisions, Baker-to-field activities, and letters to other agencies and individuals. Correspondence also includes attachments to the above.
>
> *Vital record:* one or more pieces of correspondence and related documentation that record the activities of the organization and provide proof or disproof of activities performed by, for, and within the organization. The level at which a record or set of records becomes vital is that point at which their loss or destruction would render the organization incapable of restarting its operation in a reasonable length of time, and their loss could prove embarrassing or could damage the reputation of the management team.
>
> *Loss or destruction:* correspondence and related documentation lost by being removed from a file and placed in an unknown location, or destroyed by various accidents (e.g., fire, civil disorder, tornado).
>
> *Historical record:* a *complete* file of all materials pertaining to a given activity and covering a specified period of time.

Word Processing, Correspondence Control, and Records Management 147

Correspondence Problems and Observations

Approximately 3,000 pieces of correspondence arrived at Baker Division each year. The levels of possible response ranged from immediate action to information only to long-term research and development projects requiring the coordination of one or more working components. The results of all these activities were the generation of 3,000 pieces of outgoing correspondence. This one-to-one relationship is rather typical.

Traceability of the actions of the division through the correspondence records on file depended on one or two highly efficient secretaries with unusually good memories who were able to respond to requirements for data from the files. Managers and personnel throughout the organization had recognized the problems inherent in this situation and responded by creating and maintaining their own files. The reasons for this duplicated effort are many. Among them, however, was the known possibility that secretary-with-good-memory X will be on vacation when Manager Y is called on to respond to a situation about which he wrote a letter six months ago. It is patently inefficient for a technological organization to rely on secretarial memory for information retrieval.

The existing system of correspondence control was essentially a decentralized set of files that was primarily local in content. Each unit maintained about four or five five-drawer file cabinets with approximately one-half of one cabinet devoted strictly to correspondence. Each unit head set up a file system based on his own perception of his information needs. This practice had led to the use of a different set of subject terms by each unit, sometimes for similar material. File maintenance was generally left to secretaries and there were no indexes or subject guides to file contents.

The problems that arise from such a decentralized and uncoordinated set of files fall into three main categories: security, accessibility, and flexibility. In the area of *flexibility,* the existing files could be utilized effectively only by the person who created them, which severely restricted the ability for "cross-talk" between the files in different units. In addition, files tended to grow larger over a period of time because of the difficulty of weeding, which not only added costs to storage but also made file maintenance more difficult and time-consuming. As volumes of files increased, severe problems invariably arose.

Accessibility referred to the problem of how a person knew where to find material in a given file. The fact no guides existed to help infrequent users of a file meant that, short of physical inspection of the contents of a file, there was no way to tell whether a file would contain a given piece of correspondence. This problem was further compounded by the fact that there was no way readily to tell who should see a particular piece of correspondence.

Finally in the area of *file security*, there was no assurance that a full

148   Industrial Information Systems

historical record was contained in any of the files maintained. Thus there was no assurance that any particular vital record would be retained, or, if retained, that it would be readily accessible. This lack of security resulted partly from the fact that there was no unique way to identify any particular piece of correspondence and partly from the lack of a single authoritative historical file of all correspondence. A further effect of the lack of security of existing files was their vulnerability to problems resulting from personnel turnover.

Concepts and Alternative Courses of Action

Concept of Control Numbering System. The primary element of any large publication control system—whether it be for technical reports, service requests, books or correspondence—is some method of uniquely identifying each item in the system. A publication numbering system is normally used to provide this unique identity.

A unique identifier provides several capabilities. Among these are the following:

> Each piece of correspondence has its own identity and can be referred to or asked for in a way that leaves no room for question;
>
> At any level in the organization a log can be created that completely records the input and output of a particular component in terms that permit traceability to other components;
>
> Local files can be set up in a flexible manner and at the same time eliminate the need for duplicate filing within the same file by utilizing an appropriate log and cross references;
>
> Sequential numbering permits creation of a correspondence control file since the numbering scheme provides a means of ensuring a complete file.

Concept of Correspondence Control Point. Assuming the use of a Control Numbering System, a correspondence control point can be established to serve as the first stopping point for any piece of correspondence entering the division and as the last stopping point for any piece of correspondence leaving the division. The benefits from the correspondence control point can vary according to the placement of the function within the organization, the level of automation utilized for its operation, and the responsibilities assigned to its manager.

Examples of the benefits are the following:

Vital records can be identified, isolated and protected;

Routing of correspondence to the proper point of interest will be improved;

No piece of correspondence or related material will be lost;

Retrieval of any piece of correspondence or related material can be accomplished rapidly and effectively;

A method for tracking correspondence throughout the organization will be initiated;

The efficiencies and ease of maintaining a file will probably filter down to lower components, as confidence in the centralized system grows;

The need for duplicate files of inactive material will be eliminated;

A purging and weeding mechanism will be created;

Machine-generated reports can provide a means for reducing duplication of effort and will reduce the load on secretaries;

A permanent historical record will be created with appropriate indexes for retrieval;

As confidence in a centralized system grows and the necessity for a complete record of division activities is understood, personnel will tend to generate meaningful records in the form of records of oral agreements, and so forth.

Correspondence Control Alternatives. Several postures can be taken toward the existing correspondence control system at Baker, each of which has its own set of benefits and drawbacks. At one extreme, the division can continue in the present pattern. Short-term impact will be negligible, but the long-term impact will be costly in terms of unorganized duplication of files and filing systems. At the other extreme, a fully automated centralized indexing and filing scheme can be imposed with no provision for active files within the units. The short-term impact will be high costs for design and implementation along with some savings by elimination of most of the file duplication within the organization. As in all active systems, the continuing costs of operation will be high due to the necessity of providing for all day-to-day needs of the management team. Furthermore, it is likely that local files will gradually regenerate as the needs of individual managers change.

It is therefore essential to determine a balance between the passive and active role of an automated system. It is appropriate, we believe, to leave the bulk of the active role with the operating components. The automated control system should assume the role of providing for all passive needs (i.e., historical record, vital record protection, and so forth). In the process, the indexing and filing techniques designed will improve the efficiency at the operating levels by providing for logs, file access points, indexes, microfilming policy and storage procedures, and weeding policy.

The benefits and drawbacks of these alternatives follow logically from the existing problems and are outlined in more detail below:

Retain the Present System

Benefits:
1. The individual character of each set of files is retained.
2. No additional costs are required.

Drawbacks:
1. Accessibility of files is not increased.
2. No historical record of the division's business or capability to protect the files against loss is created.
3. Duplication of correspondence is encouraged.
4. Effectiveness of the files as an information resource will decrease as the volume of the correspondence handled approaches or exceeds the capacity one person can manage (i.e., there is little room for growth).
5. Microfilming of files remains uncoordinated (i.e., some units film correspondence and some do not.

Create an Automated Centralized Correspondence Control System; Eliminate Local Files

Benefits:
1. At a minimum each unit will keep a complete set of historical correspondence files.
2. A set of logs will evolve on the date correspondence came in or went out, to whom it was sent, and how it was filed.
3. Retention in a central file of all correspondence transactions, and thereby elimination of the need for local files,
4. A defined set of access points to the material will be provided. (These could include any or all of those items shown in Table 10.1.)
5. The creation of a complete file will permit filming and subsequent protection of the file against loss by fire or civil disorder.
6. An automated system will serve as a reflection of the Division's capabilities as well as a prototype for implementation by other components of the organization.

Drawbacks:
1. Difficulties in getting people to rely on a central historical file will be involved.
2. Materials needed for day-to-day referral will not be with the working component.

Retain Local Files for Active Correspondence and Depend on an Automated Centralized Correspondence Control File for Other Needs

Benefits (in addition to those in item 2 above):
1. Local active files with the attendant benefits of responsiveness and adaptability to personal needs will be maintained.
2. A workable automated system could be packaged for usage by other components of the organization via the division's computer.
3. A complete historical record will be created and vital records will be readily identifiable and protected.

Drawbacks:
1. Costs in maintaining a system in addition to the present one will be involved.

It is evident that maintaining the status quo by retaining the present correspondence system provides neither short-term nor long-term relief. If more clerical support were added, a short-term advantage would develop in the sense that more manpower would be available to file, locate, and retrieve materials. The long-term need for an improved system would not be resolved. On the other hand, the design and implementation of a correspondence control system would require the attention of a qualified information systems specialist. The expertise of this specialist in systems design, computer storage and retrieval techniques, indexing schemes, and microfilm storage and retrieval would carry over to the other elements of this activity area including records management.

Selected Course of Action

The Baker Division accepted (1) the concept of a Control Numbering System, (2) the concept of the Correspondence Control Point, and (3) the concept of an Information System Specialist *in principle.*

The position was filled with a newly graduated Library School person who had followed the information science specialization and had some part-time work experience. The position was at something less in level than the full description outlined in Table 10.2 as being ideal. The incumbent was to report to the division's head of administration and finance. He was to "evolve" a

Table 10.1 Potential Data Elements for Automated Correspondence Control System

Data Element*	Alpha	Numeric	Multiple Field	Estimated Length
Corrsp #		x	no	6
Unit	x	x	no	2-4
Misc		x	no	4-8
Addressee	x		no	10-15
Author	x		no	4-8
Date		x	no	6
Incoming ref		x	?	6
Project #		x	no	8
Project name	x		no	15-20
Subject	x		no	15-20
Keywords	x		yes	8 each
Unit type		x	no	1
Retention code		x	no	6
Action code		x	no	1
Action date		x	no	6
Copies	x		yes	4-6 each
Local file	x		?	6 each
Acc't #		x	no	6
Serial #		x	no	6
Division		x	no	2
Subunit		x	no	2
Code for other organization	x		?	8-10 each
Job control #		x	no	6
Microfilm ref #		x	no	6

*DEFINITIONS:

1. Corrsp # -- unique sequential number.
2. Unit -- unit where item originated. (Could be either a number code or a letter code or the initials of the unit head.)
3. Misc -- space reserved for the use of the originating unit's own reference.
4. Addressee -- person or organization to whom the item is addressed.
5. Author -- original author of the item.
6. Date -- date appearing on the letterhead.
7. Incoming ref -- reference to an incoming item if applicable by 1 above; more than one if possible.
8. Project # -- in referring to work done by unit, the applicable project number.
9. Project name -- alphabetic name given the project if applicable.
10. Subject -- general topic covered in the item. (Could be considered a title field.)
11. Keywords -- terms used to characterize the content of the item.
12. Unit type -- code used to describe whether addressee is internal -- that is, another unit in the organization.
13. Retention code -- date identifying when item can be removed to an inactive file.

Table 10.1 *continued*

14. Action code -- code indicating whether further action is anticipated.
15. Action date -- time parameter for future action.
16. Copies -- names or initials of people receiving a copy of the item. (Unit code may be combined with individual initials to make identification more accurate.)
17. Local file -- file name at unit level where a copy is being kept.
18. Master file name -- file name in central file where a copy is being kept. (May not be necessary if central files are organized around Corrsp #.)
19. Acc't # -- unit to which work done described in item has been charged.
20. Serial # -- unit to which work done described in item has been charged.
21. Division # -- division of addressee.
22. Subunit # -- Subunit of addressee.
23. Microfilm ref # -- where a copy may be found in microfilm files.

correspondence control system for the division that was acceptable to the unit heads, that would involve them in the indexing terminology-generation process, that would demonstrate through performance the merits of concepts 1 and 2, that would lead to incremental automation steps, and that would positively prevent management embarrassment through missed deadlines, inconsistent responses, or lost items. Additional expenses traceable to the implementation of the new procedures were to be "more than justified" in short-term results.

A mature person with both engineering and library science degrees was hired on a part-time basis to be concerned wholly with the development of a technically acceptable list of indexing terms. Anticipated staff resistance was hoped to be considerably lessened by the use of a transparently qualified person on the crucial indexing term assignment.

Interim Results

At the time the interim results listed below were reported, the Baker Division had fully implemented and accepted the Control Numbering System and Correspondence Control Point. Acceptance of new personnel by Baker staff was largely achieved, but the Correspondence Control System remained largely in the manual mode. We found the indexing terminological effort has been illuminating.

> After initial high interest, cooperation of technical staff in units has been difficult to maintain. (Reasons cited include disenchantment with detail

Table 10.2 Ideal Information Systems Specialist Description

AREAS OF KNOWLEDGE

1. Systems analysis
2. Computer-based storage and retrieval
3. Records management
4. Abstracting and indexing
5. Technical information resources (indexes, bibliographies, and so forth)
6. Library management

ON-GOING RESPONSIBILITIES

1. Information systems development within division
2. Management of the correspondence control, reference library, and records management functions
3. Coordination with division personnel in the determination of user needs with respect to correspondence, library materials, and division records, and modification of information systems in accordance with those needs
4. Coordination with division personnel in the determination of what materials need to be controlled through the information systems
5. Serving as liaison between the division and outside information sources
6. Development of information systems for marketing to other units

---

and the basic feeling that the persons assigned to the project had sufficient background to come up with "good enough terms anyway." A contact person in each technological unit is still maintained, however.)

About 1,200 discrete and rather lengthy terms have been selected and used successfully with the annual level of 6,000 correspondence items.

About two subject index terms are assigned to each item, while origin and destination are clear from the numbering system.

Names of personal authors of items are rarely used for inquiry purposes.

Management control aspects of the system have been useful to division management. (Misroutings are significantly lowered and no instances of missed deadlines have occurred since the system became operational.)

Other priorities have delayed the onset of automation but the intention remains for an orderly implementation.

Word Processing, Correspondence Control, and Records Management   155

Summary Recommendation

Correspondence control systems should be implemented where they are currently missing or overly decentralized. As necessary characteristics, the system should: afford traceability, flexibility, and security; include a Control Numbering System; include a Correspondence Control Point; have a technically viable indexing terminology; provide the suitable functions listed for correspondence as described in Chapters 3 and 4; be capable of incremental automation; relate effectively with word processing on the one hand and records retention on the other; and provide the optimum degree of management control as required. We recommend that the ideal IIS contain a correspondence control system with the characteristics enumerated above.

RECORDS MANAGEMENT

It costs TENNECO $3 million annually to store records in the Houston area alone (or $6.23 per inch per year).[7] Such figures pale by comparison with those for the U. S. Government's annual accumulation of records: created at a cost of $15 billion and filling 28 buildings each as tall as the Washington Monument.[8]

One federal department's concise description of its program is as follows:

Documentation: What & Where

1. Air Force Documentation is briefly defined as the papers, tapes, films, maps, photographs or other documentary materials, regardless of physical form or characteristics, made or received by the Air Force in pursuance of its legal obligations or in connection with the transaction of its business and preserved (or appropriate for preservation) as evidence of organization . . . functions, policies, decisions, procedures, operations, or other activities or because of their information value.
2. The Air Force Documentation Management Program is designed to provide economy and efficiency in the creation, organization, maintenance, use, and disposition of documentation. It insures that needless documentation will not be created or kept and that valuable documentation will be preserved.
3. Documentation is located at organizational levels where effective documentation of assigned functions and responsibilities can be assured—offices that have primary interest in the subject matter documented and the primary need to use it. These locations are known as offices of record. Each office of record is responsible for the custody and maintenance of the permanent and temporary current documentation of the office it serves. The office of record

concept is a decentralized system of records maintenance and disposition. The Air Force, on 31 December 1974, had approximately 48 thousand offices of record. Their combined holdings in the current files area approximated 1.2 million cubic feet. These offices, during calendar year 1974, transferred over 64 thousand cubic feet of records to Federal record centers and destroyed over 575 thousand cubic feet. The on hand figure showed a 3.3 percent decrease over the previous year. Beginning with 1969, the Air Force, through its aggressive documentation program has effected a continued decrease in its holdings.[9]

TENNECO has the option of taking the $3 million records storage cost as a dead loss to the stockholders or "mine" it for its information content as part of the company IIS. In fact, each and every company has the same option of having a records management program that is an albatross or a swan. Suggested sources of help for the executive making the choice include workshops and/or orientation seminars held by such organizations as the American Management Association (AMA), American Records Management Association, World Trade Center, and National Micrographics Association. Due to their success and wide appeal, a number of purely commercial seminar series have arisen that need to be selected carefully.

We have participated in records management activities of our past employers largely from the periphery, but have attended enough AMA sessions on administrative service functions as well as "pure" records management sessions so as to discriminate between the "doers" and the "talkers." Included in the former are some who have come up the hard way: from file clerk to head of files to manager (and this in pre-equal opportunity days), while others were retired military personnel to whom the orderliness of materials "marching" from current use to convenient storage, to that more remote, and finally to disposal appeals.

Other sources are "controlled circulation" (i.e., free to those with an appropriate assignment) periodicals. One such source to be followed regularly is *IRM Information Records Management*, which "is available to all qualified records handling professionals," from 250 Fulton Avenue, Hempstead, N. Y., 11550. The same publisher issues *Microfilm Techniques, the Magazine for Operational Microfilm Personnel*, which is not as technical as National Microfilm Association's *Journal of Micrographics*, but it covers equipment well. The well-regarded ARMA journal is *Records Management Quarterly*.

Just What Is Records Management?

Perhaps the most straightforward way to define it is to make a composite of three 1975 orientation seminar programs, together with the published summary of a briefer workshop held by our colleague, Ammarette Roberts of

Mobil.[10] All items attributed to World Trade Institute (WTI), American Management Association (AMA), or National Microfilm Association (NMA) in this section are direct quotes from their seminar announcement brochures. The items attributed to Roberts are from an article in the Special Library Association *Bulletin.*

Records Management Includes Word Processing

    WTI (Session A)   Global Applications of Word Processing: I. The International Role of Word Processing . . . In Today's Offices . . . In the Office of the Future; II. The Word Processing Market; III. The Functional Use of Word Processing; IV. Management's Role in Word Processing; V. Selection and Training of Personnel; VI. Measuring Productivity Increase; VII. Evaluating and Selecting Equipment Applicable to Your Special Needs; VIII. Human Factors: Intangibles That Can Deliver Tangible Results; IX. Designing and Equipping Work Stations and Work Centers; X. The Global Implications of Word Processing.

    AMA (Session "A")   How Word Processing Simplifies Preparation of Business Records: High cost and slow producitivity associated with personally dictated letters processed by secretaries; Need to reduce the one for one secretary ratio; Form letters and business forms; Pattern paragraphs; Word Processing Centers; On and off line dictation systems; Interfacing word processing with EDP and printing.

    Comment: This topic has been covered earlier in this chapter where the intertwining of these topics was mentioned. Greater orderliness in the creation of the record is certain to benefit the eventual disposition of the record itself. That WTI is international in scope does cause some complicating steps, but IISs are being considered as tending to have international aspects, anyway.

Records Management Includes Forms Control

    WTI (Session B)   Forms Control in the International Organization: I. How to Establish an International Forms Control Program; II. Selecting and Working with Forms Coordinators; III. Basic Steps in Implementing a Forms Program . . . Collecting Forms Samples . . . Establishing a Forms Functional File . . . Establishing a Forms Numerical or a Forms Historical File . . . Criteria for Forms Design . . . Forms Specifications . . . Forms Warehousing and Distribution . . . Forms Staffing . . . International Graphics . . . Language Standardization; IV. Forms Procurement and Contract Buying on an International Basis; and V. The Paper Shortage—Is it Over?

AMA (Session "B") Forms Management and Its Effect on Records Management: How forms management can reduce corporate records and simplify preparation; A "crash" technique to initiate a forms management program; Establishing corporate forms policy; Analyzing existing forms; Developing a function file; Forms control to eliminate duplication and "Bootleg" forms; Elements of forms design that simplify preparation and processing of records.

Comment: This activity is another effort to regularize the created records and its success in crucial to efficient handling. However, forms are a "many-headed monster" and it is necessary to stay resolutely "on top" of this effort.

Records Management Includes Commercial and Vital Records

WTI (Session D) Commercial and Vital Records in the Multinational Corporation: I. Setting Up Commercial Archives; II. Economic Comparisons . . . In-House vs. Commercial Storage; III. Components of Service . . . Retrieval Accession Indexing . . . Security and Disposal; IV. Worldwide Record Storage Problems; V. Defining and Identifying Vital Records . . . Corporate . . . National . . . International; VI. Analysis of Vital Records Media; VII. Procedures and Responsibilities for maintaining Vital Records; VIII. Auditing and Verifying the Vital Records Program; IX. Exposure of Vital Records . . . Danger to Corporate Security . . . International Implications; X. Establishing a Retention Program for Vital Records; XI. Storage and Maintenance Planning; and XII. Destruction of Vital Records . . . Methods-shredding, burning, etc. . . . Problems with Microfilm . . . Centralized Responsibility.

AMA (Session "D") How and When to Dispose of Records No Longer Required: Establishing a records retention program; Inventory and appraisal of records; Writing a record retention schedule: Legal aspects, Government regulations, Historical aspects, Company policy; Disposing of records by: onsite destruction, storage in records center; Cost saving potentials.

AMA (Session "D^1") How to Protect Records Against Theft and Disaster: How to define or determine vital records; Developing appropriate storage for protection against disasters; How to develop controls against theft and espionage; Commercial vs. corporate facilities.

Roberts Vital Records (p. 94); Inactive Records Area (Storage), (p. 87).

Comment: The very heart of records management is to preserve the records that are needed to keep the company in being, and all other subfunctions are subservient to this goal. Balance sheets drawn up on the cost of records management programs vs. the benefits need to consider this fact.

Records Management Includes Program
Organization and Filing Systems

WTI (Session E) International Records Management and Filing Systems: I. Selling the Records Management Program to Management; II. Organization and Responsibilities; III. Designation and Selection of Coordinators; IV. The Record Survey . . . What It Includes . . . Special Problems of the International Survey; V. Determining Retention Periods; VI. Developing Policies, Procedures and Forms Acceptable in U. S. and Overseas; VII. The Records Center—Design and Operations; VIII. Developing Indexing and Retrieval Systems for Inactive Records; IX. The Records Management Manual; X. File Cleanout Days; XI. Records Program Analysis; XII. Worldwide Uniform Filing Systems; XIII. Selling the Uniform Filing Systems to Concerned Personnel; XIV. Types of Systems Other Than Uniform . . . Case Files . . . Alpha, numerica, chrono; XV. Color Coded Filing as a Convenient Global System; XVI. Analyzing and Standardizing Filing Equipment and Supplies; XVII. File Stations . . . File Room Layout . . . Supervision . . . Staffing . . . Service to Users; and XVIII. The Filing Manual . . . Procedures, Practices, Filing System, Alpha Index.

AMA (Session "E") Introduction to Records Management: Purpose of records management; Defining the records management concept and function; Scope of records management/program elements and objectives; Place of records management in the organization; Selling records management to the company.

AMA (Session "E^1") Reports Management and Its Effect on Records Management: Why reports management can reduce and simplify our most costly business records; Importance of reports to corporate objectives; High cost of reports; A crash technique to establish a reports management program. Analyzing reports for need, contents, distribution, and costs; Reports control to eliminate the unnecessary and duplication; The value of exception reporting.

AMA (Session "E^2") Records Center Administration; Company owned vs. commercial centers; Geographically locating the center; Establishing procedures for storage, retrieval, reproduction, protection, pickup and shipping, etc.

AMA (Seesion "E^3") Problem Solving Clinic (problems submitted in advance by registrants).

AMA (Session "E^4") Your Record Problems Start with the Morning Mail: Importance of recognizing new documents entering the system via mail that will have to be integrated with existing filing systems and will have to be covered in the record retention schedule; Simplified processing of incoming mail; Advantages of pinpoint routing; Sorting enroute; Self-service vs. messengers; How to save on postage; Labor saving mail processing equipment.

AMA (Session "E^5") Design and Layout of Records Management Areas: Mail rooms, centralized vs. decentralized; File rooms, centralized vs. decentralized; Record Centers, special areas for vital records; Other areas such as Word Processing Centers and Supply Rooms.

AMA (Session "E^6") The Most Important Aspect of Records Management: People! Records managers, records analysts and professional file people: a scarce talent; How and where to recruit; Staffing the department; Training; Building in a career path for promotion; Establishing a proper management and physical environment for motivation.

AMA (Session "E^7") Information Storage and Retrieval: The need for standardizing one universal file classification system within the company; Centralized vs. decentralizing filing systems; Filing substations; File management (supervision; service vs. self-service; sorting and filing; charge out and other controls; protection against unauthorized entry; subject filing; terminal digit; loose filing vs. bound filing; need for filing manuals).

AMA (Session "E^8") Using Computers to Manage Records; Selecting and controlling records; Management equipment and supplies: shelving; File cabinets: 5 drawer vs. 4 drawer, lateral vs. horizontal; Automatic filing equipment; Boxes for open-shelf filing; File folders: number of tabs/color coding; Controlling excess purchasing via appropriate disposal controls.

Roberts Where You Can Get Help (p. 82); Where to Start (p. 83); Active Records Areas (p. 84); Immediate Action Plan (p. 88); Record Storage Center (p. 88); Operating and Supervising a Records Center (p. 90); Inventory of Active Records (p. 91); Legal Aspects of Corporate Security (p. 94); Supplies and Equipment for Active Records (p. 95).

Comment: Organization of the records management program is probably the aspect where the outside consultant is a real possibility for effective "short-cutting." At the least he or she can provide a "menu" of choices from which the concerned executive may make selections for implementation in the optimum order for the particular company. Filing systems form the skeleton on which the functional organization hangs. There is need for consistency in relationships, for ability to expand or telescope as geography or status dictates, or even as the content sinks in the activity scale with the passage of time. As to staff, the function has high potential for career path development for minority groups and very long term employees. The topic of information storage and retrieval has been addressed elsewhere in this book.

Records Management Includes Microfilm and Microforms

WTI (Session C) Microfilm—An International Records Medium: I. Evaluating Records for Microfilming; II. Microfilm Applications; III. Establishing an In-House Microfilm Department; IV. Use of Service Bureaus; V. Legal

Implications—USA and Abroad; VI. Computer Output Microfilm (COM); VII. Microfilm Equipment Evaluation and Standardization; VIII. Typical Case Studies of Multinational Corporations; and IX. Technology of the Future.

AMA (Session "C") Microfilm as a Records Management Tool: Advantages and characteristics; Types of film, equipment and reduction ratios; In house operation vs. service bureaus; Applications; Estimating costs; The future of microfilm; COM, etc.

Roberts: Microfilming (p. 93).

NMA (Module 1) Fundamentals of Micrographics: I. Introduction, A. Description . . . B. Microfilm in an Information System . . . C. Microforms; II. Producing Microfilm: Methods and Equipment, A. Exposing . . . B. Developing . . . C. Inspecting . . . D. Producing various microforms; III. Duplicating Microfilm, A. Processes . . . B. Equipment for duplicating . . . C. Problems (in duplication and distribution); IV. Use of Microfilm; V. Storage and Retrieval Concepts, A. Coding Techniques . . . B. Equipment; VI. Computer Output Microfilm, A. Alphanumeric Recording . . . B. Graphic Recording; VII. Micropublishing, A. Definitions . . . B. Product Varieties . . . C. Uses; and VIII. Special Processes and Equipment.

NMA (Module 2) Retrieval and Systems Design: I. Manual Retrieval Systems, A. Roll Film . . . B. Microfiche; II. Automatic Document Storage Retrieval Systems (ADSTAR), A. Large Scale . . . B. Desk Top . . . C. Binary Coded . . . D. Computer Controlled . . . E. Scroll . . . F. Edge Notched, Semi-Automatic; III. ADSTAR Market, A. Underlying Forces . . . B. Buying Motives; IV. System Design Fundamentals, A. System Setting . . . B. Types of Information . . . C. Fact Retrieval vs. Document Retrieval . . . D. System Design by Type of Equipment . . . E. System Design Survey; V. Applications, A. Airlines . . . B. Telephone Companies . . . C. Banks . . . D. Utilities . . . E. Government . . . F. Other; VI. New Technologies, A. Add-A-Frame . . . B. Holograms; and VII. Discussion.

NMA (Module 3) Inspection and Quality Control—A Problem-Solving Microfilm Workshop: Quality—Resolution and quality index; Density—Line density, background density, base plus fog density and contrast; Archival Quality—Film bases, emulsions, processing, Ross-Crabtree, Methylene Blue and Silver Densitometric hypo tests and storage requirements.

NMA (Module 4) Computer Output Microfilm (COM): I. Computer Output Microfilm (COM) Systems, A. Microforms used in COM . . . B. COM recording techniques . . . C. COM hardware . . . D. Special features of COM recorders . . . E. COM standards . . . F. COM systems (general); II. Applications, A. Alphanumeric business applications . . . B. Graphic business, technical, and scientific applications . . . C. Graphic arts applications . . . D. COM systems in detail; and III. Future Trends, A. Computer Input Microfilm (CIM) . . . B. Microfilm for facsimile transmission . . . C. Micropublishing . . . D. COM in color . . . E. New Technologies . . . F. Industry trends.

Comment: The NMA approach is the most technical and its speakers are normally consultants or supplier-related persons. Emphasis should be placed on procedures and equipment that are not over elaborate yet lend themselves to upgrading. Further, they should adhere most closely to promulgated standards to avoid expensive re-do. If equipment seems equivalent, buy from the company with the most knowledgeable representative.

(Note: WTI had a Session F on Information Availability to Users Worldwide, but it is excluded here as not being in records management. The topics listed in F are included in the considerations in Chapter 12 on IIS International Operations.)

Summary Recommendation

It is clear from the preceding composite definition that records management is a widely diversified subject. We recommend the program for a given corporation be custom tailored to its precise situation and specific goals. Ample sources have been suggested for continuing education in this field.

NOTES AND REFERENCES

1. "Executive Briefing . . . The Office of the Future, an In-depth Analysis of How Word-Processing Will Reshape the Corporate Office," *Business Week* **2387**:48-84 (June 30, 1975).
2. Ibid., p. 49.
3. Ibid., p. 49.
4. Ibid., p. 72.
5. Typical articles include:

    McGlynn, John J., "IBM's Conversion to Word Processing," *Professional Management Bulletin* (October 1971), 3 pp.

    Word Processing Management, a bi-monthly section in *Administrative Management*.

    John H. Caison, "Your Secretary: Robot or Management Aide?" *Industry Week* (July 12, 1972), 6 pp.

    Edgar G. Williams, "Changing Systems and Behavior," *Business Horizons* (August 1969), 6 pp.

    Michael V. Fiore, "The Secretarial Role in Transition," *Supervisory Management* (November 1971), 22-27.

R. Alec Mackenzie, "Are Executive's Secretaries Obsolete?" *Personnel* (September/October 1971), 60-64.

Alexander S. Biller, "Much More Than Hardware," [Suggested parallel career paths through Document Production or Secretarial Administration], *Word Processing Magazine* (IBM Office Products Division) 1972, 3 pp.

6. In association with Dr. R. E. Wyllys.
7. Statement by TENNECO to Special Libraries Association Texas Chapter, National Microfilm Association Joint Seminar "Focus on Micrographics," September 27, 1975.
8. "Uncle Sam still the Records Management Champ," *Information and Records Management* **9**(12):6 (December 1975).
9. Ibid., p. 33.
10. Ammarette Roberts, "Starting a Records Management Program," in Texas Chapter, Special Libraries Association *Bulletin* **26**(3):82-96 (April 1975); American Management Association, [Announcement brochure for] Fundamentals of Records Management Seminar, Royal Coach Motor Hotel, Atlanta, October 6-10, 1975 (Course #12535-48); World Trade Institute, [Announcement brochure for] International Records and Information Processing Conference, World Trade Center, PONY/NJ, New York City, November 17-19, 1975; National Microfilm Association, [Announcement brochure for seminar on] Module 1—Fundamentals of Micrographics; Module 2—Retrieval and Systems Design; Module 3—Inspection and Quality Control; Module 4—Computer Output Microfilm (COM), Airport Marina Hotel, San Francisco, September 9-11, and Barbizon Plaza Hotel, New York City, October 7-9, 1975.

Chapter 11

Bell Laboratories Library Network

Robert A. Kennedy*

INTRODUCTION

The community which the Bell Laboratories Library Network serves is a large, geographically dispersed, industrial research corporation deeply involved in high technology and vitally dependent upon effective information transfer. Bell Labs is the R&D unit of the Bell System and is jointly owned by American Telephone and Telegraph, parent company of the system, and Western Electric, the System's manufacturing and supply unit. The work of Bell Labs, done at sixteen locations in eight states, is directed primarily to scientific research in fields relevant to telecommunications, the design and development of communication equipment and systems, systems engineering of network services and components, and the development of business information systems programs to help the twenty-three Bell System operating companies handle expanding business information needs.

Of the 17,000 Bell Labs employees, more than 7,900 are scientists and engineers and some 3,500 are assistant technical staff. A large number of staff members have advanced degrees: 2,100 at the Ph.D. level and 3,500 at the Master's. Their need for and consumption of information is high, principally in the fields of physics, chemistry, materials, computing, mathematics, behavioral sciences, electronics, electrical and mechanical engineering, management

---

*Libraries and Information Systems Center, Bell Laboratories, Murray Hill, N. J. 07974.

Authors' note: We consider this Network to be the most advanced, most centralized industrial information system operating today. This chapter is by a leading participant in its development and is offered as a case study of what *can* be done.

and, of course, telecommunications. Their output of information is also substantial; for example, in the public sphere alone, Bell Labs scientists and engineers contributed some 1,800 papers and 2,400 talks in 1976. In the final analysis, both the raw material and the end product of Bell Labs is information.

It is not surprising, therefore, that much attention is paid to information transfer or that the numerous information sources and channels available to an R&D community are heavily used. Discourse with coworkers, conferences, and symposia, seminars by visiting scientists, invisible colleges, personal files, and departmental book and journal collections are among the helpful information mechanisms and avenues. The role of the technical libraries in Bell Labs is, however, major—in resources, services, traffic and corporate support. In fact, Bell Laboratories has had a technical library operation since its formation in 1925, and even before then, technical library services were available to Bell System scientists and engineers.

THE LIBRARY NETWORK AND ITS SERVICES

The present library system is composed of twenty libraries serving all Bell Laboratories locations from New Jersey to Colorado and from Georgia to Massachusetts. Seven of the libraries are at Western Electric locations where Bell Labs has laboratories to facilitate the transition of its designs into manufacturing by the Western Electric Company; these libraries are operated jointly with Western Electric and serve both companies. The library of the Western Electric Engineering Research Center at Princeton, New Jersey, a facility primarily concerned with manufacturing processes, is also a fully integrated component of the library system.

The system reflects a number of management philosophies and operational practices developed over the years in an effort to provide high quality service at reasonable cost to all employees, whether located at Bell Labs headquarters (Murray Hill, N. J.) or 1,800 miles away at Denver. Some of these management perspectives will be noted later. Most important, however, is the concept of networking, the persuasion that a multi unit, geographically dispersed library operation should be structured and managed as a total activity. This concept implies a high degree of functional interdependency, resource pooling, responsibility sharing, and commonality of systems, standards, and goals.

To help make networking work, the Bell Laboratories Library Network employs a mix of centralized special services and decentralized standard services supported by extensive management information, computer, communications and delivery systems. Decentralization is preferred for the basic "bread-and-butter" library functions—that is, circulation and reference services, and on-site supply of the book, journal, and other information resources necessary to handle promptly the majority of local information needs. Collection building, however, is not limited to local needs; as will be noted later, coordinated resource management is one of the targets and operational realities of networking.

Centralized services encompass functions and resources needed throughout the network that would be inefficient or uneconomical or impossible to provide on a local level. Centralization also offers opportunities for insuring common high standards and system-wide service monitoring, as well as supplying the critical mass and economies of scale necessary to justify certain specialized competencies. Among the operations that are centralized, but not all at one location, are:

Acquisitions, classification, and cataloging, including preparation of computer-composed and -printed catalogs of the network's books, journals, microforms, and audio/video tapes.

Current awareness services, including the regular publication of twelve major announcement bulletins, and a computer-aided system for selectively disseminating technical documents.

Publication of a wide spectrum of specialized information directories, catalogs, indexes, pathfinders, and so forth.

Literature searching services using highly trained subject specialists who are skilled in machine and manual searching to undertake the more demanding information searches, compile specific and continuing bibliographies, and supplement reference librarian services.

Translation services providing oral and written translations by on-site staff or external assignment of all the major languages of science.

Computing information services, including specialized announcement and index services, the handling of external requests for Bell Labs software, and the operation of libraries specializing in computer programs, related documentation, machine manuals and other literature supporting numerous computing activities.

Technical report services furnishing centrally a full range of acquisition, announcement, request processing, and search services on domestic and foreign technical reports of interest to Bell Labs.

Management information services supplying to library management an extensive series of computer-compiled reports on library operations and performance.

Information systems design and development services charged with the primary responsibility for defining, programming, and establishing new and improved information handling systems for the whole Network.

Additional aspects of several of these services will be examined later. The large publication activity merits particular note here, however, because it exemplifies a strong conviction and commitment of network management: the essence of special library services is outreach directed to need. The emphasis is on projection rather than reaction, which implies going to the desk of the users, making it easy to learn about, request and get information, marketing the library image and the repertoire of library services, and researching and developing information alerting and access packages addressed both to known and anticipated needs. The twelve different current awareness bulletins, for example, are designed to offer fast announcement of information selected and organized for particular audiences. Supplementing these network bulletins are a number of local library bulletins that focus on specific interests of a given laboratory location. The bulletins cover separately, or in combination, internal documents, external reports, Bell Labs talks and papers, books and serials, audio/videotapes, and publishing papers in all the major fields of interest to Bell Labs technical and management people. Each of the library network's special publications (to cite three: the BTL Information Sources and Consultants, Magnetism Literature Index, Computer Program Index) is produced for the same service objective: to put directly into the hands of the prospective user an information access instrument, a minilibrary, which may be the more consulted because it is designed to meet a particular information need and is on site at the point of that need.

To state that librarianship is too important to be left to the librarians is merely to observe that a user-sensitive, full-service information operation requires a work force with a range of specialized training and talents. The nearly 130 members of the Bell Labs Library Network include not only librarians (a majority of whom have technical backgrounds) but other specialists as well. The staff includes information scientists with Ph.D.'s in science and expertise in one or more foreign languages who handle complex literature searching and bibliographic responsibilities for the whole network. Other specialists competent in various technologies and foreign languages are translators and literature analysts. Others are specialists in system analysis, programming, and information system design. Others are expert in computing information and technical report services. Finally, complementing the network staff of librarians, specialists and support personnel are many specialists in technical and scientific departments who contribute advice and direct help to the Libraries' information programs.

USE OF MACHINES

Machines are vital partners in a dynamic information service. The influence of the computer is particularly profound, but other machines, though less dramatic in impact, are important or essential in a modern library. Extensive microform resources, including a large collection of microfiche upon which technical report service operations turn, require a variety of equipments in the Bell Labs Network; an efficient, highly automated microfiche blow-back device is especially helpful in this respect. Audio/video tape libraries of educational programs, technical talks, seminars and so forth must be supported with appropriate playing and recording hardware. Telecommunication services are, of course, immensely important, especially in a widely dispersed library network where the effect of distance on the availability and quality of information services must be minimized. The role of the telephone (which is, after all, the single most powerful on-line facility for conquering distance) need hardly be stated; long-distance teleconferencing and data transmission become a way of life in library networking. A teletype network is also available to the Bell Labs libraries, as is a long-distance facsimile system for transmitting small, urgent documents between company locations. Telecommunication services also include a Telereference facility in the largest libraries. This message recording system is available to any employee at any time from anywhere. Thus a scientist working at home late at night or away at a technical conference can dial the Telereference service and request that a specific paper or item of information be supplied. This "express" service, used about a thousand times a month, gives a response to the requester within twenty-four hours.

The present and predictable importance of the computer to the Bell Labs Library Network can hardly be overstated. Almost every facet of Library operations and services has been touched or materially affected by the computer. Networking as a large-scale, everyday operating reality is crucially dependent on computer-aided systems for acquiring, organizing, announcing, retrieving, supplying, controlling, and managing information. In all, over fifty information services or functions in the network are now computer aided. Work to exploit computer powers continues, for two basic goals: (1) to provide new and improved information services to the user and (2) to improve, extend, and make more efficient the library operations upon which these services depend.

W. K. Lowry has described the background and principal features of the computer systems used by Bell Labs libraries.[1] We shall note here, therefore, only some highlights of six major systems: the BELDEX indexing system; MERCURY dissemination system; BELLPAR/BELLTAB bulletin systems; on-line searching systems; BELLREL circulation system; and BELLTIP acquisition-cataloging system.

BELDEX is the current version of a machine-indexing system developed in 1959 to generate keyword-in-context, author, and numerical indexes of technical documents for current awareness bulletins and retrospective catalogs. The powers and uses of the program have been expanded far beyond original concepts. In addition to standard permuted-title and other indexing, BELDEX offers numerous options including keyword-out-of-context indexing, several book-like indexes, "sideslipping" (i.e., secondary and additional index arrangements within a given keyword cluster), identification of significant contextual "chunks" of information, semiautomatic cross-referencing, synonym conversion, and so forth. These and other features have made BELDEX a multipurpose, workhorse program used extensively in Bell Labs both within and outside the libraries. Both Honeywell 6000 and IBM 370 versions are in use. Library applications include a variety of directories, bibliographies, bulletins, indexes, catalogs, and serial lists. In other areas of Bell Laboratories and elsewhere in the Bell System the program is routinely used for correspondence file indexes, catalogs of projects and standards, equipment inventory control, and many other purposes.

MERCURY is a computer-aided system for selectively disseminating internal technical reports, seminar announcements, computer documents, and other information to interested employees.[2] The system, in use since 1966, operates on a Honeywell 6000 computer. Prior to MERCURY, an author distributed his or her technical report to a relatively small circle—to the people known or thought to be interested. In a large, dispersed organization this practice clearly results in imperfect early communication. MERCURY provides much improved information coupling. By using MERCURY, an author may distribute a new paper not only to named colleagues or departments as in the past, but also to all Bell Labs people who have expressed an interest in receiving papers on specified subjects, or projects, or from specified authors or departments.

MERCURY provides important user options. A reader, for example, may choose between receiving an abstract sheet, complete document, or only a title listing. All papers included in a given subject area may be selected or only those designated by the author as comprehensive or panoramic. A major emphasis in MERCURY is involvement of the users and responsiveness to them. The heart of the system, for example, is a number of technical vocabularies, developed collaboratively with the users, for each subject area of significance to Bell Labs. These mnemonic, hierarchically structured vocabularies are deliberately compact and well supplied with scope notes for direct use by both authors and readers. Over 5,700 Bell Labs people are now enrolled in the MERCURY service, and it has been found to be useful for many purposes. Announcements of new library bibliographies, for example, are sent to readers whose interest profiles match the bibliography subject. The responses suggest the print runs needed to meet demands.

Two other systems, BELLTAB and BELLPAR, which are sufficiently alike to be considered jointly, are also focused on alerting services. Both are used to compile twice-monthly current awareness bulletins using data from external magnetic tapes and internal keyboarding. BELLTAB, a PL/1 program run on an IBM 370-168, produces *Current Technical Reports*, a subject-structured announcement of about 6,000 technical reports per year. The bulk of the report citations, with abstracts, are selected by BELLTAB from magnetic tapes supplied by the National Technical Information Service; additional items are input locally using an interactive computer edit system. The BELLPAR program, written largely in FORTRAN for the Honeywell 6000 computer, produces *Current Technical Papers*, five different subject bulletins listing about 50,000 journal papers annually. For this purpose BELLPAR selects citations of papers of interest from the INSPEC tapes produced by the Institution of Electrical Engineers and SPIN tapes prepared by the American Institute of Physics. Citations selected by the libraries' literature analysts from journals not covered by the tape services are input to BELLPAR files from computer terminals. Both the BELLTAB and BELLPAR systems are complemented by request processing and management information programs.

Except for regular batch searches of INSPEC tapes in support of a number of continuing bibliographies, computer-aided searching of the published literature at Bell Laboratories is now done entirely on such external interactive systems as the Lockheed Corporation's DIALOG, the National Library of Medicine's MEDLINE, the System Development Corporation's ORBIT, the New York Times Information Bank, and Bibliographic Retrieval Services. Bell Labs experience with on-line searching systems has been substantially favorable.[3] Speed, search power, search effectiveness, bibliographic convenience, and moderate costs (relative to scientists' time and manual searches) are factors that have contributed to the rapid growth of on-line searching by information scientists and reference librarians throughout the library network; from 1975 to 1977 for example, the number of searches increased some 700 percent from approximately 400 to over 3,400. The use of interactive searching systems for bibliometric studies[4]—that is, making quantitative analyses of the bibliographic features of a body of literature, identifying the leading journals in a specific field[5], determining contributions of various organizations to a discipline, and so forth—is also growing in volume and importance.

On-line circulation control has been a reality in Bell Laboratories libraries since the BELLREL system[6] began operating in 1968. In its initial configuration BELLREL linked the three largest libraries, all in New Jersey, to a central computer; now fourteen libraries in eight states are completely on-line to the system and six other libraries, are significantly serviced by the system. BELLREL's primary objective is to improve the total response of the libraries to the users by pooling the widely dispersed resources of the network, by following up on borrowers' reservation queues automatically, by automating clerical functions, and by providing enriched feedback for effective management of resources and services. BELLREL, written largely in COBOL and operating on an IBM 370-155 computer, is currently handling over 1,200 transactions per day.

As an on-line circulation and file query system electronically consolidating remote libraries, BELLREL is a major mechanism in making networking work.

All of the library network's book and journal resources—currently 160,000 book copies and 3,200 journal titles—are recorded in BELLREL disk files that offer up-to-the-minute accountability for any need arising in any library. Supplementing the terminal and file query facilities are some thirty batch-mode products and reports that help greatly in monitoring the needs of library users and in managing network information resources appropriately. Several of these reports are discussed below.

Complementing the BELLREL system, and closely correlated with it, is the BELLTIP book acquisition, accounting and cataloging system[7] operational since January 1972. In this system, input terminals coupled to a Honeywell 6000 computer submit order information, receipt and invoice data, cataloging details, file changes, and various queries. Outputs include order forms, cancellation and claim notices, financial summaries, "in-process" reports, and much additional management data that enable the library to monitor purchases, work processes, collection building and other areas. BELLTIP also maintains the publication files for BELLREL as well as producing library bulletin copy.

Most importantly, BELLTIP maintains and compiles the library network's book catalog, an electronically photocomposed printed catalog covering the book resources, monographs in microform, and audio/video collections of the entire network. This catalog, which totally replaced large card files in 1973 and for the first time provided all Bell Labs Libraries with information about all books in the system, has been a major force in improving network communications and services. Copies of the catalog are also supplied to Bell Labs user groups having a local need for the set. The catalog currently comprises ten annual volumes, covering over 265,000 entries, and a monthly cumulated supplement.

Two additional systems contribute to and are integrated with BELLTIP cataloging operations. One is a computer-aided system that maintains authority lists for the catalogers (generating automatically much done manually hitherto) and produces subject headings for the printed book catalog.[8] The other is the Ohio College Library Center (OCLC) on-line query and cataloging system of which Bell Labs is a member. In this application, selected cataloging information displayed on the on-line terminal is shunted into BELLTIP in machine-readable form for further processing there; this melding reduces both cataloging and keyboarding efforts. BELLTIP-derived cataloging submitted to OCLC is also a feature of the coordinated system. Additional major uses of the OCLC system and its large information files are in prospect.

As may be concluded, there is a substantial degree of interdependency and coordination in the design and use of the Libraries' family of computer systems. The production of a bibliography, for example, may involve: an on-line search of an external data base or a batch search of a BELLPAR tape internally; computer conversion of machine-readable output from these searches into BELDEX system records; BELDEX compilation, printing, and indexing of the bibliography; on-line composition of prefatory material using one of Bell Labs computer-editing and text-composition systems; announcement through both the MERCURY and current awareness bulletin programs; cataloging in BELL-TIP; and automatic hand-off to BELLREL files for circulation purposes.

MANAGEMENT OF INFORMATION PROGRAMS

Good management information is basic to the good management of information. A responsive and effective information service requires adequate information for its own control, growth, and adjustment. This concept implies a cultivated understanding of the needs of the populations to be served and their reactions to the services provided; it also implies continued monitoring of information handling operations, technical alternatives, costs, and the like.

The sources and mechanisms used to acquire information to help manage Bell Labs libraries include ad hoc and continuing user committees, interviews and laboratory visits, periodic user questionnaires, on-line system monitoring, and statistical analyses and reports of great variety and richness. Much reliance is placed on computer aid in compiling and analyzing data; indeed, the provision of management information is an important design objective of the majority of the computer systems. Some examples follow.

Two major imperatives apply to collection building in a library network that operates as an integrated system rather than a loose consortium of essentially separate enterprises: meeting local needs *and* coordinating total resources in a service- and cost-effective way. Both these requirements have been significantly aided by a computer-supported selection system implemented in Bell Laboratories several years ago.[9] In this system, used both for selection and weeding purposes, selection profiles have been established for each library that define by explicit classification number and verbal descriptor a degree of coverage or "collection level" for each subject of interest at that location. Much pertinent management information, including extensive statistical data supplied by the BELLREL circulation system on subject usage by technical departments and locations, contributed to the determination and refinement of the profiles for each library. A Selection Advisory Committee, an on-going review and policy-making group of librarians, reviewed all individual library profiles to ensure that level assignments were realistic and compatible, overall network interests were properly represented, and no unnecessary redundancy resulted. Profile review and various other aspects of the system as a working reality rely heavily on computer support. For example, the overall subject interests of the network are recorded and maintained in a master matrix showing the profile level for each library in each subject class; individual library profile statements and subject heading indexes to all profiles are among the additional aids produced.

The profile levels provide library management with confirmed and coordinated indicators for collection building and maintenance. To help further, a computer-compiled report is produced annually to document each library's performance in following its profile. This report, which utilizes data from the profile system and the BELLTIP acquisitions-cataloging system, identifies the number of books and dollars spent by classification number, library and profile level. Expenditures in areas for which a library has no profile assigned are marked for particular attention. The profiles, of course, must change as interests and programs change.

Acquisition operations are monitored and supported by a number of important management reports from the BELLTIP system. An "In-Process List," compiled weekly for each library, tracks all incoming books from initial order through centralized processing and final delivery to the requesting library. Problem situations are pursued automatically or flagged for particular action. A network version of the list is also produced to alert each library to what others are ordering, thereby helping to coordinate acquisitions. Fiscal accountability that is provided on-line gives the current status of any library budget or supplier account. Other on-line queries report on particular orders or workflow situations. Supplier performance is periodically tabulated in a vendor performance analysis report. This document gives insights on order costs, discounts, delivery times, claims, cancellations, and so forth; its usefulness to management is substantial.

Prompt and proper response to demonstrated or predicted need is the goal of a series of on-line and batch reports supplied by the BELLREL circulation system. Brief mention of three will suffice. A "Titles in Demand" list is produced weekly to identify all book titles for which there are five or more people waiting anywhere in the Network. The number of copies held and on order by each library and the number of people waiting at each location are among the important facts reported. Using this list, library supervisors hold a weekly teleconference to decide what additional purchases or other action should be taken to help meet demands as promptly as practicable. Counterbalancing this "hot" list is a "cold" list, the "Zero Activity Report," which identifies titles that have had little or no recorded use in a specified time span. This list, along with other data, is helpful in purging the collection and keeping it attuned to need. Still another computer report put to good use in managing information resources is the "Loan History" report; for example, when a technical department moves to another laboratory location, a subject listing of the materials borrowed by the department is helpful in establishing an appropriate collection at the new location.

The importance of current awareness bulletins to the library program was noted earlier. For the editors of these bulletins, the tasks of keeping coverage on target and selecting the best of the new information competing for space are greatly aided by continuing analyses of the uses made of specific subjects and materials. In the technical reports area, for example, quarterly computer analyses of requests for reports in each subject category are systematically used to adjust coverage of the bulletin. The result is a hit rate of 80 percent or better.[10]

CONCLUSION

Some features of a library-based information network serving a large industrial research organization have been noted in this chapter. The approaches taken are in no way suggested as models; clearly, the structure, services, and systems of any library must be shaped to its own purpose and public. Large differences in scale, level of support, and operational detail abound in special libraries. Yet industrial and other librarians may be expected increasingly to share many management perspectives and practices. Advances in information technology and the common need for good, cost-effective services compel it.

The electronic library is a rapidly developing fact of life. As noted, the Bell Labs library system is already heavily committed. This involvement is bound to increase in scale and sophistication. Information service excellence, as a sustained achievement rather than an occasional aberration, is becoming increasingly dependent on technological support—that is, computers, telecommunications, reprographic processes, micrographics, audio/video devices. Indeed, it is technology that is making possible a development of enormous importance to all libraries—that is, the emergence of large-scale library networking as a true resource- and work-sharing enterprise. The advantages of networking are coming to be realized on a state, regional and national level, as well as within industry and academe.

Machines and networking alone do not make a library. A healthy and responsive information service requires a proper (substantial) investment in people, publications, *and* systems. Conventional bibliographic resources and apparatus are necessary in depth, and they should be imaginatively and vigorously promoted. Specialized collections and competencies may be no less important to the information welfare of an organization; in Bell Laboratories, the heavy use made of the special materials, tools, and services furnished by the libraries' Computing Information Service is a case in point.

Perhaps the most important factor in achieving good library service is user involvement. A high degree is beneficial to all. Users who are asked to give advice, or serve on committees, or react to specific services, or aid in surveys and analyses (but not to direct or control) not only help to correct and perfect library performance, they also become library publicists and ambassadors of good will.

NOTES AND REFERENCES

1. W. K. Lowry, "Use of Computers in Information System." *Science* **175**(4024):841-846 (1972).

2. W. S. Brown and J. F. Traub, "MERCURY—A System for the Computer-Aided Distribution of Technical Reports." *J. Assoc. Comp. Mach.* **16**(1): 13-25 (1969).
3. D. T. Hawkins, "Impact of On-Line Systems on a Literature Searching Service," *Special Libraries* **67**(12): 559-567 (1976).
4. D. T. Hawkins, "Unconventional Uses of On-Line Information Retrieval Systems, or, On-Line Bibliometric Studies," *J. Amer. Soc. Info. Sci.* **28**(1): 13-18 (1977).
5. D. T. Hawkins, "Semiconductor Journals," *J. Chem. Info. and Comp. Sci.* **16**(1): 21-23 (1976).
6. R. A. Kennedy, "Bell Laboratories' Library Real-Time Loan System (BELLREL)," *J. Lib. Automat.* **1**(2): 128-146 (1968); and "Bell Laboratories On-Line Circulation Control System: One Year's Experience," *Proceedings of 1969 Clinic on Library Applications of Data Processing*, April 27-30, 1969 (Urbana: University of Illinois, (1970), pp. 14-30.
7. W. K. Sipfle, "Bell Laboratories Book Acquisition, Accounting and Cataloging System (BELLTIP)," 1975, 43p. ERIC Report IR 005 105, November 1977.
8. I. C. Ross, "A Cataloger's Authority List Maintenance System," *J. Amer. Soc. Info. Sci.* **27**(4): 224-229 (1976).
9. F. H. Spaulding and R. O. Stanton, "Computer-Aided Selection in a Library Network," *J. Amer. Soc. Info. Sci.* **27**(5-6): 269-280 (1976).
10. Eileen W. English, "Hits and Misses," *Special Libraries* **66**(5-6): 237-240 (1975).

Chapter 12

Scope of IIS Operations

IIS EXTENT IN *FORTUNE* 500 CORPORATIONS AND THE IMPLICATIONS

The distribution of industrial information systems is not uniform in quantity, resources, or support over the industrial community. However, we learned in the late 1950s that industrial management has an insatiable appetite for comparative data on "How are we doing?" in comparison to other industrial organizations on most functions, including the IIS. Although there is a paucity of reliable data, recognized directories do exist whose information we have been manipulating for some time. Further, practitioners are generally aware of "benchmark" IISs, such as the Bell Laboratories Library Network described in the preceding chapter, they can suggest to their managements for confidential inquiry.

It seemed obvious to us some time ago that cross-checks should be made between the annual listings of *Fortune* 500 corporations and the previously mentioned directories. We have now successfully done so, and the results that are of interest to managements to whom the IISs report will be highlighted in this chapter with references made to detailed unique tables in Appendix B and to two of our articles, one published in *The Journal of the American Society for Information Science* and one announced by the *ERIC Clearinghouse* at Syracuse University.

The JASIS article was intended for our information science colleagues and its abstract gives the essence of the content on the initial page:

> The "heart" of the industrial technical library universe is encompassed in the library systems of 311 of *Fortune* 500 Corporations. Of the 30+ variables used to delineate these 311 systems, the number of professional librarians, libraries and corporations were most important. A "Library Penetration" ratio was evolved from the three measures. To meet the budget-setting need for cross industry comparison, *Fortune* 29 industry classifications were used, with *Chemicals* and *Petroleum Refining* [being] most important. Systems including overseas units, or Internationally-operating systems, were statistical leaders in every measure. Twenty-four pairs of measures were found to have correlation (R) of 0.80 (or higher) with significance R of 0.00001. How the remaining 189 of *Fortune* 500 operate without formal information service requires study.[1]

178   Industrial Information Systems

Some of these phrases will be elaborated after the abstract is cited for the *ERIC* report that was done for our fellow library professionals.

> An in-depth study of the *Fortune* 500 Corporations' libraries has revealed consistent characteristics across 27 industrial classifications, some of which parallel Special Libraries Association Divisions. Partial profiles for Pharmaceutical, Aircraft and Food Libraries are given as examples.... Best estimates are that the 311 corporations spend between $108.8 and $145 million for library materials and services annually.[2]

While the next section of this chapter highlights the most significant of the variables we studied in elucidating the extent and character of the "universe" of IIS's maintained by the *Fortune* 500 corporations, a considerable body of unique tabular data is also included in abridged form as Appendix B and in full form as microfiche in a pocket attached on the inside of the back cover. The cooperation of the publisher in making this detail available will enable readers to make comparisons and subanalyses of their own for very specific management purposes, and this data is in itself worth the cost of the book.

The title of Appendix B, Summary Data on the Industrial Library Systems of the *Fortune* 500 Corporations, is rather descriptive of its content. Special attention is invited to Table B.1 where the 311 corporations with libraries are aggregated on the vertical divisions by the 29 industry classifications suggested by *Fortune* supplementary material to their original listings. This grouping proved to be statistically reliable in our study and much of our reporting is on these classifications. The horizontal columns in the table are the variables we found to be most useful and where they are unique, we so state. The order of columns is thought to be easily grasped visually and is used for all subsequent tables in Appendix B, including both Table B.2 (covering the 189 *Fortune* 500 corporations without formal IIS's) and subsequent tables on each of the industrial classifications.

Appendix C is devoted to the alphabetical listing of the names of the 311 corporations given in Table B.1 plus their industrial classifications assigned, followed by a similar listing for the 189 corporations in Table B.2.

The most important variables in our study turned out to be: I. Corporations with libraries divided by industrial classification; II. Number of libraries; III. Number of international systems as contrasted to domestic-only systems; IV. Number of professional librarians employed; and V. Materials possessed, particularly periodical subscriptions. The following sections consider these variables in turn—each with its subsidiary variables under it.[3]

Variable I: Corporations with Libraries by Industrial Classification

Our study makes clear that the industrial classification is the common "building block"—that is, a library/information service can be evaluated to determine how it ranks with the mean *in its industrial classification*. Further the means of the several variables we studied serve to form the profile or "typical" situation in an industry category—that is, if a company falls below the mean, it can decide whether it should be satisfied with the reasons therefor or take remedial actions forthwith. On the other hand, if a company doesn't have any IIS, it can aspire to the mean or profile library/information service—as a minimum planning figure. (Recall, however, that all functions included in the earlier chapters—such as on generation and production of information—are not typically included in the figures cited here, so that an upward adjustment is indicated.) Finally, if in these days of conglomerates that almost defy classification, a company feels that *Fortune* has classified it in the wrong industry, it can aspire to the means in the higher classification of the two. Note that the industrial classification of *Food* (#18) leads the industrial classifications with 33 corporations, followed by *Chemicals* (#16) and *Appliances, Electronics* (#28), while two of the smaller classifications have no corporations with libraries at all.

At the second level of criticality are the rank in Assets (written here as "*R*Assets"), Number of Employees, and *R*Sales. The *Fortune* article cited earlier is replete with tables showing rank order of the corporations on various measures, with *R*1 always being the most desirable and *R*500 the least desirable. Figure 12.1 shows the mean ranks of the twenty-nine industrial classifications, and the corporations with libraries consistently outperform those without libraries on the means of measures. Further, there is considerable stability in the means of the business-related measures and among the library-related measures. Interestingly the overall means of all library-related measures clustered around *R*170, whereas the arithmetic mean is *R*250.

Following through on these second level measures under variable I, we find corporations in *Rubber* (industrial classification #35) lead measure IA, *R*Assets, with a mean of *R*70.5, followed in turn by the categories of *Petroleum Refining* (#32) and *Tobacco* (#39). For measure IB, Number of Employees, the total of nearly 13 million employees in the 311 corporations is led by *Appliances, Electronics* (#13) with 2.1 million employees in that industrial classification followed by *Motor Vehicles and Parts* (#28) and *Food* (#18). For IC, *R*Sales, *Rubber* (#35) leads with *R*71.2, while *Petroleum Refining* (#32) and *Motor Vehicles . . .* (#28) trail.

Two measures are at the third level of criticality. IC1, Mean Rank of Number of Employees, finds *Rubber* (#35) again leading, *Office Machinery (includes Computers)* (#30) having its first mention, and *Motor Vehicles . . .* (#28) again being included. Also at the third level is IC2, Corporations *without* libraries. The full table is included in Appendix B and includes the relevant second level measures for this group of 189 corporations. *Food* (#18) also leads IC2 with 36 corporations without formal library/information center services, followed by *Metal Manufacturing* (#24) and *Farm and Industrial Machinery* (#17).

180   Industrial Information Systems

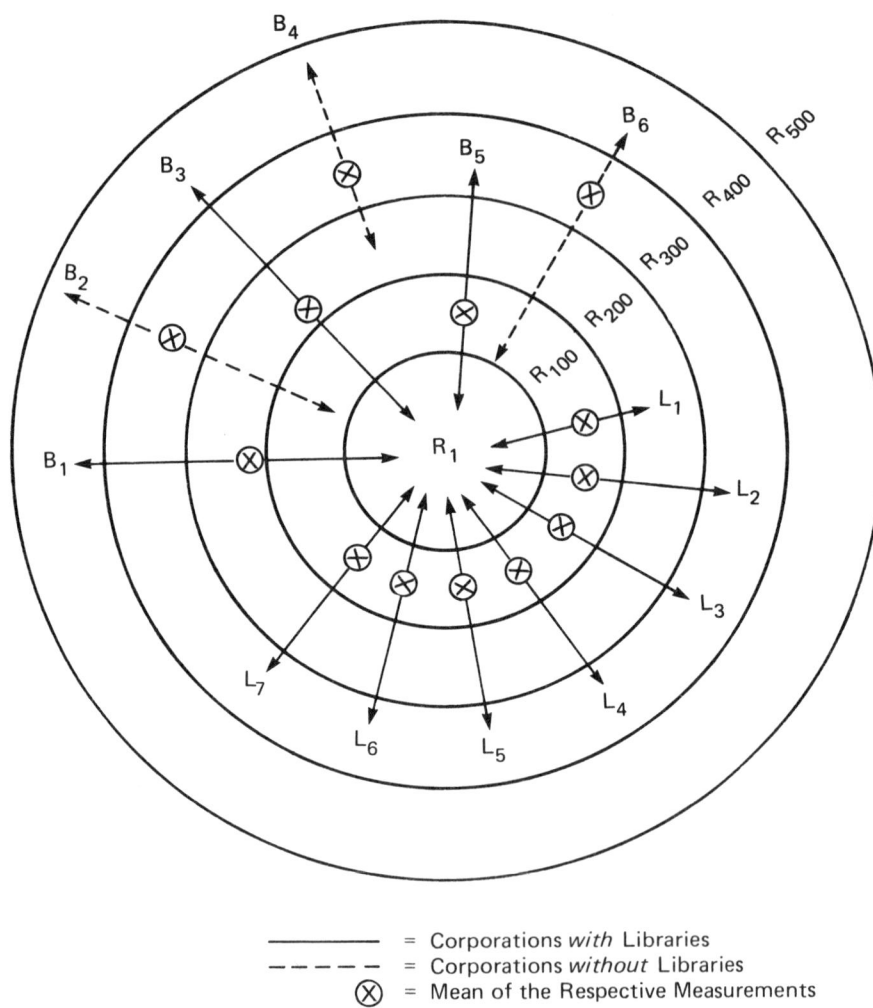

——————— = Corporations *with* Libraries
– – – – – = Corporations *without* Libraries
⊗ = Mean of the Respective Measurements

Business-related measures
B_1 = REmployees
B_2 = REmployees
B_3 = RSales
B_4 = RSales
B_5 = RAssets
B_6 = RAssets

Library-related measures
L_1 = RLibraries
L_2 = RProfessional Librarians
L_3 = REmployees/Professional Librarians
L_4 = RHoldings
L_5 = RHoldings/Employee
L_6 = RVolumes
L_7 = RSubscriptions

Figure 12.1 Comparison of the Commercial Measurements and Library-Related Measurements of the *Fortune* 500 Corporations—Ranges of the Means of the 29 Industry Classifications.

Scope of IIS Operations 181

Variable II: Number of Libraries

This variable represents the next of the first priority measures, and needs no elaboration on its importance at this stage. The total listed in the standard directories consulted and attributed to the 311 corporations are 1,175.2 libraries/information centers. As expected, *Chemicals* (#16) leads with 182.2 libraries, while *Appliances, Electronics* (#13) has 164.5 libraries and *Petroleum Refining* (#32) includes 124.8 libraries. There is a long drop to the fourth and subsequent industrial classifications.

The second priority level under Variable II begins with IIA, Mean *R*ank in Number of Libraries for that subject category. *Pharmaceuticals* (#33) has Mean *R*87.4, with *Aircraft* (#11) and *Chemicals* (#16) trailing. Most of the libraries are science/technology in orientation and subject content. Measure IIB, Sci/Tech Libraries, is led by the now-familiar *Chemicals* (#16) with 158.7 such libraries, trailed by *Appliances, Electronics* (#13) and *Petroleum Refining* (#32), with the latter having nearly twice the number of the fourth subject category. The final second priority here is number of domestic (U. S.) libraries, IIC. The same industrial classifications are represented here, with leading *Chemical's* (#16) having 158.2 U. S. libraries.

At the third level of priority under Variable II are the number of business/financial-biased libraries, IIB1. To vary the pattern slightly, *Chemicals* (#16) with 11.5 such libraries are followed by *Petroleum Refining* (#32) and *Pharmaceuticals* (#33). Other Libraries, IIB2, includes those oriented to news, legal, historical, and other orientations. *Publishing and Printing* (#34) earns its first mention here with 72 such libraries, followed by the familiar *Pharmaceuticals* (#33) and *Petroleum Refining* (#32).

Variable III: Internationally Operated Industrial Library Systems

This first priority measure again emphasizes the asymmetric distribution of strength among the industrial library systems. While certain industrial classification names repeatedly appeared in the previous pages on number of corporations and on number of libraries, the firms operating internationally consistently (with the major exception of *Aircraft* (#11)) led the domestic-only firms in their subject classifications in the important measures. The *JASIS* and *ERIC* articles mentioned earlier show this domination graphically. (The following section on IIS International Operations is thus concerned with "the cream of the crop,"—though not so stated because of our previous association with certain of them—because of the evidence in this section.) The exemplary industrial classification of *Chemicals* (#16) leads with 10 firms operating international industrial library systems, closely followed by *Pharmaceuticals* (#33) with 9 such companies and *Petroleum Refining* (#32) with 7.

Second-level priority measures under this rubric are the number of such firms with domestic-only operations, number of Canadian libraries, and finally number of United Kingdom, European, and other Continent libraries. For the first-mentioned, IIIA, this *negative* measure shows *Food* (#18) with 28 domestic-only firms, while *Appliances, Electronics* (#13) and *Metal Manufacturing* (#24) have large totals as well. IIIB, Canadian Libraries, is led by *Chemicals* (#16) and *Petroleum Refining* (#32) with 14 libraries each, and *Appliances, Electronics* (#13) has 9. The next priority item, U. K. and Other Libraries, IIIC, we believe from personal information to be seriously under-reported in the standard directories. On the basis of published information, though, *Petroleum Refining* (#32) leads with 11 such libraries and is trailed by *Chemicals* (#16) with 10 and *Pharmaceuticals* (#33) with 9.

*Variable IV: Number of Professional Librarians/
Information Officers Employed*

In this fourth measure we found to be of first priority in assessing excellence, we have grouped all professionals listed in the several directories, since the use of designations such as "Translator," "Systems Officer," and "Literature Scientists" were not consistently used. Some few libraries were listed that had *no* professional staff, but they were exceptions. Presumably there is a straight-line relationship between the number of professional librarians in a library, a firm, and an industrial classification with the level of excellence of IIS service provided, and we found no contrary evidence.

The reader would have guessed correctly that the leaders in Variable IV would be *Chemicals* (#16), *Petroleum Refining* (#32) and *Appliances, Electronics* (#13). The respective totals found are 313.7, 239.0, and 216.0 out of the 2,504.2 professional librarians in the 311 corporations.

The most crucial second-level priority measure in this section of the findings is IIA, Mean Number of Professional Librarians Per Corporation Library. The lead appears to belong to *Metal Products* (#25) on the basis of an unresolved discrepancy in reporting from a single firm. More believable are the 3.35 professional librarians/corporation library for the category *Pharmaceuticals* (#33) and 2.67 professional librarians for *Publishing and Printing* (#34). Interestingly, the overall mean is 1.71 professional librarians per company library as opposed to the 1 professional per such library as folklore has it.

IVB, Mean Rank in Number of Professional Librarians Employed, finds *Pharmaceuticals* (#33) with Mean *R*61.6, trailed by *Rubber* (#35) and *Chemicals* (#16). The remaining second-level priority, IVC, Employees per Professional Librarian, is a *unique* measure reported in this study of the *Fortune* 500 corporations. There is a very wide divergence in these figures, and we would much prefer to have the figures for "Professional Employees/Professional

Librarian," but they are unavailable now and for the forseeable future. Perhaps the *change* in these figures from that reported in our table and those reported in future studies will be the really significant consideration. Currently, the industrial classification that is the leader is *Pharmaceuticals* (#33) with 2,606 employees/professional librarian with *Chemicals* (#16) following with 2,781 and *Publishing and Printing* (#34) at 4,506. The mean is somewhat over 13,000 persons/librarian.

The measure at the third priority here is IIIC-1, Mean *R*ank, Employees/ Professional Librarian. *Pharmaceuticals* again leads at $R44.8$, with *Publishing and Printing* (#34) finishing ahead of *Chemicals* (#16).

Variable V: Materials—Periodical Subscriptions

In industrial technical libraries/information centers, the number and importance of periodical subscriptions far outweigh all other forms of bibliographic information. They are treated here as the main part of Variable V, with the others being subsidiary. The 311 corporations receive 308,679 periodicals, with *Petroleum Refining* (#32) leading industrial classifications with 49,481. Close behind are *Chemicals* (#16) with 44,986 subscriptions and *Appliances, Electronics* (#13) with 32,678 titles. Variable V', Mean Subscriptions/Corporation Library, shows the same three industrial classifications leading with the typical library in each receiving 437, 385, and 319 subscriptions, respectively. Variable V", Mean Rank of Subscriptions Received, shows the following "finish": *Petroleum Refining* (#32) with $R57$, *Pharmaceuticals* (#33) with $R99.2$, and *Measuring, Scientific, and Photographic Equipment* (#23) with $R107.2$.

The next important group of materials are Volumes, VA. Among the 9,899,878 held by the 311 corporations, *Chemicals* (#16) leads with 1.6 million volumes, while *Petroleum Refining* (#32), *Appliances, Electronics* (#13), and *Office Machinery (includes Computers)* (#30) each exceed one million volumes. VB, Mean Volumes for Corporation Library, sees *Aircraft* (#11) leading with 13 thousand volumes in the typical library, while *Publishing and Printing* (#34) and *Pharmaceuticals* (#33) trail somewhat. VC, Holdings, represents an effort on our part to give "credit" for large collections of technical/research reports, security classified reports, and microforms held in certain industrial libraries. The formulae we used is detailed in the *JASIS* article, so it seems sufficient to note here that *Aircraft* took a substantial lead of nearly 3 million bibliographic items, with *Appliances, Electronics* (#13), *Chemicals* (#16), and *Petroleum Refining* (#32) being over a million behind *Aircraft.* VD, Mean Holdings/ Corporation Library, has *Aircraft* in a comfortable lead with 43 thousand items, *Motor Vehicles and Parts* (#28) at 21,000 items, and six industrial classifications in the 13,000's. Since "Holdings" is itself a unique measure with this study, then VE, Holdings per Corporation Employee, is necessarily also unique. The overall figure is just over one bibliographic item for each and every company employee (1.18 to be more exact). The standings show both *Aircraft* (#11) and *Publishing and Printing* (#34) having four times as much.

At a lower level of priority in this section V Materials are the mean ranks of these last mentioned measures. VB1, Mean Rank of Volumes features *Pharmaceuticals* (#33) and *Aircraft* (#11) at $R76.5$ and $R86.4$, respectively. VD1, Mean Rank of Holdings, shows the places reversed, with *Aircraft*'s Mean $R57.8$ comfortably leading *Pharmaceuticals*' $R82.6$. The listing for Mean Rank of Holdings per Corporation Employee, see *Appliances, Electronics* (#13) and *Aircraft* (#11) in a virtual tie at $R56.8$ and $R57.1$.

To summarize the implications of Appendix Table B.1, the most important considerations are that the *Fortune* 500 corporations represent the important segment of the industrial special library universe, that the analysis by industrial classifications is the most fruitful approach, and that of the 20-odd variables studied, the first priority ones are: I. Number of corporations with libraries; II. Number of libraries maintained; III. Number of internationally operating systems; IV. Number of professional librarians employed; and V. Materials (especially periodical subscriptions).

Relationships between Measures

Table 12.1 answers the question that logically next comes to mind: Are there "couplings" among these measures that are statistically significant? There are indeed and Table 12.1 lists twenty-four pairs of measures from seven industrial classifications with significant linkages. The leading categories are *Measuring, Scientific and Photographic Equipment* (#23) and *Office Machinery (includes Computers)* (#30) with six pairs each. "Assets" is a repeatedly mentioned measure in these pairs, which is surely another reason for using as select a population as the *Fortune* 500 corporations for the study reported here.

A graphical look at each of the twenty-four pairs of relationships is provided by the so-called "Scattergrams" generated under the SPSS (Statistical Program for the Social Sciences) we used. The machine diagrams for the first two pairs of measures on Table 12.1 are given as Figures 12.2a and 12.2b. The remainder of the pairs on Table 12.1 are included in Appendix B following Table B.31. (Note that where numerals appear within the boundaries of the "scattergrams" they stand for two or more superimposed data points.) An interesting (but nonvalid statistically) picture was provided by a set of each measure ran versus RAssets.

The meaning of these couplings is that the IIS director can consider fewer variables than in Table B.1 and thus concentrate in the near term on company assets, company employees, professional librarians, number of libraries, and the holdings (or periodical subscriptions).

Table 12.1 Relationships between Measures of the Fortune 500 Corporations and Their Library Resources (in Order of Certainty within Category)

CATEGORY TITLE/MEASURES	Correlation (R)	Significance (R)
11 Aircraft and Parts		
Measures:		
Libraries vs Employees	0.863	0.000
16 Chemicals		
Measures:		
Holdings vs Assets	0.931	0.000
Libraries vs Assets	0.913	0.000
Libraries vs Employees	0.896	0.000
Professionals vs Assets	0.854	0.000
Professionals vs Employees	0.838	0.000
20 Glass, Cement, Gypsum, Concrete		
Measures:		
Professionals vs Assets	0.925	0.000
23 Measuring, Scientific and Photographic Equipment		
Measures:		
Holdings vs Assets	0.941	0.000
Holdings vs Employees	0.913	0.000
Libraries vs Employees	0.882	0.000
Professionals vs Assets	0.850	0.002
Professionals vs Employees	0.849	0.002
Libraries vs Assets	0.834	0.003
28 Motor Vehicles and Parts		
Measures:		
Libraries vs Employees	0.912	0.000
Libraries vs Assets	0.891	0.000
Professionals vs Employees	0.888	0.000
Professionals vs Assets	0.864	0.001
30 Office Machinery (including Computers)		
Measures:		
Holdings vs Assets	0.990	0.000
Holdings vs Employees	0.966	0.000
Professionals vs Assets	0.965	0.000
Professionals vs Employees	0.948	0.000
Libraries vs Employees	0.894	0.001
Libraries vs Assets	0.871	0.001
38 Textiles		
Measures:		
Holdings vs Employees	0.838	0.005

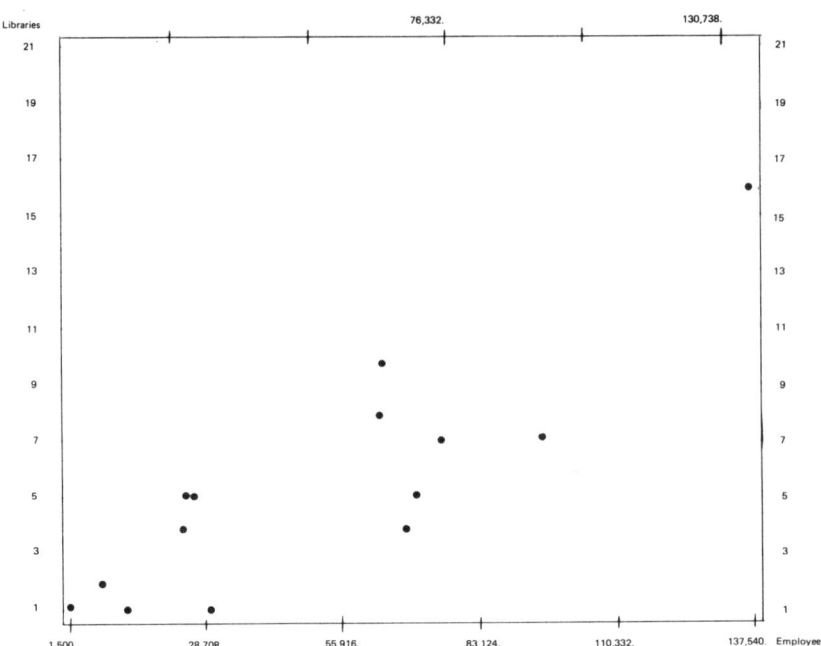

Figure 12.2a "Scattergram" of AIRCRAFT Industrial Classification—Number of Libraries vs Number of Company Employees

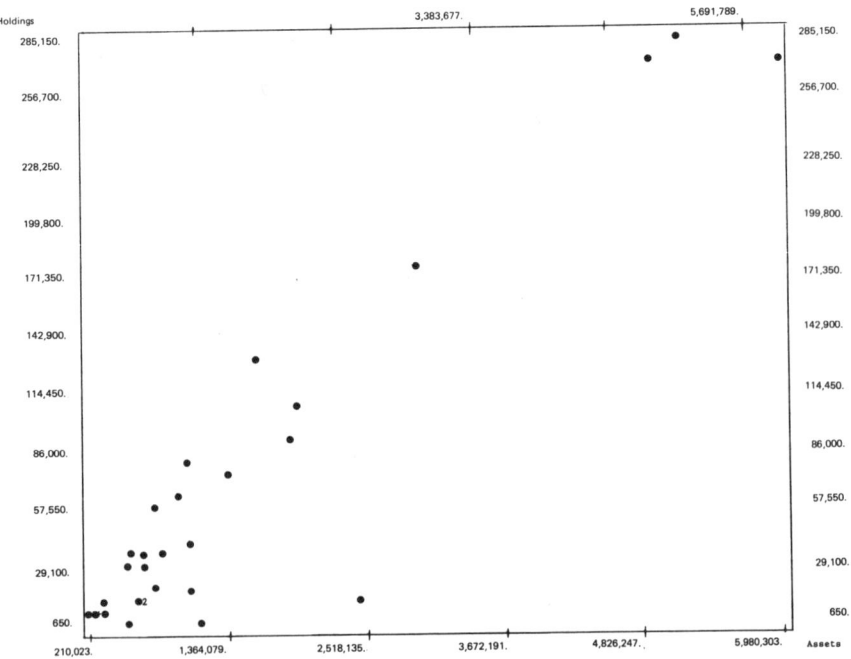

Figure 12.2b "Scattergram" of CHEMICALS Industrial Classification—Number Holdings vs Assets (in $ thousands)

Financial Implications

Personnel costs are the major component of the IIS and are normally more than 50 percent of the IIS total costs and sometimes as high as 75 percent. Quite recent figures are provided in the Special Libraries Association's Salary Survey, 1976.[4] We considered the median figure of $16,000 was too low for industrial special librarians as a group and the 75th percentile of $18,800 was too high. Thus the *Fortune* 500's 2,054.2 professionals would cost $34.9 million annually. Considering that clericals would cost about $7,500 each and that their proportion to professionals was about 1:1.50, they would cost about $23.1 million annually. Using fringe benefits at 25 percent would give total personnel costs of $72.5 million annually.

Taking costs of materials next, a very recent study by King shows that periodical subscriptions cost $45 each annually.[5] This figure would give a cost of $13.9 million for the 311 *Fortune* 500 corporations' 308,679 subscriptions. Using 1/3 of that cost for book purchases would give $4.6 million. (Note that this proportionality and several of the others in this section are based on formulae included in Chapter 9.) In the experience of certain major industrial systems, "other costs" covering reports, pamphlets, some equipment, and so forth is 1/10 of the total budget cost or $14.5 million. Then there is the case of bibliographical materials (periodicals, books, and so forth) that are bought by the firm for use outside the library and in the technical departments themselves. Instances are known where these costs are 25 percent of the total library budget, or $36.2 million in the case being quantified here.

Using the above assumptions and calculations, we see for the first time that *Fortune* 500's personnel costs for library services and materials are $141.7 million for 50-50% assumption or $10.98 for each and every company employee. If we assume that a 60 percent for personnel and 30 percent for remaining costs is more reasonable, then the annual cost is $105.5 million or $8.18 per employee. (Note that occupancy and utility costs are excluded from these figures.)

Summary Recommendation

While each subsection on the IIS extent in the *Fortune* 500 corporations and the implications has been summarized separately, it is probably wise to reiterate that 311 of these corporations form the bulk of the IISs extant, and that we do not know—but are willing to study—how the remaining 189 corporations manage without formal library services. We recommend a limited list of variables be determined to compare the company to the means of the industrial classification it belongs to as well as the means of the entire population; that the company be compared with companies perceived as competition; and that

188   Industrial Information Systems

the prevailing personnel and materials costs as well as proportions found useful elsewhere in this book to formulate library budgets be used to arrive at a suitable course of action.

IIS INTERNATIONAL OPERATIONS

A geographically centralized IIS is the easiest to administer, then the geographically dispersed domestic system, the U.S.-Canadian combination, the U.S.-Overseas with English as the common working language, and finally the U.S.-Overseas where several working languages are employed. While it is true that leased telephone, telegraph, and cable lines remove many impediments in communication, it is still better to resolve matters face-to-face (the supersonic company plane is not yet common) and so geographic concentration merits first mention. Where there is a large concentration (or nucleus) of company libraries (i.e., DuPont around Wilmington, GM around SE Michigan, Bell Labs in northern New Jersey, BOEING around Seattle), the IISs interact as good company operational management procedures dictate.

In performing its acquisitions functions, the geographically dispersed domestic system starts to encounter the problem of which informational elements should be secured from in-company sources and which from external sources. (For example, when should the IBM Burlington facility use the University of Vermont or the Vermont State Library in preference to other IBM libraries for nonproprietary materials?) By extension of this thought, the IBM Hursley (Winchester) library should use the Lending Division, The British Library, Boston Spa, Yorkshire, or the Science Reference Library (National Reference Library of Science and Invention), The British Library, Chancery Lane or Queensway, London, as appropriate, instead of cabling continental or U.S. IBM libraries. There may be public relations considerations in addition to operational considerations that dictates support of national library resources-sharing networking systems.

In the case of purchasable information items available only in an overseas country, very successful use has been made of leased-cable requests to the overseas corporation library, with full reimbursement by interlocational funds transfer. (It is normal to charge the requesting location for extraordinary messenger or taxi expenses to expedite action.) On occasion, subscriptions might be placed through the overseas location to take advantage of the subsidiary's corporate membership in a professional, trade, or government-sponsored research association. Of course, there are two points of view on this potential saving, one of which is that the generous company would want to pay full price invariably so as to show its full support of that national professional or trade group.

Sometimes items can *only* be obtained through intervention of the overseas operation or persons. The circumstance is recalled where we had ordered so many preprints from a distinguished engineering society overseas that it was clearly desirable to start a blanket order for *all* preprints as issued, which, however, turned out to be "impossible" because there was no policy permitting such orders. On inquiry, we found that only a council member could suggest a new policy be set up. The solution was to ask a council member who was one of the subsidiary's senior technical staff to introduce such a motion, which he was pleased to do. Now a number of U.S. corporations have standing orders for those preprints.

Overseas operations are also useful intermediaries in arranging for expeditious translations from their national language of both "open" and company publications. One device is to permit national employees to do such translations on their personal time. This practice serves the twofold purpose of insuring technical accuracy while giving the employee a chance to practice English.

It goes without saying that all transmission of information and data between domestic and overseas operations should be in full compliance with applicable national government and security regulations. However, do beware of inertia in such approval channels and focus the appropriate legal staff attention on total or near blockages.

The above-mention of company legal resources recalls the earlier injunction for the IIS to use effectively *all* company resources for information purposes. That these resources are considerable was hinted in the previous section on the *Fortune* 500 corporations. It is made explicit in Table 12.2, which is entitled "Comparison of 240 Domestic-Only and 71 International Industrial Library Systems for Nine Variables." While this table shows clearly the dominance of the internationally operating IISs, Figure 12.3 shows how great a proportion of the total volumes in IISs are in the latter systems. Appendix A on the General Motors Research Laboratories Library contains a helpful flow diagram on information input.

While the discussion thus far could be taken to imply that the major industrial library resources are in the United States and the lesser overseas, the fact is that informal communication with certain systems where the reverse is true have led us to the conclusion that the principles given here work equally well either direction.

Turning from the acquisitions functions to the cataloging functions, the key consideration is the sharing of catalogs and indexes internationally, which calls for agreement on input standards, format, and terminology within the IIS or machineable tables to transfer from one system to the other. (We know of at least one case where language differences were ignored.) The libraries of the IBM British, French, and German Laboratories did a pioneer KWIC (keyboard-in-context) index to all their monograph (books) down to chapter titles by mixing the three languages alphabetically and the product was

Industrial Information Systems

found useful. Thus there can be a tendency where English is the working language of the company for bibliographical tools to develop overseas where, atleast in the developmental stage, both the national language and English are used. In fact, in overseas library meetings of more than one corporation, the option offered to make any comments on the meeting floor in their national language

Table 12.2 Comparison of 240 Domestic-Only and 71 International Industrial Library Systems for Nine Variables

HOLDINGS

Holdings (Thousands)	Domestic-Only #Corps.	%	International #Corps.	%
200+	8	2.6	11	3.5
175-200	0	0	3	1.0
150-175	2	0.6	1	0.3
125-150	3	1.0	3	1.0
100-125	4	1.3	7	2.3
75-100	6	1.9	3	1.6
50-75	18	5.8	7	2.3
25-50	31	10.0	16	5.1
1-25	161	51.8	18	5.8
Unknown	7	2.3	0	0

HOLDINGS PER EMPLOYEE

Holdings/ Employee	Domestic-Only #Corps.	%	International #Corps.	%
3+	26	8.4	13	4.2
2.5-3	7	2.3	5	1.6
2.0-2.5	9	2.9	6	1.9
1.5-2	13	4.2	9	2.9
1.0-1.5	27	8.7	10	3.2
0.5-1	46	14.8	14	4.5
0 -0.5	105	33.8	14	4.5
Unknown	7	2.3	0	0

VOLUMES

Volumes (Thousands)	Domestic-Only #Corps.	%	International #Corps.	%
150+	2	0.7	11	3.5
125-150	2	0.7	3	0.1
100-125	1	0.3	3	0.1
75-100	3	0.1	7	2.3
50-75	10	3.3	7	2.3
25-50	43	14.1	17	5.6
0-25	172	56.6	23	7.6

Table 12.2 *continued*

RANK IN EMPLOYEES

REmployees	Domestic-Only #Corps.	%	International #Corps.	%
Top 50	25	8.0	22	7.1
51-100	30	9.6	17	5.5
101-150	34	10.9	10	3.2
151-200	30	9.6	8	2.6
201-250	26	8.4	5	1.6
251-300	28	9.0	1	0.3
301-350	24	7.7	6	1.9
351-400	15	4.8	0	0
401-450	16	5.1	2	0.6
451-500	11	3.5	0	0
Unknown	1	0.3	0	0

RANK IN ASSETS

RAssets	Domestic-Only #Corps.	%	International #Corps.	%
Top 50	26	8.4	24	7.7
51-100	37	11.9	10	3.2
101-150	31	10.0	12	3.9
151-200	28	9.0	9	7.9
201-250	34	10.0	2	0.6
251-300	23	7.4	7	2.3
301-350	22	7.1	3	1.0
351-400	20	6.4	2	0.6
401-450	17	5.5	2	0.6
451-500	1	0.3	0	0
Unknown	1	0.3	0	0

PROFESSIONAL LIBRARIANS

Professional Librarians	Domestic-Only #Corps.	%	International #Corps.	%
20+	9	2.9	14	4.5
11-19	18	5.8	22	7.1
7-10	19	6.1	4	1.3
6	11	3.5	4	1.3
5	13	4.2	4	1.6
4	21	6.8	1	0.3
3	21	6.8	5	1.6
2	32	10.3	10	3.2
1	87	28.0	6	1.9
0	9	2.9	0	0

Table 12.2 *continued*

	RANK IN SALES			
	Domestic-Only		International	
RSales	#Corps.	%	#Corps	%
Top 50	26	8.4	22	7.1
51–100	35	11.3	13	4.2
101–150	33	10.6	11	3.5
151–200	29	9.3	5	1.6
201–250	28	9.0	6	1.9
251–300	22	7.1	6	1.9
301–350	21	6.8	4	1.3
351–400	23	7.4	1	0.3
401–450	12	3.9	2	0.6
451–500	11	3.5	1	0.3

	LIBRARIES			
	Domestic-Only		International	
Libraries	#Corps.	%	#Corps.	%
20+	0	0	5	1.6
15–20	0	0	8	2.6
13–14	0	0	1	0.3
11–12	4	1.3	3	1.0
9–10	5	1.6	3	1.0
7–8	9	2.9	9	2.9
5–6	17	5.5	15	4.8
3–4	50	16.1	13	4.2
1–2	155	49.8	14	4.5
0	0	0	0	0

	EMPLOYEES PER PROFESSIONAL LIBRARIAN			
Employees/	Domestic Only		International	
Professional	#Corps.	%	#Corps.	%
40+	8	2.6	2	0.6
35–40	3	1.0	0	0
30–35	5	1.6	0	0
25–30	8	2.6	4	1.3
20–25	15	4.8	2	0.6
15–20	27	8.7	3	1.0
10–15	42	13.5	7	2.3
5–10	52	16.7	19	6.1
0–5	71	22.8	34	10.9
Unknown	9	2.9	0	0

Scope of IIS Operations 193

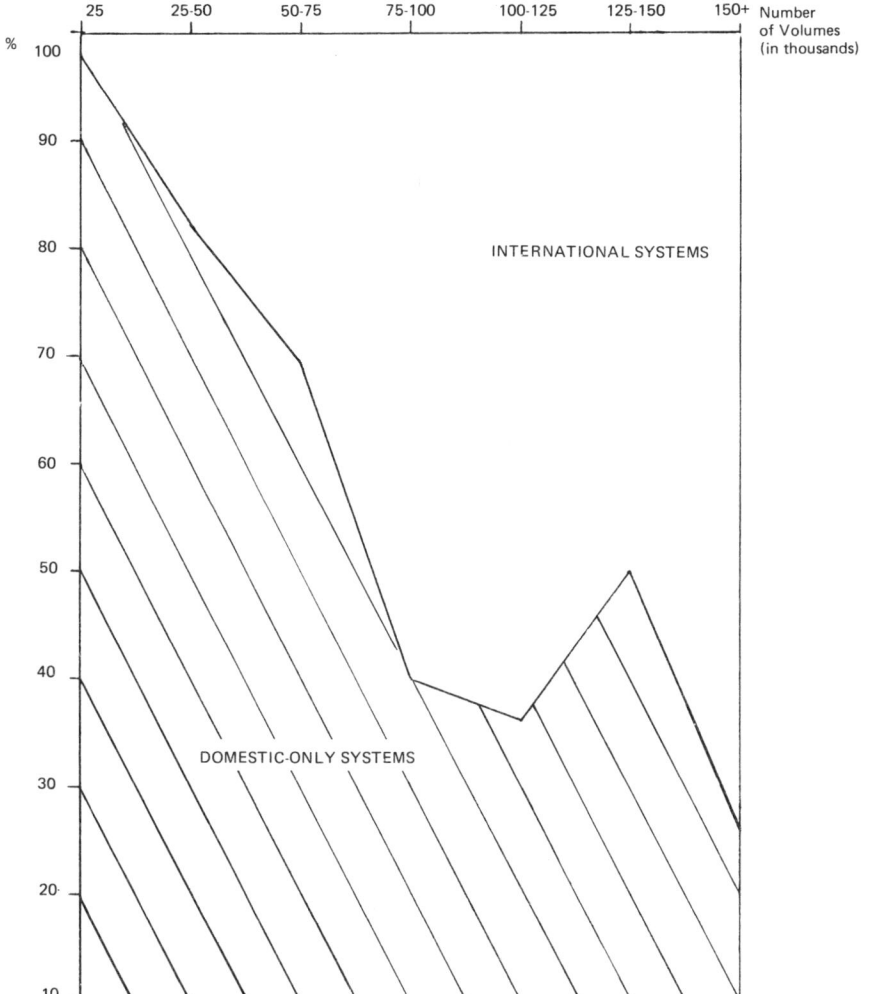

Figure 12.3 Relative Proportions of Volumes in Domestic-Only and International Industrial Library Systems

or English has been appreciated but not utilized (even though the national language was the dominant one at the subsequent "refreshment oasis" session). To summarize, terminology and format are the main concerns in international processing functions.

The generation and production of information functions can lead to different national styles, organs, and manners of presentation. While there is a paramount need overseas for the national technical staffs to present a favorable image to their countrymen on the company's technical competence, someone should be charged to see that overseas-generated information is "plugged-in" to the company IIS in an appropriate manner and to an appropriate extent. Military security documents, the covers of which were seen in the library of an IBM Scandinavian subsidiary, have no business in the company except within that nation; however, it is incumbent on the appropriate person to insure that generalized findings that would be of assistance to other units of the company become aggressively sought out and recorded in "cleared" form.

The dissemination and utilization functions of course are the "payoff" ones of the IIS. Overseas operations of GM were receiving "Current Engineering Information," the Research Laboratories' Library list of new accessions and new periodical articles since before World War II. Requests for listed material from GM Overseas Operations or directly from overseas subsidiaries were received in significant quantities and handled routinely with those from domestic plant cities, irrespective of whether the facility had a formal library or not. A member of the domestic reference staff should regularly scan lists received from subsidiary libraries for overlooked items requiring purchase.

Sometimes the most difficult reference questions do not require the finding of a book or periodical article; instead the question is one of "Who knows what in this corporation?" In the absence of a formal "yellow pages" sort of tool within the company, frequently the services of an IIS staff member in the overseas company are utilized by transoceanic phone to pinpoint the "knower" of a particular crucial fact or process. While it is universally true that the quickest way to answer a reference question is to ask directly the person who knows the answer, the next best thing is to ask the person's IIS staffer, wherever he or she may be.

The archetype of the international operating in-company information service is IBM's ITIRC (IBM Technical Information Retrieval Center), Armonk, New York, 10504. A brochure on that service, which is visitable by suitable arrangements with the appropriate IBM Data Processing Division representative, may be requested by writing ITIRC. Briefly, the service operates on internally generated and externally procured data bases and provides current awareness (or SDI) and retrospective dissemination and search services in a dual mode—from Armonk and from La Gaude, France. Articles on ITIRC appear from time to time in the professional literature, but a visit is recommended.

There have been administrative functional implications in several of the previously mentioned suggestions. In essence, all domestic IIS personnel should communicate with an overseas staff person in the same way they would like to be communicated with—that is, clearly, reasonably, precisely, and with due regard to existing cultural and language differences. The appearance of overbearing, unappreciative, unreasonable masters summoning a slave should be carefully avoided.

Scope of IIS Operations 195

Summary Recommendation

We recommend that IISs operating internationally do so within the framework of the home company/subsidiary modus operandi. The main differences are in the number of items involved, the urgency of the need for information exchange, and the possible vacuum of clear-cut company and/or national procedure for the exchange. Certain key concerns with the several functions have been outlined here, and we recommend that good international business procedures be used to handle nontechnical problems. This chapter has also included some hints on technical IIS problems, in which, for example, an informal meeting with the IIS director of an international-operating *Fortune* 500 company in a different industrial classification could be useful. A longer-term benefit could be the involvement of a professional consultant that the 500 company has found useful in the past.

PREDICTABLE IIS VARIATIONS

It is clear from the preceding section on IIS extent in *Fortune* 500 corporations that there are some large systems holding a significant proportion of the total bibliographic and staff resources that industry as-a-whole devotes to technical information services. Further, the section on IIS international operations shows that the international systems have a large percent of *that* large percent. To follow this point on skewed resource distribution to its ultimate conclusion, it is clear that *within* the leading such international systems, some few company locations typically have the lion's share of the company's literature/service resources. For example, a leading multidivisional, multinational corporation had 80 percent of its IIS resources concentrated in 20 percent of its IIS locations. We have thus revealed the first predictable variation within IISs is the nonuniform distribution of resources among the system's elements/locations.

The second variation is that due to the differences in the *functional assignments* of the several locations. Research locations will typically have complex, capable IIS elements while production or field service operations may have minimal information service facilities. The probable rank order for a company's divisional IIS units in descending order is:

Research (sophisticated service to sophisticated users, long time frame, sympathetic management);

Advanced Military Development (sophisticated users, access to government data bases, extremely short time frame needs mixed with longer-term needs, IIS expenses chargeable to contract to extent negotiated with government's contract officer);

Advanced Commercial Development (mixed-mode services ranging from near-Research to near-Systems Proving for variety of users, varying time frames, high project mortality, premium on flexibility);

Systems Proving and/or Pilot Plant Activities (narrower-focused services, short time frame, results orientation);

Sophisticated Subsystem Production (slightly broader focus than preceding but for relatively few key users, high stakes involved, short time scale);

Marketing Support (diffuse needs over broad spectrum, indefinite time-frame, personality dependent);

Main Systems Assembly and/or Product Production (crisis-sensitive program for clear needs of key users plus reassurance back-up for broad population of short-term users);

Maintenance and Customer Support (fairly low level or even parasitic information requirements and services, possible crisis-handling increase with trend of consumer legislation).

Presumably this "pecking-order" has received sufficient parenthetical elaboration, but we cannot resist two examples of the unusual: the marketing director of the chemical division of a nonchemical based corporation who rates the divisional library as a prime asset in his marketing efforts and actively solicits questions from customers that the divisional library can handle for him as his "extra service"; and the on-line information retrieval system for an extensive customer field maintenance and up-grading service that has a panel of three or four heavily experienced engineers on duty at all times to respond when the nation-wide system is "up" for direct inquiry by users because the IR system response was unclear or insufficiently detailed.

The third variation within IISs is the *subject matter* on which the company's products/services is based. The section on *Fortune* 500 corporations showed the most reliable measures were those based on industry (subject matter) classifications: Chemical (and chemistry-related), electronics, and transportation companies led the extractive and food processing groups by substantial margins. Another way to phrase this finding is *high technology* divisions *vs. medium technology vs. low technology* divisions. While still highly visible differences between divisional information needs/services exist now, there will be an inevitable "smearing" of these distinctions in the future as environmental and societal concerns conmingle with the company's technical concerns. For example, the problem of disposal of carcasses of sacrificial animals accumulated at Mecca during the Holy Year turns out to require highly complex mathematical modeling for the solution proposed by a high technology company.

The fourth source of variation is whether the company is a *single- or*

Scope of IIS Operations 197

multi-industry endeavor. Conceivably this variation could be considered as a subcategory under the third variation mentioned above, but is separately listed for emphasis. Both organizational and financial implications for the IIS exist, and their extent depends on the peculiar situation existing within the company. The need to maximize the advantages and minimize the disadvantages of the situation for the IIS is a challenging managerial concern.

Geographic spread of IIS elements forms the *fifth* variational possibility. Its extreme form, the international operating system, was covered in the preceding chapter, and the points raised there should be reviewed for domestic applicability. Otherwise some reasonable variations on the existing interlocational relationships currently employed in the company should serve to minimize the effects on the IIS of geographic spread.[6]

Scale Effect should be considered the *sixth* source of variability. We should be aware that possibilities exist for cost-savings on jobber placement of periodical subscriptions; company contracts for binding, microfilming, microfiching, and color slide production; and other useful forms of leverage. However, it is a mistake, for example, to uncritically move IIS procedures from a complex installation in the San Francisco bay area to a tiny facility in Nashua, New Hampshire. The recommended phrase to use is "Well, if there is no persuasive local reason to the contrary, why not do it in the following standard IIS company way . . . ?"

All companies are not uniformly homogenous: some divisions have special relationships to certain trade associations; some have subcontractor relationships to outsiders; others have patent agreements; the government security relationships are well known and complex in administration. We call this *seventh* variation source as *outside interdependence*. Its existence can lead to "compartmentalization" within the IIS. In its best form, this compartmentalization serves to limit the company exposure and focus the company's benefits from participation in the referenced relationship; at its worst this tendency in organization can be extremely counterproductive. Higher management has the clear responsibility to insure only the optimum level of compartmentalization exists in the company's IIS operations.

Summary Recommendation

The differences among the IISs between industries has parallels in the differences among divisions and locations within the same company. Six categories of the foreseen differences have been particularized to aid *in situ* identification. Assuming that a wholly decentralized IIS is not the pattern for the company, we recommend rationally required variations be employed along with the management attention necessary to keep them to an optimum level. Appropriate use of professional consultants may be desirable and/or essential.

NOTES AND REFERENCES

1. Eugene B. Jackson and Ruth L. Jackson, "The Industrial Special Library Universe—A 'Base Line' Study of Its Extent and Characteristics," *Journal of the American Society for Information Science* **28**(3): 135-152 (May 1977).
2. Eugene B. Jackson and Ruth L. Jackson, "The Personnel, Material and Financial Resources of the Library Systems of 311 Industrial Corporations," Submitted to *ERIC Clearinghouse*, Syracuse University, October 1977 (ERIC No. IR005-222).
3. The seminal reference here is: *"Fortune's* 500 Largest Industrials in U.S., 1975," *Fortune* **91**(5): 208-235 (May 1975). The standard library directories used are cited in full in the JASIS article.
4. "SLA Salary Survey, 1976," *Special Libraries* **67**(12): 597-624 (December 1976).
5. Donald W. King et al., *Statistical Indicators of Scientific and Technical Communication, 1960-1980,* Vol. 1, A Summary Report for National Science Foundation, Division of Science Information (Rockville, Md.: King Research, Inc., Center for Quantitative Sciences, 1976), 99 pp. (Sold by the Superintendent of Documents, Washington, D. C.)
6. GE's handling of the geographical spread matter is concisely covered in a February 7, 1977 communication from Walter Grattidge: ". . . enclosed is a brochure of the International Access Directory of the Company responsible for offering worldwide timesharing and other information access services . . . the company (also) has an extremely comprehensive telephone communication system, I understand the largest outside the government, by which any office in GE can direct dial any other company office within the U.S. or abroad. In addition, contact is possible with many external companies and organizations through the direct dial system. There is also a corresponding extensive internal company mail system, including company trucks taking mail between major GE centers such as Schenectady to N.Y.C., Philadelphia, Erie, Cleveland, Pittsfield, and Boston. The company still relies on U.S. mails for communication with points west of the Mississippi . . . ."

Chapter 13

Considerations in Mechanizing the IIS Functions

This chapter is inevitable in a book on IISs written in the late 1970s; however, it suffers from the need to be either an extremely long tutorial or a relatively short recital of "musts" to do and pitfalls to be avoided. We have opted for the latter to cover our involvement with the topic since the time of our invited talk to the Library of Congress' Staff Forum, December 5, 1951, on "Suitable Applications for Rapid Selection Devices."

What a far cry from that time to the comment on fourth generation computer systems that arrived in the ASIS *Bulletin* the day this section was in the typewriter. Ira W. Cotton writes:

> We can already see pieces of such a [fourth generation] system in the modern packet-switched networks which are in operation and being expanded, and in private corporate networks, such as that operated by the Singer Company. This latter network is organized into four hierarchical levels: 1) a small number of large, centralized hosts; 2) a modest number of regional minicomputers; 3) large numbers of special-purpose intelligent terminals; and 4) a large number of unintelligent teletypewriter-compatible user terminals. These components are interconnected in hierarchical fashion from highest to lowest through communications facilities.[1]

NINE "COMMANDMENTS" FOR MECHANIZATION

How does a current state of IIS nonmechanization proceed toward the inevitable fourth generation state just described? The purpose of this chapter is to provide a guide through the quicksand that abounds. (Please note that we use the old-fashioned word *mechanize* rather than the newer term of *automation* because we see much more hard work in the procedure than magic, and "automation" implies application of too much magic for our taste.) The steps listed below are necessary to mechanize the IIS properly:

1. Identify *all* the functions in the IIS. (Previous chapters in this book should aid in this process.)
2. Read critically the extant literature on IIS mechanization.
3. Determine which functions can, should, or must be mechanized either in whole or in part.
4. Determine the optimum combination of functions to be mechanized in view of (a) the state of sophistication in computer hardware in the company; (b) the state of sophistication in computer software in the company; (c) the level of computer expertise available from in-house sources; and (d) the availability of creditable computer/library science advice from outside sources.
5. Initiate action causing pilot studies to be made "in house" or "out-of-house" on major elements of the proposed IIS system(s).
6. Initiate parallel functional operations in the old and new modes.
7. "Cut-over" to the new method of mechanized operation.
8. Share the "hard" results of mechanization endeavors with other IIS directors in professional forums.
9. Plan for the next enhancements of the IIS.

Starting with the first step, identification of all the IIS functions, these "nine commandments" of library mechanization should be fleshed out. The listing of functions in Chapters 3 to 5 and the tables in Chapter 6 should be a head start on inventorying the existing IIS functions. The next elaboration could be the relevant sections of the Alexander list detailed later on in this chapter.

Step 2, critical reading of the extant literature, can lead to increased general awareness of the issues involved in library mechanization, but a more desirable objective is the identification of authors and/or projects worth emulating and those to be avoided. While each director's list will vary in detail, they all will include the review chapters from the ASIS *Annual Review of Information Science and Technology*, the articles originating with the Bell Laboratories Technical Libraries (see the references in Robert Kennedy's Chapter 11 in this book), the works of Lancaster (see the references in the Bibliography section of this book), Grattidge, Licklider, Epstein, and the current columns of Williams and Brandhorst in the ASIS *Bulletin*. Works by persons identified with major manufacturers or information jobbers may appear under their own names in the professional press or with or without attribution in publications issued by their respective companies. We think of such names as Baxendale, Black, Furth, Sammet, and Warheit right off. There are also writers of inadverent "science fiction" to be carefully avoided.

Under Step 3, determining those functions that can, should, or must be mechanized in whole or in part, there is the school of thought that says begin with the functions causing the most trouble currently ("the shoe that pinches" principle), while we advocate beginning at the start of the functional "pipeline" and building on previously processed records. (Don't redo or re-input information without compelling reasons. Among other reasons for this dictum is the fact that input is characteristically slow and affords endless opportunities for "typos" to be introduced.)

The landmark effort in library mechanization under R. W. Alexander epitomizes the use of the computer for functions it could best do and came closest to reflecting complete understanding between the systems analysts and the professional librarians.[2] The findings were embodied in a comprehensive statement of technical specifications, detailed flow charts, and masses of coding sheets for an on-line, real-time, integrated library system (i.e., instant, continuous, and "intelligent" response). The list of Alexander's topics in Table 13.1 illustrates the comprehensiveness of the effort and the relative levels of emphasis. Each of the functions in the list could be searched instantaneously and shown on a terminal screen or placed in a queue to be printed at a later time. The system operated in either an "expert" or "novice" mode. The only flaw was that the system was coded for an experimental monitor that the company decided not to market as a standard monitor. A partial "reincarnation" of the system will be mentioned under Step 4d.

There are a variety of considerations under Step 4 on deciding the optimum combination of functions to mechanize. Taking Step 4a, computer hardware available in the company, we are reminded that there was a stage in the past where IIS functions were put on the computer because the machine was not busy, or it was a prestige matter to use a computer, or that one had to be "up-to-date." Fortunately these considerations no longer force inappropriate applications of computers to IIS functions. These days, in fact, a *spectrum* of computers may be available. Further, the IIS is not limited to computers physically in the company, since service centers and jobbers are only too happy to offer computer services for a fee; beware, though, that a "black box" service is not being touted merely because it is the only "black box" not now completely committed. This caution does not mean that no sharing can be considered at all; one prestigious on-line circulation system costs the IIS nothing for machine time as the large capacity machine is needed only seldom by the comptroller (and he foots the machine bill). We do know of other systems that come to a grinding halt when payrolls have to be run or a government contract proposal has to get in. A point to remember is that IIS files differ radically in character from normal data processing files. The latter call for relatively small storage and repetitive manipulation, while bibliographic data calls for huge amounts of storage and relatively infrequent access of individual data items.

The state of computer software (Step 4b) depends importantly on the monitors and/or file management systems resident on the computers. While some of the software is necessary just to operate the central processing unit (CPU), other packages are conscious choices between alternatives and may be quite costly "to exercise" and still others are on a flat rate and the greater the use, the less the unit cost.

Table 13.1 An On-Line, Real-Time, Integrated Library System

TOPIC	EMPHASIS LEVEL*
I. INTRODUCTION	3x
A. PROBLEM DEFINITION	3x
B. OBJECTIVES	5x
C. GUIDELINES FOR REVIEWING THE SPECIFICATIONS	4x
II. PROJECT DESIGN CONSIDERATIONS	x
A. SYSTEM OVERVIEW	5x
1. File Review & Maintenance	x
2. Ordering	2x
3. Receiving	x
4. Cataloging	2x
5. Circulation	x
6. Searching	x
B. CONCEPTS	x
1. On-Line	3x
2. Real-Time	8x
3. Data Capture	4x
4. Reminder Lists	2x
5. Access-Point Files	2x
6. Printing Queues	10x
C. PROGRAMMING STRUCTURE	2x
D. TIMING	x
E. HUMAN FACTORS	x
F. DISPLAYS	x
G. FILES	3x
H. SYSTEM STATISTICS	x
III. FILES	2x
A. FILE INPUT	8x
B. INPUT FORMS	4x
C. INTERNAL CONTROL	12x
D. FILE OUTPUT	4x
IV. FUNCTIONS	12x
A. ORDERING	2x
1. New Orders	3x
2. Reorders	2x
3. Additional Orders	3x
4. Ordering Special Periodical Issues	x
5. Ordering Periodical Indexes	x
6. Claims for Nonperiodicals and Missing Periodical Issues	3x
7. Claims for Periodical Indexes	2x
8. Cancellation of Outstanding Orders	2x
9. Automatic Orders	2x
10. Interlibrary Loans	x

* Note that "x" = one vertical inch or narrative matter on diagrams

Table 13.1 *Continued*

TOPIC	EMPHASIS LEVEL*
11. Periodical Renewal	2x
12. Cancellation of Subscriptions before Termination	2x
13. Claims Cancellation	2x
14. New Item Entries Without Ordering	2x
15. Standing Orders	2x
16. Blanket Purchase Orders	3x
17. Bindery Orders	3x
18. Orders from Machine-Readable Input	2x
19. Replacement Orders	2x
20. Requesting Price Quotations	2x
21. Cancellation of Subscription Renewals	2x
22. Reviewing Periodical Renewals	3x
B. RECEIVING	17x
1. Receipt of Undamaged Non-periodicals	4x
2. Receipt of Damaged Non-periodicals	2x
3. Receipt of Interlibrary Loans	4x
4. Receipt of Bindery Orders	x
5. Receipt of Ordered Periodicals	12x
6. Receipt of Unordered Periodicals	2x
7. Receipt of Blanket Purchase Order Items	x
8. Receipt of Replacement Orders	2x
9. Cancellation of Price Quote Requests	x
C. CATALOGING	7x
1. Initial Cataloging of New Items	3x
2. Revising Detail of Accessions	2x
3. Transferring Document Detail	3x
4. Purging Accessions	3x
5. Requesting Proof Sheets	2x
6. Changing Periodical Titles	4x
7. Replacing Subscriptions	4x
8. Cataloging from Machine-Readable Input	5x
9. Printing Book Catalogs	4x
D. CIRCULATION	6x
1. Check-Out	2x
2. Check-In	x
3. Placing Reserves	3x
4. Cancelling Reserves	x
5. Borrower Replacement for Item in Circulation	2x
6. Reviewing Status of Documents	x
7. Handling Payment of Fines	2x
E. FILE REVIEW & MAINTENANCE	14x
1. Accessing the Files	2x
2. File Display	6x
F. SEARCHING	x
1. Features	x
2. Modes of Operation	2x
3. Program Logic	4x
V. FILES	2x
A. ACCESS-POINT FILES	x
1. Authors	4x

Table 13.1 *Continued*

TOPIC	EMPHASIS LEVEL*
2. Non-periodical Titles	5x
3. Call Numbers	3x
4. Descriptors	7x
5. Library of Congress Subject Headings	3x
6. Publishers	4x
7. Vendors	6x
8. Purchase Order-Item Numbers	2x
9. Report Numbers	3x
10. Contract Numbers	3x
11. Patent Numbers	3x
12. Periodical Titles	3x
13. Codens	4x
B. ACCOUNTING FUND FILE	3x
C. DEPOSIT ACCOUNTS	2x
D. PATRON IDENTIFICATION FILES	4x
E. DATE REMINDER LISTS	11x
F. PRINT QUEUES	22x
G. CODE TRANSLATION FILES	17x
VI. OFF-LINE STORAGE	--
A. ORDER DETAIL	2x
B. CIRCULATION DETAIL	2x
APPENDIX A. FILE DEFINITIONS	5x
A. BIBLIOGRAPHIC INFORMATION	x
1. Author Name	6x
2. Title	4x
3. Descriptors	4x
4. Title Analytics	5x
5. Document Type	3x
6. Document Form	2x
7. Call Number	19x
8. Periodic Title Link	3x
9. Subject	3x
10. Patent Number	2x
11. Series Identification	3x
12. Accession Number	2x
13. Report Number	2x
14. Contract Number	2x
15. Report Number Source	4x
16. Contract Number Source	3x
17. Language Indicator	4x
18. Collation	3x
19. Library of Congress Card Number	2x
20. Library of Congress Subject Headings	3x
21. Dates	3x
22. Publisher/Source	4x
23. Place of Publication	4x
B. OTHER INFORMATION	x
1. Reference/Routing Code	3x
2. Document Classification	3x
3. Location Code	3x
4. Cataloging Source	2x

Table 13.1 *Continued*

TOPIC	EMPHASIS LEVEL*
5. Requester's Identification	2x
6. Status & Date	4x
7. Delay Date	2x
8. Source of Information	2x
9. Notes	5x
10. Acquisition Code	3x
11. Owner Code	3x
12. Ordering Library Name	4x
13. Donor's Name	2x
14. Exchange Identification	2x
15. Missing Issues Identification	4x
16. Date to Initiate Automatic Order	2x
17. Date to Expect Standing Order	2x
18. Type of Order	2x
19. Index Service	3x
20. Index Characteristics Code	2x
21. Index Receipt/Order Code	2x
22. Bindery Vendor Code	x
23. Index Vendor Code	x
24. Lettering Code	3x
25. Bindery Condition Code	2x
26. Bindery Color Code	2x
27. Bindery Label (or Ticket)	2x
28. Bindery Inclusion Code	2x
29. Bindery Code	x
C. ON-ORDER INFORMATION	x
1. Price	2x
2. Vendor	3x
3. Vendor Item Number	2x
4. Purchase Order Number	2x
5. Purchase Order Item Number	2x
6. Type of Payment	2x
7. Deposit Account	3x
8. Deposit Account Order Number	2x
9. Account Identifier within Vendor	2x
10. Date to Expect Receipt of this Order	2x
11. Order Form Name	2x
12. Fund Account Number	3x
13. Shipping Instructions	3x
14. Claim Initiation Date	x
15. Quantity	2x
16. Invoice Number	2x
17. Account Number (within Vendor)	2x
18. Library of Congress Card Order Code	2x
D. PERIODICAL RECEIPT INFORMATION	x
1. Expected Receipt Date	2x
2. Date of Last Order	2x
3. Date of Last Issue of Subscription	2x
4. Date of First Issue of Subscription	3x
5. Receipt Frequency Code	3x
6. Number of Issues Expected	3x
7. Oldest Issue Identification	5x
8. Most Current Issue Identification	2x
9. Claims Delay Interval	2x

Table 13.1 *Continued*

TOPIC	EMPHASIS LEVEL*
E. PERIODICAL RENEWAL INFORMATION	x
1. Renewal Indicator	x
2. Renewal Date	2x
APPENDIX B. CODE TRANSLATION TABLES	2x
A. CODE TABLE IDENTIFICATION	5x
B. BIBLIOGRAPHIC INFORMATION	34x
C. OTHER INFORMATION	37x
D. ON-ORDER INFORMATION	10x

The level of computer expertise (Step 4c) available "in house" is truly crucial, especially when there is a relevant component in that expertise. (Handling differential equations well does not guarantee transferability to periodical check-in records, for example.) Difficulty of communication between the systems analyst/programmer and the IIS professional is blamed by Stephen E. Furth, information retrieval pioneer, for the slow rate of progress in past IIS mechanization efforts.[3]

The availability of creditable computer/library science advice from outside sources (Step 4d) changes somewhat from time to time with priority needs and variant circumstances (not to mention available financial resources). For example, a decision to "buy in" to the on-line interactive system offered for a brief time as the successor to the Alexander work would not only have represented a substantial investment in funds to underwrite the vast recoding and recommendation required, but also required finding *nine* other organizations to share the costs or it was "no go." Despite certain horror stories information science colleagues are delighted to share (or even provide unasked), we suggest the closest possible liaison with the representatives of hardware and software suppliers,[4] as well as sensitivity to "the track record" of consultants from library/information science used at this stage of the mechanization process.

Step 5, initiating pilot studies either "in house" or "out-of-house," is the next logical step and a very important one. It permits an "orderly retreat" if required, with minimum of dislocation or embarrassment. Presumably no additional discussion is required here.

Step 6, initiating parallel operations using both the old and new modes is necessary because of the urgent necessity to preserve the integrity of the bibliographic records (scrambled records are too high a price to pay for haste, and a record misfiled is a body of data unavailable to handle a user's crucial inquiry). At an early stage of IIS mechanization the time period for parallel operation would need to be significantly longer than at a later stage when confidence and skill are available to a higher degree.

Step 7, inauguration of the new mechanized IIS function, needs to be done carefully (just as one lets go the tail of a tiger gingerly). At this stage, photographers and communications specialists should be handy so that maximum in-company exposure can result from this stride forward in the evolution of an IIS primed to handle the crucial needs of critical users in exemplary fashion.

Steps 8 and 9, sharing factual experiences and comparable procedures with noncompany professional colleagues and planning for the next enhancements of the brand-new system, may seem somewhat anticlimatic now, but the steps are necessary and concluding portions of the complete mechanization cycle.

It is well in passing to note that the IIS might consider participating in a network operating on a regional or trade associationwide basis, as a tenth "commandment." Sharing of bibliographic data bases that mechanization makes possible is a trend to be watched in the future.[5] Of course, only "open" sources could be shared, with the proprietary or security classified material withheld entirely or run on the same programs internally. For some divisions, this limitation to only open literature in the network would be no handicap, and in divisions close to the commercial product, the *only* important information is "closed" company information.

Summary Recommendation

We recommend that current resources in and available to the company in both hardware and software be explored, evaluated, and exercised for their proper contributions to the mechanization of appropriate IIS functions; further, that other resources outside the company be exploited so that the "mix" leads to feasible operational procedures and that these be tested in pilot and parallel modes, and if affirmative results are obtained, full operation follow. Significant findings should be shared with other IIS directors and studies continued to look for inevitable improvements. The possible role that networking has for the future in enhancing your IIS system resources should also be considered so that the ultimate service may be provided and the company's prime missions be achieved.

NOTES AND REFERENCES

1. Ira W. Cotton, "Protocols, Competition, and Fourth-Generation Systems," *Bulletin of the American Society for Information Science* 3(3): 31-32 (February 1977).
2. Robert W. Alexander, personal communication.
3. Stephen E. Furth, personal communication.
4. Information at this stage of the mechanization process is very dynamic. Items received in April 1977 included: IBM United Kingdom Limited, *Guide for Application Programming, Dortmund Library System—DOBIS*, 1st ed. (Feltham, Eng.: IBM, October 1975), in 3 vols.: GE15-6068— Executive Guide, GE15-6069—Application Guide, GE15-6070—System and Implementation Guide; and The Institute for Graphic Communication, [Announcement Brochure for conference on] *Advances in Bibliographic and Document Storage and Retrieval Systems*, IGC's Fifth Annual Analysis of New Developments and Trends, IGC Conference Center, Andover Inn, Andover, Mass., April 5-7, 1977.
5. Special Libraries Association, *Networks and Special Libraries: Why and How?* (New York: SLA, 1976), 6 pp.

Chapter 14

The True Worth of the IIS

It would be desirable to begin this final chapter with a nomogram upon which a straight edge could be laid and the true value of the IIS and of information itself be read off. Unfortunately, doing so is not possible. Further, it may be that the value of information and of systems for handling it might be like "beauty"—that is, visible only in the eye of the beholder—and the reader of this book should be an educable beholder.

Be that as it may, the IIS must provide information that is not only accurate, but also timely and in a form useful to the patrons. If the patrons use the service on another occasion, the implication is that they found the earlier response to be useful. If they are willing to pay a charge for it, the evidence is that of the marketplace. The ultimate measure is when a patron proposes the budget of the IIS be increased at the expense of his or her own unit's allocation.

Costing. A first step in calculating worth is *counting,* while the second step is attributing the right *charges* to the things/services counted. There is rather poor agreement on these basics, despite such steps as the holding of *Ad Hoc* sessions on "Measuring Impact" and on "Economic Assessment" at the August 1977 Engineering Foundation Conference on "Innovative Management of Technical Information Functions in Industry," Franklin Pierce College, Rindge, New Hampshire.

One leading IIS that struggles with internally comparable IIS statistics finds that division comptrollers do not interpret Standard Expense Classification (SEC) Codes identically; hence, the figures reported for expenditures for books and journal (periodical) subscriptions are not fully comparable from location to location. That IIS establishes ratios such as between salaries and total budgets, loans per borrower, loans per item acquired, and so forth to smooth out some of the inconsistencies. Thus, the main point we wish to make is to count consistently and define the bases for counting so that other locations can see whether the figures are or are not consistent with theirs (and see the rationale for any differences).

Some suggested grounds rules include: (1) Count as professionals only those exempt under the Labor Standards Act; all others are nonprofessionals (clericals); (2) include fringe benefits in salaries; (3) do *not* include charges for utilities and company-leased communications; (4) do *not* include rental of space; (5) count as reference inquiries those that *exceed twenty minutes* to answer (others are "quick answers"); (6) weight circulation by messenger to user's office *higher* than personal circulation within the IIS quarters; (7) weight processing of internal company bibliographic items *higher* than those for similar items commercially procurable; (8) weight *discarded* items higher than similar items acquired (since more effort is involved in "weeding"); (9) show *totals* for charged services to all other units, rather than identifying individual units served. The list could be endless but the parameters are outlined by these nine. Rereading the Chapter 9 on budgeting would also help.

Cost Reporting is a thought somewhat repetitive of the foregoing, but is included to emphasize the IIS's obligation to make established costs known both within the company and outside to the extent that the information does not compromise proprietary interests. Our past experiences show that there are numerous well-meaning people in each company that advise the following of the example of the "Three Monkeys," and it is up to the IIS Director to be the advocate for sharing for the professional good. At the present time, companies report their expenditures for R&D as a separate item in their Annual Reports; we foresee the time when expenditures for information services are similarly "called out."

Required reading in cost reporting is Grattidge and King's JANUS seminar paper.[1] (The only error found in it was the date of typing, which should have read January 12, 1977.) Grattidge not only cites costs as experienced by GE's corporate R&D, but cites the corrective steps taken and forecasts necessary ones for the future. Table 14.2 further on in this chapter is from this source.

Cost Effectiveness is most frequently thought of in connection with the consideration of whether or not to mechanize functions within the IIS (see the preceding chapter). In general, the "housekeeping" and production functions are more readily cost justified than the utilization functions.

Planning-Programming-Budgeting (PPBS) was in an eclipse for awhile as a budget formulation technique, and IIS managers were just as glad, since the system cut across functional lines. However, first-hand evidence suggests that President Carter's administration views that system with high regard, and government contractors will have to consider its implications for them. Management literature is full of explications of this technique. Most of the examples we have covered with budget evolution have used other more traditional approaches than PPBS. Zero-based budgeting also has strong advocates, and the IIS could conceivably follow that technique as well.

Cost Benefits from effective use of information are mostly expressable in time saved by expensive company personnel. We owe much to pioneering efforts in these directions by IIS people in the pharmaceutical houses and other chemically related industries. One basic psychological problem inherent in cost benefit analysis is that whatever makes the IIS look *good* makes the patron and his or her unit look *bad* (they are no longer all-knowing technically and are publically admitting it. . .).

Representing sort of a "negative cost benefit" is the widely held folklore that if it will cost $25,000 to *find* the answer via an IIS or in the extant literature, it is better to do the research over again in the laboratory. This assertion has not been proven to our knowledge, and it is interesting that the belief seems impervious to the effects of inflation.

There needs to be much more careful work like that just reported by Ben Weil for Exxon Research and Engineering Company.[2] He uses the device of reporting dollar benefits as "X" and multiples of "X". In this way he is able to show that Exxon realizes a benefit of *eleven times the cost of the open literature purchased*—surely a good investment by anybody's standards.

Economics of Information is a relatively new specialty, although Walter Carlson[3] and a few others have been known to hold forth from time to time on it. The general thrust is that information is a "perishable commodity," and any monopoly its possession earns is time dependent. As the impression that present-day society is no longer a goods-producing one, but is a knowledge-producing one, grows, it is inevitable that the perceived economics of the "Knowledge Society" will gain an increasing attention from top echelons. Works by Baumol and Machlup have the most credibility, and a major report by the latter for the National Science Foundation should be watched for in the summer of 1978.[4]

Marketing the IIS has been mentioned from time to time as a clear necessity. Ferber's[5] bibliography has some interesting leads, and marketing forms a principle "ingredient" in the much praised/maligned SCATT report.[6] Although the latter's opacity is probably unnecessary and surely was *not* a contract requirement, the book merits "plowing through."

Summary Recommendation

As must be evident by this time, we are advocating exploration of additional readings on elements that go into establishing the "True Worth of the IIS," since the answer for each company must be phrased in manner and quantities that will be meaningful to its executives. We see Costing, Cost Reporting, Cost Effectiveness, Budget Formulation Technique (Traditional, PPBS, Zero-Based, or other), Cost Benefits, Economics of Information, and Marketing as being useful subcategories of worth. Table 14.1 shows some readings under these headings. To conclude on an "upbeat" note, we cite as Table 14.2, Grattidge's view of necessary actions for the IIS of the Future, and we heartily agree with these steps.

NOTES AND REFERENCES

1. Walter Grattidge and M. King, Information for Industrial R and D—Prices,

Table 14.1 Suitable References for Topics in "True Worth of the IIS"

AUTHOR	COST REPORTING	COST BENEFITS
Grattidge*	s.p.	s.p.
Heiliger*	s.p.	
Hodge*		
King*	s.p.	s.p.
King*	s.p.	
Palmer*	p. 205-211	p. 205-211
Rees*	p. 177-179	p. 182-183
Weil*	all	
Wessel*	s.p.	
Annual Review of Information Science & Technology, v. 9, 1974	see index	p. 182-187; 308-309
Annual Review... v. 10, 1975	see index	p. 53-61
Annual Review... v. 11, 1976	see index	s.p.
American Chemical Society. Sub-Committee on the Economics of Chemical Information. *Cost Effectiveness of Information Systems.* Washington, D. C.: The Society, 1969.		
Sagarra, Carlos A. *An Approach to Cost Effectiveness of a Selective Mechanized Document Processing System.* Ft. Belvoir, Va.: 1967 (ATLIS Report No. 12).		
Veazie, Walter H. & Thomas F. Connolly. *The Marketing of Information Analysis Center Products and Services.* Washington, D. C.: American Society for Information Sciences, 1971 (ERIC/CLIS).		

NOTE: s.p. = scattered pages in the work.
*Listed in Bibliography to this volume.

Table 14.1 *continued*

COST EFFECTIVENESS	MARKETING	ECONOMICS OF INFORMATION	BUDGET PROCESS	PLANNING, PROGRAMMING AND BUDGETING (PPBS)
s.p.	s.p.		s.p.	
	s.p.			
s.p.				
p. 179–180	p. 181–182	p. 183	p. 179–180	p. 180–181
s.p.				
p. 234, 250	s.p.	p. 57–80		p. 350–351
s.p.	p. 80, 256		see index under Mgt.	p. 53–61
s.p.	s.p.	p. 27–54	p. 383, 388–389	p. 27–28, 310, 313–314, 384
13p.				
66p.				
		28p.		

Table 14.2 Necessary IIS Actions for the Future

PRICES AND COSTS

Recognize increasing price levels and associated in-house costs

Choose Responsive Strategies:
  Increased selectivity
  Increased productivity through mechanization
  Direct project support
  Enhance value of services
  Broaden range of resources

ROLE

Establish Tighter Interrelationship with Organizational Mission:
  Closer subject coverage with R&D programs
  Broaden reference capability

METHODS

Assess Application of New Technology and Services:
  Experimentation and evaluation
  Market promotion, user education
  New capabilities for staff

Source: Grattidge, Walter, and M. King, "Information for Industrial R and D--Prices, Cost, Choices and Responses," Preprint for *Janus* Seminar, New York, January 12, 1976 [sic], p. 45.

    Cost, Choices and Responses, Preprint for JANUS Seminar, New York January 12, 1976 [sic], 34 pp.
2. Ben H. Weil, *Benefits from Researcher Use of the Published Literature at the EXXON Research Center*, Presented before the Information Industry's Association, National Information Conference and Exposition, Washington, D. C., April 20, 1977, 4 + 7 pp. (Preprint).
3. Walter M. Carlson, *The Economics of Information Transfer.* Prepared for presentation March 12, 1969, to the Division of Engineering, New York Academy of Sciences in New York (Armonk, New York, 1969), 30 pp.
4. W. J. Baumol, *On the Economics of Library Operation*. Final report submitted to the National Advisory Commission on Libraries, Mathematica (Princeton, 1967), 120 pp.; Fritz Machlup, "Production and Distribution of Scientific and Technical Information" in *National Perspectives for ARL Libraries* (Washington, D. C.: Association of Research Libraries, 1975?), pp. 18-35; Fritz Machlup, "Our Libraries: Can We Measure Their Holdings and Acquisitions?" *AAUP Bulletin* **62**: 303-307 (1976).

5. Robert Ferber, Comp., et al., *A Basic Bibliography on Marketing Research*, 1974 Revision (New York: American Marketing Association, 1974), 299 pp.
6. Russell L. Ackoff et al., "Designing a National Scientific and Technological Communication System," The SCATT Report (Philadelphia: University of Pennsylvania Press, 1976), 173 pp.

Appendixes

Appendix A:

The General Motors Research Laboratories Library: A Case Study

EUGENE B. JACKSON

THE GENERAL MOTORS CORPORATION in its institutional advertisement in August 1965 issues of national periodicals featured librarians under the legend "Answer Ma'am" and revealed that among its resources are twenty-two company libraries in the United States with seventy-eight persons on their staffs.[1]

The capstone of this library "system" is the General Motors Research Laboratories Library, housed at the beautiful 600 acre Technical Center in suburban Warren, Michigan. This Library (abbreviated as the "GMR Library") has existed since 1917, has carried out an interloan service for other company divisions since 1927, has prepared a current awareness bulletin since 1933, has a larger total collection and staff and receives more current periodical titles than many of the public library departments of technology and science responding to the questionnaire by Daniel Pfoutz and Jackson Cohen.[2] Yet it is far from self-sufficient.

It borrows about 1,100 items on interlibrary loan a year (equivalent to one-sixth of the total interlibrary loans supplied to all industry in a year by the Massachusetts Institute of Technology libraries,[3] has deposit accounts in several of the libraries mentioned by Ralph Phelps,[4] William Budington,[5] Dwight Gray and J. Burlin Johnson,[6] and still cannot answer all the demands placed upon it by its three "publics."

These are, first, the Research Laboratories staff of 500 professional scientists and engineers; second, the several hundred engineers and scientists in other staffs and groups at the Technical Center site (some of whom have their own professional library support); and,

---

The author is Director of Information Retrieval and Library Services, International Business Machines Corp., Armonk, N.Y., and was formerly Librarian, General Motors Research Laboratories, Warren, Mich.
Reprinted, with permission, from *Library Trends* 14(3):353-361 (1966).

third, the thirty-three Divisions of the Corporation located all over the world. Using communications terminology, the GMR Library serves as a "switching function" between the needs of a substantial portion of the Corporation's literature users and the library community. (For descriptions of the GMR Library and the Corporation's "library system," two earlier articles may be read.[7-8]) Further, it serves as a switching function between these users and the documentation services of the Department of Defense, Atomic Energy Commission, and others. This last function is also exercised by certain Division library services having broader access to more highly classified military documents than the "need to know" of the Research Laboratories permits; see Fig. 1.

It seems inevitable that there is a triangle associated with the availability of information to an industrial firm. At the apex is a small area representing material physically located at a given location; below this, there is an area larger in size representing material elsewhere in the Company; and finally the far larger area in the remainder of the triangle represents the material available on the outside. Interlibrary loan is the catalyst that permits a decentralized industrial library system to work under these circumstances.

Although the accurate keeping of statistics suffers by the pressure of business to get the job done, the figures on interlibrary loans (*from* non-GM Libraries) and interloans (*to* other parts of the Corporation) are more accurate than most which were kept. Table 1 shows that they have been fairly constant at the respective levels of 1,100 interlibrary loans and nearly 6,000 interloan requests per year during the period 1957 to 1964.

As interloans initiate a certain percentage of GMR interlibrary loan requests, they will be considered first. It is to be noted that Table 1 excludes all activities contiguous to the Research Laboratories, as employees of a transportation manufacturer are highly mobile and accustomed to taking advantage of "cafeteria" service of the kind offered by GMR Library. On the other hand, photocopies and duplicate periodical issues mailed in response to a preprinted American Library Association Interlibrary Loan form from a distant Corporation technical literature activity are easily included in statistics and form the main source for Table 1.

The implications of Table 2 seem to be that there is a broad scatter of technical literature needs throughout the Corporation, that those Divisions manufacturing accessories for inclusion in the Corporation's

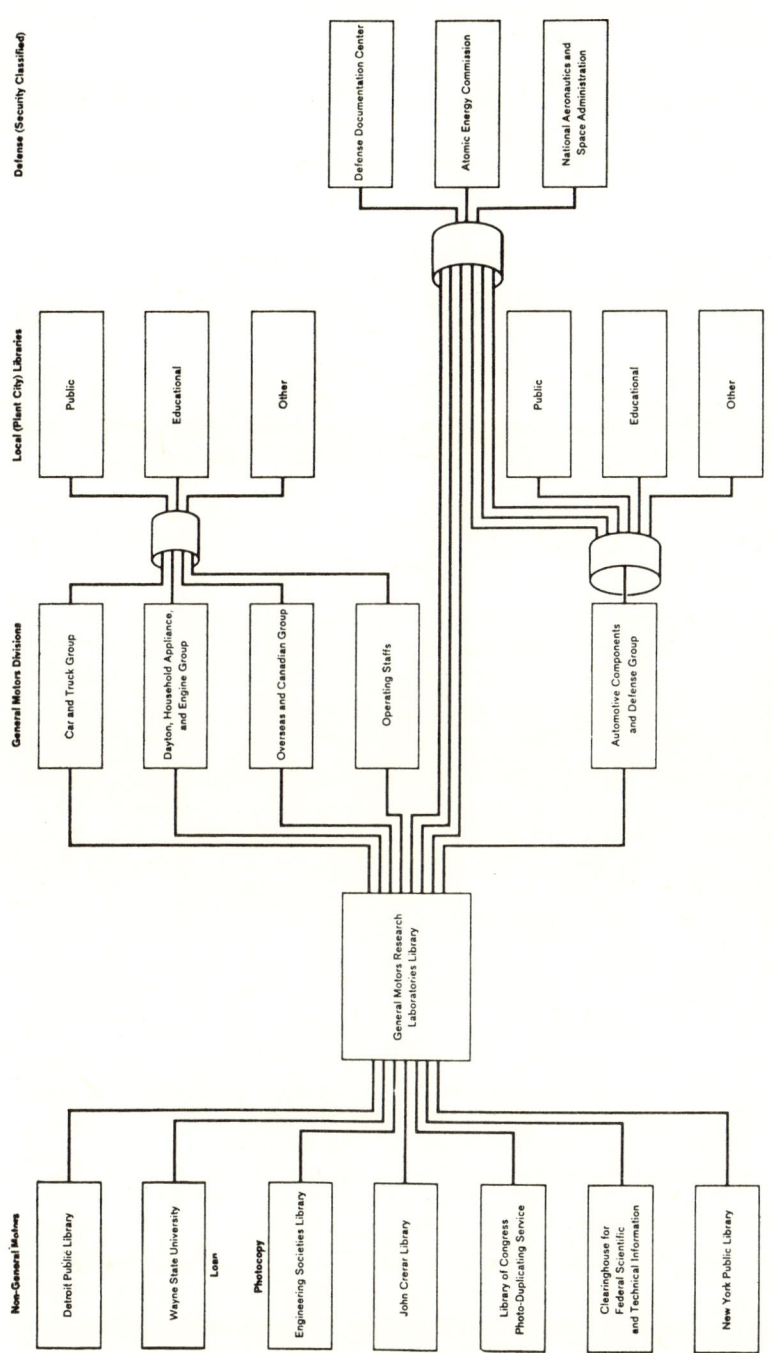

Figure 1. Technical Literature Sources Utilized by General Motors Corporation.

assembled products have engineering problems susceptible to literature-aided solution, and further that transfer of Research Laboratories' staff members to Divisional positions is reflected in the figures.

TABLE 1

Total GMR Interloans and Interlibrary Loans, 1957-1964

Activity	1957	1958	1959	1960	1961	1962	1963	1964
Interloans sent	4,750	5,056	6,368	6,615	7,180	4,975	5,515	6,565
Interloans returned for direct procurement				230	350	500	405	325
Total interloans handled	4,750	5,056	6,368	6,845	7,530	5,475	5,920	6,890
Interlibrary loans requested	1,125	1,310	1,027	1,215	1,050	870	1,130	1,205

TABLE 2

Major Users of GMR Interloan Services
(Excluding All Technical Center Site Activities)
1957-1964

Major Users	1957	1958	1959	1960	1961	1962	1963	1964
DHA&E Gp Div 1[a]	12%	12%	11%	10%	6%	5%	5%	10%
C&T Gp Div. 1[b]	0	2	2	1	1	3	7	8
O&C Gp Div 1[c]	1	1	1	3	5	8	8	5
AC&D Gp Div 1[d-e]	1	3	3	4	7	7	3	5
AC&D Gp Div 2	5	2	1	1	1	3	1	4
AC&D Gp Div 3	1	3	5	8	10	11	7	4
DHA&E Gp Div 2	13	8	8	7	5	4	3	4
AC&D Gp Div 4[d]	10	12	10	6	4	7	5	3
C&T Gp Div 2	5	4	4	2	2	3	3	3
AC&D Gp Div 5[d]	8	11	12	10	5	4	5	3
OPER STAFF 1[f]	1	3	3	2	2	2	4	3
C&T Gp Div 3	4	1	2	2	2	1	2	2
All other divs. and staffs	39	38	38	44	50	42	47	46
Total	100	100	100	100	100	100	100	100

[a] DHA&E Gp Div = Dayton, Household Appliance and Engine Group Division.
[b] C&T Gp Div = Car and Truck Group Division.
[c] O&C Gp Div = Overseas and Canadian Group Division.
[d] Have now or at one time had professional librarians in the Division.
[e] AC&D Gp Div = Automotive Components and Defense Group Division.
[f] OPER STAFF = Operations Staff activity.

The growth of interloans has been subject to restraints imposed by the staff and budget limitations of the GMR Library. This is understandable in view of the Library's organizational status as one department in a staff activity of this decentralized corporation, having no line relationship to the other libraries or technical literature activities in General Motors. Divisional cooperation in keeping the interloan totals down has taken such forms as establishment of photocopy accounts at principal outside technical libraries, assumption of photocopy costs for materials in the GMR Library collection, granting authority to charge the Division with literature procured to handle its requests, and willingness of a Division to procure its own literature after GMR Library verification of bibliographic references.

It will be recalled that Table 2 excluded any usage from other activities at the Technical Center site. To gain some idea of the division of staff time among other company activities, the GMR Library Staff maintained usage statistics for July-August 1964 and in November 1964 for the purposes of the present article. Records kept were of three kinds. First were the substantive reference questions answered by telephone; these questions were defined as those requiring some subject competence and required more than twenty minutes each to answer. Second were locative reference questions answered by telephone; these were the simple factual directory or handbook type and involved less than twenty minutes to answer. Third was a count of material circulated outside GMR during these periods on specific requests. Table 3 shows the results of these studies and of a similar one done in May 1957 at the request of the GMR administration.

Some implications of Table 3 are that the nearby technical personnel freely call on the GMR Library for factual information, but that equal quantities of material have to be circulated to the two groups to handle their combined reference inquiries. The encouragement given at the annual meeting of the GM Committee on Technical Literature, to use local city resources, appears to be effective for locative type reference questions. Proprietary considerations insure that crucial substantive reference questions are answered within the Corporation's resources. (Each of the above mentioned annual meetings has included a presentation by a major official of the public library in a city where General Motors has facilities, with mutual benefits to participants.)

The all-important 1,100 items borrowed on interlibrary loan will be considered next. These are largely for material required by the professional staff members of GMR. The mechanics are that the loaned items are picked up on a daily messenger trip to the city of Detroit's Cultural Center. The GMR messenger picks up at the same time interlibrary loans for other Technical Center site activities that have been telephoned in by their librarians or technical literature specialists but they do not appear in these tabulations.

The results shown in Table 4 were as expected inasmuch as the scientists normally require literature broader in scope and of more depth than engineers. The mathematical scientists are few in number but are avid literature users, even though the GMR Library's mathematical collection was not as large as for other fields.

TABLE 3

Comparative Usage of GMR Library by Non-GMR Personnel

Types of Use	1957 May	1964 Jul.–Aug.	1964 Nov.
Substantive reference questions	(N = 25)	[a]	(N = 99)
Non-tech. center site	28%	66%	37%
Tech. center site	60	34	57
Non-GM	12		6
Locative reference questions	(N = 183)		(N = 318)
Non-tech. center site	20	24	27
Tech. center site	70	76	69
Non-GM	10		4
Material circulated	(N = 181)		(N = 535)
Non-tech. center site	17	49	48
Tech. center site	75	48	51
Non-GM	8	3	1

[a] Number of transactions is not available for this period.

TABLE 4

Origin of 577 Interlibrary Loan Requests

Origin of Requests	313 Requests for Period ending Nov. 1, 1964		264 Requests for Period ending May 31, 1965	
	%	No.	%	No.
GMR Executive Office	—	1	4	9
GMR Engineering Research Depts.	19	58	26	68
GMR Basic and Applied Sciences Depts.	37	116	41	110
GMR Mathematical Sciences Depts.	16	51	12	31
GMR Administrative Services Depts.	17	54	11	30
GMR Personnel Dept.	1	2	—	1
Other Divisions and Staffs				
Non-Tech. Center site	6	18	1	3
Tech. Center site (lacking own information facilities)	4	13	5	12

It is not surprising that the major fields of GMR Library competence (physical science and engineering) represent respectively 83 per cent

TABLE 5

Subject Matter of 577 GMR Interlibrary Loan Requests

(Based on Dewey Decimal Classification)

Subject Matter	313 Requests for Period ending Nov. 1, 1964		264 Requests for Period ending May 31, 1965	
	%	No.	%	No.
000 General Works	—	1	1	2
100 Philosophy	4	13	1	4
200 Religion	1	3	—	—
300–330 Social Sciences, Economics	3	10	3	8
370–380 Education, Public Services	1	4	3	8
400 Language	—	1	—	1
500–509 Pure Science	2	5	3	7
510 Mathematics	12	38	3	7
520 Astronomy	2	5	—	1
530 Physics	12	36	10	26
540 Chemistry	13	40	15	38
550 Earth Sciences	3	10	2	6
560–590 Paleontology—Zoology	1	3	4	10
610 Medical Sciences	3	10	7	18
620 Engineering	16	49	13	34
660 Chemical Technology	14	45	15	39
Other 600's Technology	5	16	13	34
700 Arts	1	3	4	10
800 Literature	2	5	1	4
900 History	5	15	1	3
Fiction and Biography	—	1	1	4

and 85 per cent of the totals. However, the fact that the remaining 17 per cent and 15 per cent cover the entire spectrum of knowledge shows the difficulty an industrial library faces in attempting to become completely self-sufficient.

TABLE 6

Format of Publications of 577 GMR Interlibrary Loan Requests

	313 Requests for Period ending Nov. 1, 1964	264 Requests for Period ending May 31, 1965
Periodicals	60%	52%
Books and monographs	37	45
U. S. Government Documents	2	1
Annual Reviews	1	2

The crucial importance of periodical literature mentioned by several of the authors in this issue of *Library Trends* is strongly supported by this case study. The twenty-three indexing and abstracting services currently received by GMR Library and its set of the Library of Congress' printed book catalog insure the accuracy of references forwarded for interlibrary loan. (In those rare cases where partially verified requests were forwarded, notation was made of sources searched.)

TABLE 7

Date of Original Publication of 577 GMR Interlibrary Loan Requests

	313 Requests for Period ending Nov. 1, 1964	264 Requests for Period ending May 31, 1965
1960–1965	60%	60%
1950–1959	24	30
1940–1949	7	6
1930–1939	5	1
1920–1929	3	—
Prior to 1920	1	3

This dramatic illustration of the current nature of information actively sought by industrial researchers in fulfilling their literature needs still includes a chronological scatter of between 10 per cent and

TABLE 8

Loaning Libraries for the 577 GMR Interlibrary Loan Requests

	313 Requests for Period ending Nov. 1, 1964	264 Requests for Period ending May 31, 1965
Detroit Public Library	*84%*	*78%*
Technology and Science	66	56
Sociology and Economics	1	5
Philosophy, Religion and Education	2	4
Other Departments	15	13
Wayne State University Library	*15*	*20*
Kresge-Hooker Science	13	17
Medical	1	2
Other Departments	1	1
Other local area libraries	*1*	*2*

15 per cent of earlier important works. There is an implication that cooperative industrial library support of acquisition action by a major regional library would be more advantageous than their separate efforts to secure pre-1949 materials.

The superior collections of scientific periodicals in the Detroit Public Library's Technology and Science Department and in the Wayne State University Kresge-Hooker Science Library are clearly revealed in the sources of the materials borrowed by the GMR Library. There was a scatter of 20 per cent and 25 per cent of references sought in the other departments of the two main loaning libraries. The cooperative spirit evidenced by all levels at these libraries was of great assistance.

From the foregoing tables, it would appear that the usual request for an interlibrary loan from the GMR Library was from a member of the GMR Basic and Applied Science Departments on either a physical science or engineering subject, located in a periodical issued in the 1960's, and met by a loan from the Technology and Science Department of the Detroit Public Library.

The realization that the GMR Library was dependent upon the resources of the library community was accompanied by a conviction that all industrial special libraries must be good citizens of that community with corresponding responsibilities, rights, and privileges. This led to active participation in the drafting of the metropolitan area proposal by Katharine G. Harris, Robert E. Runser and this author; and in the affairs of the Associates of the Kresge-Hooker Science Library, the Advisory Committee on Libraries to the Macomb County (Mich.) Planning Commission, the meetings identifying the reference resources of the State called by the Michigan State Librarian, and other educational and recruiting endeavors.

References

1. "Answer Ma'am," Harper's, 231:29, Aug. 1965.
2. See pp. 236-261.
3. See p. 268.
4. See pp. 273-287.
5. See pp. 288-294.
6. See pp. 332-346.
7. Jackson, Eugene B. "Enter at Your Own Risk," *Library Journal*, 82:1146-1151, May 1, 1957.
8. ———— ————. "Portrait of a Special Library System," *Library Journal*, 87:3962-3965, Nov. 1, 1962.

Appendix B:

Summary Data on the Industrial Library Systems of the *Fortune* 500 Corporations

Table B.1 Fortune 500 Corporations with Libraries (Arranged in order by Number of Libraries in Each Fortune Industrial

Industrial Classification		No. of Corps.	RAssets	Libraries	International Systems		Professional Librarians		Subscriptions	Employees	RSales
					Yes	No	No.	Mean/Corp. Lib.	No.	No.	Mean
			Mean	No.					No.		Mean
#16	Chemicals	29	183.2	182.2	10	19	313.7	1.51	44,986	872,286	199.9
#13	Appliances, Electronics	28	211.0	164.5	6	22	216.0	1.11	32,678	2,090,400	211.9
#32	Petroleum Refining	24	71.4	124.8	7	17	239.0	1.78	49,481	823,675	71.3
#33	Pharmaceuticals	17	195.0	77.0	9	8	202.0	3.35	27,398	429,434	235.5
#11	Aircraft	14	197.0	76.0	3	11	194.0	2.19	23,449	700,834	180.0
#30	Office Machinery (includes Computers)	9	107.3	66.0	4	5	89.0	1.16	17,383	808,411	145.8
#18	Food	33	235.1	60.5	5	28	77.5	1.27	13,907	907,060	169.4
#23	Measuring, Scientific and Photographic Equipment	9	193.6	52.0	3	6	94.0	1.57	20,810	436,823	231.6
#24	Metal Manufacturing	20	117.8	49.2	0	20	58.2	1.23	10,063	799,224	138.2
#28	Motor Vehicles and Parts	10	105.6	48.0	2	8	92.0	1.48	12,267	1,819,980	99.2
#17	Farm and Industrial Machinery	18	219.2	45.0	5	13	63.0	1.20	14,473	542,543	234.1
#25	Metal Products	14	199.5	40.8	4	10	124.8	6.28	7,183	447,746	192.2
#20	Glass, Cement, Gypsum, Concrete	16	262.0	39.0	3	13	63.0	1.53	7,155	408,456	281.8

Table B.1 *Continued*

#31	Paper and Wood Products	17	179.2	34.0	2	15	40.0	1.16	6,618	453,132	202.2
#34	Publishing and Printing	9	316.3	33.7	1	8	72.0	2.67	4,196	109,178	359.2
#37	Soaps, Cosmetics	7	235.4	24.0	3	4	21.0	1.19	5,225	169,263	218.0
#35	Rubber	5	70.2	15.5	1	4	34.0	2.14	3,573	425,983	71.2
#14	Beverages	6	185.0	9.0	1	5	10.0	1.08	1,758	19,593	198.0
#38	Textiles	8	263.3	8.0	0	8	11.0	1.38	990	252,320	263.7
#39	Tobacco	4	91.8	6.0	0	4	15.0	2.75	1,770	132,164	118.8
#36	Shipbuilding, Railroad Equipment, Mobile Homes	3	177.3	5.0	1	2	4.0	0.83	1,213	49,188	265.7
#15	Broadcasting and Motion Picture Production and Distribution	3	219.7	5.0	0	3	8.0	1.56	538	52,546	198.7
#27	Miscellaneous Manufacturing	2	312.0	4.0	1	1	7.0	1.75	742	35,328	324.0
#26	Mining	2	123.0	2.0	0	2	2.0	1.00	375	13,832	244.0
#12	Apparel	2	291.0	2.0	0	2	2.0	1.00	253	44,520	318.5
#29	Musical Instruments, Toys and Sporting Goods	1	185.0	1.0	0	1	2.0	2.00	195	33,573	197.0
#21	Jewelry and Silverware	1	339.0	1.0	0	1	0	0	−1	8,098	436.0
#19	Furniture	0									
#22	Leather and Leather Products	0									
	TOTALS (27 of the 29 Categories)	311		1,175.2	71	240	2,054.2		308,679	12,912,590	
	MEANS (27 Categories)		195.8					1.71	11,872		215.0

Table B.2 *Fortune* 500 Corporation without Libraries

Industrial Classification		No. of Corps.	Employees		RSales	RAssets
			No.	Mean R	Mean	Mean
#16	Chemicals	4	7,126	413.5	315.3	333.3
#13	Appliances, Electronics	14	228,050	294.4	330.4	320.0
#32	Petroleum Refining	9	29,318	476.4	247.6	284.1
#33	Pharmaceuticals	0				
#11	Aircraft	0				
#30	Office Machinery (includes Computers)	1	6,300	433.0	388.0	289.0
#18	Food	36	355,796	400.6	324.2	426.6
#23	Measuring, Scientific and Photographic Equipment	2	19,800	359.5	484.0	387.5
#24	Metal Manufacturing	20	234,750	357.5	335.1	321.0
#28	Motor Vehicles and Parts	8	142,779	262.8	273.3	282.4
#17	Farm and Industrial Machinery	20	298,048	308.8	365.6	339.3
#25	Metal Products	15	152,403	358.3	413.5	414.3
#20	Glass, Cement, Gypsum, Concrete	2	21,847	343.5	302.5	295.0
#31	Paper and Wood Products	15	160,513	353.4	351.4	316.8
#34	Publishing and Printing	0				
#37	Soaps, Cosmetics	0				
#35	Rubber	1	14,100	289.0	382.0	395.0
#14	Beverages	3	29,891	361.3	392.7	339.3
#38	Textiles	5	77,779	271.2	387.6	376.2
#39	Tobacco	2	23,703	325.0	302.5	331.5
#36	Shipbuilding, Railroad Equipment, Mobile Homes	5	38,593	407.4	443.6	433.2
#15	Broadcasting and Motion Picture Production and Distribution	1	4,900	457.0	263.0	175.0
#27	Miscellaneous Manufacturing	0				

232

Table B.2 *Continued*

#26	Mining	7	54,297	399.0	341.6	261.1
#12	Apparel	12	299,880	197.6	333.3	353.8
#29	Musical Instruments, Toys and Sporting Goods	2	38,300	244.0	339.5	326.5
#21	Jewelry and Silverware	0				
#19	Furniture	2	34,100	249.5	365.0	403.0
#22	Leather and Leather Products	3	89,100	156.7	271.0	332.3
TOTALS (29 Categories)		189	2,361,373			
MEANS			102,668	335.6	350.1	340.1

Table B.3 *Fortune* 500 Corporations in Category 11, Aircraft (Arranged in Order by Number of Libraries)

Corporations with Libraries	RAssets	Libraries	International Systems		Professional Librarians		Subscriptions	Employees	RSales
			Yes	No	No.	Mean			
		No.					No.	No.	
Rockwell International	36	16	X		32	2.0	4,063	137,523	35
General Dynamics	133	10	X		19	2.0	2,645	63,575	98
Lockheed	-1	8		X	46	5.75	2,942	62,100	49
Boeing	82	7		X	23	3.80	4,091	74,400	39
United Aircraft	76	7	X		16	2.29	2,095	95,031	46
Avco	114	5		X	10	2.0	1,177	27,027	283
McDonnell	56	5		X	22	4.40	2,552	70,739	54
Northrop	301	5		X	5	1.0	1,220	26,200	236
Martin Marietta	139	4		X	12	3.0	817	24,584	168
Textron	104	4		X	4	1.0	848	68,000	89
Thiokol Chemicals	463	2		X	2	1.0	300	7,904	468
Cessna Aircraft	393	1		X	1	1.0	-1	1,500	393
Grumman	284	1		X	1	1.0	550	29,651	175
Rohr Industries	387	1		X	1	1.0	140	12,600	391

234

Table B.4 *Fortune* 500 Corporation in Category 12, Apparel (Arranged in Order by Number of Libraries)

Corporations with Libraries	RAssets	Libraries No.	International Systems Yes	International Systems No	Professional Librarians No.	Professional Librarians Mean	Subscriptions No.	Employees No.	RSales
Northwest Industries	144	1		X	1	1.0	200	30,000	182
Warnaco	437	1		X	1	1.0	53	14,520	455
Corporations without Libraries									
U.S. Industries	152							38,800	127
Genesco	249							57,000	166
Levi Strauss	278							30,141	222
Kayser-Roth	297							27,000	301
Cluett, Peabody	359							26,694	322
Blue Bell	382							25,000	329
Hart,Schaffner,Marx	355							20,500	341
VF	445							18,000	416
Kellwood	398							17,544	396
Jonathan Logan	408							11,520	413
Phillips-Van Heusen	462							15,300	470
Hanes	461							12,381	496

Table B.5 *Fortune* 500 Corporations in Category 13, Appliances, Electronics (Arranged in Order by Number of Libraries)

Corporations with Libraries	RAssets	Libraries No.	International Systems Yes	International Systems No	Professional Librarians No.	Professional Librarians Mean	Subscriptions No.	Employees No.	RSales
General Electric	10	32	X		52	1.63	6,134	404,000	8
RCA	29	19	X		22	1.16	2,933	116,000	31
Western Electric	18	15	X		18	1.29	3,778	189,972	15
Raytheon	174	12		X	17	1.42	2,141	54,410	100
Westinghouse Electric	24	12		X	21	1.75	3,094	199,248	19
Bendix	97	11		X	12	1.09	1,977	82,100	77
International Telephone & Telegraph	9	10		X	5	.50	566	409,000	10
Singer	67	10		X	10	1.00	1,466	111,000	66
Texas Instruments	171	6	X		13	2.17	2,143	65,524	126
Varian Associates	414	4.5	X		3.5	.78	924	10,392	492
Motorola	148	4		X	4	1.00	590	51,000	149
North American Phillips	179	4		X	4	1.00	500	31,577	204
Teledyne	138	4		X	8	2.00	600	50,300	116
Hewlett-Packard	223	3		X	5	1.67	1,160	28,900	225
Cutler-Hammer	417	2		X	4	2.00	477	14,400	427
ESB	364	2		X	2	1.00	250	17,000	380
Gould	260	2		X	6	3.00	730	22,468	259
Hoover	317	2	X		1	.50	655	27,452	334
AMP	299	1		X	2	2.00	500	13,573	348
Bunker Ramo	379	1		X	1	1.00	200	10,604	467
Fairchild Camera	380	1		X	1	1.00	250	18,092	421
Harris	300	1		X	0	0.00	180	16,800	335
Lear Siegler	314	1		X	1	1.00	125	20,768	272
Square D	372	1		X	1	1.00	150	16,800	365

Table B.5 *Continued*

Studebaker Worthington	143	1	X	1	1.00	215	29,370	150
Whirlpool	200	1	X	2	2.00	500	26,950	122
White Consolidated Industries	205	1	X	1	1.00	150	24,900	199
Zenith Radio	258	1	X	1	1.00	290	27,800	218
Corporations without Libraries								
Emerson Electric	209						34,500	172
McGraw Edison	230						26,000	220
Eltra	264						27,384	250
Sunbeam	259						26,304	258
Scovill Manufacturing	327						16,659	275
Reliance Electric	323						19,800	298
Avnet	356						9,500	302
I-T-E Imperial	313						14,944	340
General Signal	340						11,700	358
Champion Spark Plug	319						13,800	381
General Instrument	329						4,713	386
Fedders	344						8,500	445
Roper	401						6,765	446
Scott and Fetzer	467						7,481	495

Table B.6 *Fortune* 500 Corporations in Category 14, Beverages (Arranged in Order by Number of Libraries)

Corporations with Libraries	RAssets	Libraries No.	International Systems Yes	International Systems No	Professional Librarians No.	Professional Librarians Mean	Subscriptions No.	Employees No.	RSales
Coca-Cola	99	2		X	3	1.00	350	31,755	74
PepsiCo	108	2		X	2	1.00	453	49,000	90
Seagram (Joseph E.) & Sons	107	2	X		2	1.00	325	12,500	257
Anheuser-Busch	173	1		X	1	1.00	350	12,205	143
Pabst Brewing	378	1		X	1	1.00	75	5,200	384
Schlitz Brewing	245	1		X	1	1.00	205	6,900	240
Corporations without Libraries									
Heublein	216							18,123	210
General Cinema	455							9,318	482
Southdown	347							2,450	486

Table B.7 *Fortune* 500 Corporations in Category 15, Broadcasting and Motion Picture Production and Distribution (Arranged in Order by Number of Libraries)

Corporations with Libraries	RAssets	Libraries	International Systems		Professional Librarians		Subscriptions	Employees	RSales
		No.	Yes	No	No.	Mean	No.	No.	
Columbia Broadcasting	146	3		X	5	1.67	403	30,030	111
American Broadcasting	236	1		X	1	1.00	60	12,516	206
MCA	277	1		X	2	2.00	75	10,000	279
Corporations without Libraries									
Warner Communications	175							4,900	263

Table B.8 *Fortune* 500 Corporations in Category 16, Chemicals (Arranged in Order by Number of Libraries)

Corporations with Libraries	RAssets	Libraries	International Systems		Professional Librarians		Subscriptions	Employees	RSales
			Yes	No	No.	Mean			
		No.					No.	No.	
Dupont	17	29	X		71	2.54	8,162	136,866	17
Union Carbide	20	21	X		29	1.38	6,163	109,566	22
Monsanto	39	17	X		23	1.35	4,116	60,926	43
Dow Chemical	19	15	X		26	1.73	4,230	53,325	27
American Cyanamid	96	11.5	X		22	1.91	3,001	38,024	107
Olin	170	9		X	20	2.22	1,957	23,000	161
Celanese	73	8	X		12	1.50	1,307	38,000	101
NL Industries	156	7.5		X	6.5	0.87	1,490	25,800	124
Allied Chemical	69	7	X		18	2.57	1,620	32,167	85
Cabot	247	5	X		6	1.20	756	6,357	404
Grace (W. R.)	50	5		X	5	1.00	895	74,800	44
Hercules	115	5		X	18	3.60	1,534	24,958	133
Diamond Shamrock	159	4		X	7	1.75	675	9,793	211
Pennwalt	262	4	X		5	1.25	684	14,800	280
SCM	228	4		X	4	1.00	615	29,600	165
Airco	219	3		X	6	2.00	790	14,021	251
Akzona	234	3		X	4	1.33	350	19,515	254
Chemetron	343	3		X	4	1.33	79	9,031	379
Ethyl	189	3		X	5	1.67	1,323	17,497	198
Stauffer Chemical	197	3		X	6	2.00	955	12,451	233
Witco Chemical	368	2.2		X	2.2		256	5,183	314
Air Products and Chemicals	220	2		X	2	1.00	425	13,013	308
Ferro	444	2		X	2	1.00	396	7,770	457
Koppers	227	2		X	4	2.00	700	15,763	217

Table B.8 *Continued*

Rohm and Haas	161	2		X	1	.50	1,180	19,247	196
Sherwin-Williams	263	2	X		2	1.00	100	22,081	241
Dart Industries	141	1		X	0	0.00	-1	29,566	164
International Minerals & Chemicals	202	1		X	2	2.00	775	5,689	234
Lubrizol	385	1		X	1	1.00	156	3,479	426

Corporations without Libraries

Williams Companies	120							9,100	205
Clorox	411							6,400	312
Reichhold	427							4,050	347
Inmont	375							8,952	397

Table B.9 *Fortune* 500 Corporations in Category 17, Farm and Industrial Machinery (Arranged in Order by Number of Libraries)

Corporations with Libraries	RAssets	Libraries No.	International Systems Yes	International Systems No	Professional Librarians No.	Professional Librarians Mean	Subscriptions No.	Employees No.	RSales
Babcock & Wilcox	151	7	X		13	1.86	2,593	40,073	156
FMC	89	7		X	17	2.43	1,678	48,320	91
Caterpillar Tractor	40	3		X	7	2.33	875	80,144	36
Deere	66	3		X	5	1.67	5,700	56,000	75
Ingersoll-Rand	109	3		X	3	1.00	428	45,582	142
Midland Ross	354	3	X		1	.33	250	10,000	396
Carrier	188	2		X	2	1.00	400	27,079	207
Cincinnati Milicron	303	2		X	1	.50	100	14,840	373
Dresser Industries	119	2		X	2	1.00	430	39,000	146
Foster-Wheeler	312	2	X		2	1.00	440	17,464	228
Sunstrand	271	2		X	2	1.00	135	13,869	367
Timken	254	2	X		1	.50	180	22,196	270
USM	255	2	X		2	1.00	650	26,840	281
A-T-O	370	1		X	1	1.00	63	16,440	351
Allis-Chalmers	167	1		X	1	1.00	320	27,440	158
Clark Equipment	160	1		X	1	1.00	125	32,767	148
Outboard Marine	318	1		X	1	1.00	-1	15,042	350
Wheelabrator-Frye	420	1		X	1	1.00	106	9,447	440
Corporations without Libraries									
Otis Elevator	194							50,700	179
Walter Kidde	180							37,000	180

Table B.9 *Continued*

Alco Standard	311	13,000	203
Cummins Engine	213	20,364	237
Black and Decker	240	20,700	278
Tecumseh Products	434	9,168	303
Rexnord	357	14,134	342
Trans Union	130	10,000	344
Cooper Industries	362	12,482	407
Joy Manufacturing	345	11,217	408
Trane	349	10,900	417
Ex-Cell-O	367	11,730	419
Koehring	358	9,083	425
Federal Mogol	383	13,572	428
Hobart	381	11,615	432
Dover	460	8,880	447
Gardner-Denver	361	10,873	452
Briggs and Stratton	471	8,601	463
American Hoist and Derrick	413	7,829	469
Amtel	476	6,200	478

Table B.10 *Fortune* 500 Corporations in Category 18, Food (Arranged in Order by Number of Libraries)

Corporations with Libraries	RAssets	Libraries	International Systems		Professional Librarians		Subscriptions	Employees	RSales
		No.	Yes	No	No.	Mean	No.	No.	
LTV	65	6.5		X	9.5	1.46	1,155	66,000	29
General Foods	74	6	X		6	1.00	684	47,000	58
CPC International	112	5	X		5	1.00	1,405	42,500	71
Greyhound	110	5		X	6	1.50	705	54,482	45
General Mills	140	3		X	7	2.33	1,087	46,398	94
Borden	90	2	X		2	1.00	212	46,700	47
Esmark	124	2		X	3	1.50	600	33,500	30
Heinz	163	2	X		2	1.00	1,125	32,206	139
Nabisco	153	2		X	2	1.00	230	47,000	106
Norton Simon	132	2		X	2	1.00	545	28,000	123
Pet	280	2	X		2	1.00	290	17,700	226
Pillsbury	226	2		X	6	3.00	465	26,300	202
Agway	282	1		X	1	1.00	300	32,100	193
Amstar	275	1		X	2	2.00	100	6,538	191
Anderson, Clayton	315	1		X	1	1.00	170	19,000	227
Archer-Daniels-Midland	291	1		X	1	1.00	600	4,052	128
Campbell Soup	182	1		X	1	1.00	120	32,291	136
Campbell Taggart	426	1		X	1	1.00	92	15,522	294
Carnation	169	1		X	1	1.00	160	21,709	103
Castle and Cooke	231	1		X	1	1.00	150	23,308	255
Central Soya	294	1		X	1	1.00	120	9,713	112
Green Giant	449	1		X	2	2.00	350	6,382	423
Hershey	389	1		X	1	1.00	510	7,200	328
Kraftco	84	1		X	1	1.00	162	50,410	33
Libby, McNeill & Libby	374	1		X	1	1.00	100	6,190	363

Table B.10 Continued

Lipton (Thomas J.)	422	1	X	2	2.00	250	6,144	378
Oscar Mayer	376	1	X	1	1.00	190	13,329	209
Peavey	431	1	X	1	1.00	150	3,665	339
Quaker Oats	191	1	X	1	1.00	400	25,400	163
Ralston Purina	113	1	X	1	1.00	480	51,000	55
Staley (A.E.) Manu-facturing	388	1	X	1	1.00	250	3,791	287
Standard Brands	172	1	X	1	1.00	150	21,900	120
United Brands	136	1	X	2	2.00	600	50,000	84

Corporations without Libraries

Beatrice Foods	105	65,000	42
Consolidated Foods	137	71,000	80
Iowa Beef Processors	457	5,790	131
Associated Milk Producers	451	3,561	141
Land O'Lakes	390	6,780	183
Del Monte	229	32,100	192
Kellogg	266	17,000	200
Hormel (Geo. A.)	454	8,698	215
American Beef Packers	482	3,104	223
International Multi-foods	386	7,891	256
MBPXL	492	2,500	261
Gold Kist	402	7,600	262
Kane-Miller	468	5,168	271
General Host	448	9,938	277
ConAgra	453	5,466	282
Di Giorgio	428	6,000	333
Ward Foods	477	20,000	353
Hygrade Food Products	494	3,600	356
Cook Industries	261	7,000	368
Federal Co.	480	11,600	369

Table B.10 Continued

Corporations without Libraries (Continued)	RAssets	Libraries No.	International Systems Yes No	Professional Librarians No. Mean	Subscriptions No.	Employees No.	RSales
Riviana Foods	435					6,300	389
Spencer Foods	499					1,500	394
Fairmont Foods	478					7,630	395
Savannah Foods and Industries	465					1,111	398
American Bakeries	486					9,462	405
Stokely-Van Camp	447					5,000	409
Interstate Brands	484					11,384	412
Rath Packing	497					4,498	415
Dairylea Cooperative	493					1,900	435
Southern Industries	483					2,001	441
Idle Wild Foods	498					901	442
Bluebird	495					1,600	450
Monfort of Colorado	481					1,750	460
Brewer (C.)	371					5,895	461
Seaboard Allied Milling	489					604	476
Flavorland Industries	496					701	494

Table B.11 *Fortune* 500 Corporations in Category 19, Furniture (Arranged in Order by Number of Libraries)

Corporations without Libraries	RAssets	Libraries	International Systems		Professional Librarians		Subscriptions	Employees	RSales
		No.	Yes	No	No.	Mean	No.	No.	
National Service Industries	409							20,000	354
Simmons	397							14,100	376

247

Table B.12 *Fortune* 500 Corporations in Category 20, Glass, Cement, Gypsum, Concrete (Arranged in Order by Number of Libraries)

Corporations with Libraries	RAssets	Libraries No.	International Systems Yes	International Systems No	Professional Librarians No.	Professional Librarians Mean	Subscriptions No.	Employees No.	RSales
PPG Industries	87	6.5		X	11.5	1.77	1,621	38,000	113
Corning Glass Works	164	5.5	X		10.5	1.91	1,455	45,000	190
GAF	210	4	X		5	1.25	395	72,213	214
Norton	298	4	X		3	.75	655	20,437	311
Owens-Illinois	75	3		X	13	4.33	939	66,155	88
Carborundum	308	2	X		2	1.00	450	18,249	313
Libbey-Owens-Ford	243	2		X	3	1.50	190	18,761	273
Lone Star Industries	256	2		X	3	1.50	45	13,319	276
Owens-Corning Fiberglas	224	2		X	1	.50	106	19,621	238
U.S. Gypsum	201	2		X	3	1.50	604	20,600	232
Anchor-Hocking	396	1		X	1	1.00	150	14,900	400
Brockway-Glass	443	1		X	1	1.00	-1	10,500	487
Flintkote	302	1		X	1	1.00	60	8,343	349
General Refractories	425	1		X	0	0.00	30	9,863	459
Johns-Manville	165	1		X	4	4.00	400	26,600	181
Vulcan Materials	394	1		X	1	1.00	55	5,895	385
Corporations without Libraries									
National Gypsum	274							13,577	295
Certainteed Products	316							8,270	310

Table B.13 *Fortune* 500 Corporations in Category 21, Jewelry and Silverware

Corporations with Libraries	RAssets	Libraries No.	International Systems Yes	International Systems No	Professional Librarians No.	Professional Librarians Mean	Subscriptions No.	Employees No.	RSales
Insilco	339	1		X	0	0	-1	8,098	436

Table B.14 *Fortune* 500 Corporations in Category 22, Leather and Leather Products

Corporations without Libraries	RAssets	Libraries	International Systems		Professional Librarians		Subscriptions	Employees	RSales
		No.	Yes	No	No.	Mean	No.	No.	
Interco	252							43,500	174
Brown Group	342							27,600	264
U. S. Shoe	403							18,000	375

Table B.15 *Fortune* 500 Corporations in Category 23, Measuring, Scientific and Photographic Equipment (Arranged in Order by Number of Libraries)

Corporations with Libraries	RAssets	Libraries No.	International Systems Yes	International Systems No	Professional Librarians No.	Professional Librarians Mean	Subscriptions No.	Employees No.	RSales
Minnesota, Mining and Manufacturing	43	15	X		20	1.33	4,066	83,609	59
Xerox	26	11		X	35	3.18	8,486	101,380	41
Eastman Kodak	21	10	X		16	1.60	4,182	124,100	32
Johnson & Johnson	106	8	X		15	1.88	1,910	54,300	99
Bell and Howell	309	3		X	2	.66	320	13,115	372
Sybron	306	2	X		1	.50	370	17,000	343
Bausch & Lomb	407	1		X	1	1.00	560	12,900	484
Becton, Dickinson	332	1		X	1	1.00	56	17,400	402
Polaroid	192	1		X	3	3.00	860	13,019	253
Corporations without Libraries									
Talley Industries	440							9,800	477
Cenco	335							10,000	491

Table B.16 *Fortune* 500 Corporations in Category 24, Metal Manufacturing (Arranged in Order by Number of Libraries)

Corporations with Libraries	RAssets	Libraries No.	International Systems Yes	International Systems No	Professional Librarians No.	Professional Librarians Mean	Subscriptions No.	Employees No.	RSales
U. S. Steel	12	6		X	8	1.33	2,320	187,503	12
AMAX	80	5		X	7	1.40	632	12,417	167
Armco Steel	49	5		X	6	1.20	508	52,121	51
Anaconda	71	4		X	4	1.00	375	24,760	118
Reynolds Metals	52	4		X	5	1.25	812	39,300	95
Bethlehem Steel	23	3		X	10	3.30	1,547	121,623	21
Inland Steel	81	3		X	2	.67	467	34,928	78
National Steel	53	3		X	3	1.00	465	37,785	64
Kennecott Copper	58	2.7		X	2.7	1.00	311	32,300	119
Allegheny Ludlum	222	2.5		X	2.5	1.00	316	18,799	208
Aluminum Co. of America	33	2		X	3	1.50	400	50,151	65
Asarco	116	1		X	1	1.00	225	15,300	151
Cyclops	346	1		X	1	1.00	50	10,200	274
General Cable	330	1		X	1	1.00	140	6,700	325
Kaiser Aluminum & Chemical	62	1		X	5	5.00	655	26,910	114
Kaiser Industries	123	1		X	1	1.00	240	23,300	186
Lykes-Youngstown	91	1		X	0	0.00	100	30,000	105
Republic Steel	64	1		X	1	1.00	300	44,230	63
UV Industries	283	1		X	0	0.00	-1	12,637	355
Wheeling-Pittsburgh Steel	206	1		X	0	0.00	200	18,260	194

Table B.16 *Continued*

Corporations without Libraries

Ogden	177	34,000	104
Illinois Central	59	14,491	145
Phelps Dodge	102	14,941	195
Chromalloy American	251	23,900	244
Cerro	193	8,579	252
St. Joe Minerals	272	11,180	267
Interlake	270	13,391	286
NVF	338	7,076	324
Revere Copper Brass	269	8,438	327
McLouth Steel	360	5,075	338
Amstead Industries	436	11,700	359
Alumax	322	7,069	364
Howmet	286	9,546	392
Signode	392	6,497	403
Handy & Harman	470	2,750	413
Porter (H. K.)	474	7,712	433
Penn-Dixie Industries	429	5,000	453
Copperweld	469	4,654	458
Northwestern Steel	419	4,351	472
Keystone Consolidated	432	7,400	474

253

Table B.17 *Fortune* 500 Corporations in Category 25, Metal Products (Arranged in Order by Number of Libraries)

Corporations with Libraries	RAssets	Libraries No.	International Systems Yes	International Systems No	Professional Librarians No.	Professional Librarians Mean	Subscriptions No.	Employees No.	RSales
American Can	79	8.5		X	11.5	1.35	1,585	47,400	67
Combustion Engineering	166	6	X		12	2.00	1,630	40,765	140
Gillette	162	6	X		5	0.83	888	33,100	160
American Standard	134	3	X		2	0.67	343	57,700	117
Colt Industries	190	3		X	3	1.00	445	23,700	171
Universal Oil Products	287	3		X	9	3.00	572	11,281	243
Whittaker	246	3		X	3	1.00	385	14,600	216
National Distillers	158	2		X	2	1.00	170	14,345	185
Gulf & Western Industries	45	1.3	X		1.3	1.00	185	75,000	83
Chicago, Bridge & Iron	292	1		X	1	1.00	150	12,000	362
Continental Can	68	1		X	2	2.00	600	65,070	52
Crane	238	1		X	1	1.00	50	24,725	170
Emhart	391	1		X	1	1.00	180	12,560	437
Indian Head	337	1		X	71	71.00	-1	15,500	289
Corporations without Libraries									
Crown, Cork & Seal	253							15,266	248
National Can	305							14,200	265
Stanley Works	326							16,671	318
Harsco	363							14,900	337
Parker-Hannifin	404							13,462	406
Norris Industries	438							9,893	411

Table B.17 *Continued*

Eagle-Picher	442	9,800	430
Robertson (H. H.)	456	8,481	444
Wallace-Murray	452	7,858	462
American Chain & Cable	423	8,200	466
Ceco	475	7,886	471
Allied Products	459	8,600	475
Butler Manufacturing	473	4,636	479
Microdot	479	6,100	490
Tyler	466	6,450	500

Table B.18 *Fortune* 500 Corporations in Category 26, Mining (Arranged in Order by Number of Libraries)

Corporations with Libraries	RAssets	Libraries	International Systems		Professional Librarians		Subscriptions	Employees	RSales
		No.	Yes	No	No.	Mean	No.	No.	
Pennzoil	78	1	X		1	1.00	200	9,487	184
Texasgulf	168	1	X		1	1.00	175	4,345	304
Corporations without Libraries									
Pittston	214							17,125	169
Newton Mining	145							12,000	317
Eastern Gas & Fuel	232							10,100	319
Utah International	176							4,509	336
Cyprus Mines	268							4,713	387
Westmorland Coal	472							4,500	390
Belco Petroleum	321							1,350	473

Table B.19 *Fortune* 500 Corporations in Category 27, Miscellaneous Manufacturing (Arranged in Order by Number of Libraries)

Corporations with Libraries	RAssets	Libraries No.	International Systems Yes	International Systems No	Professional Librarians Nos.	Professional Librarians Mean	Subscriptions No.	Employees No.	RSales
Armstrong Cork	203	2		X	6	3.00	646	24,102	224
Bath Industries	421	2		X	1	.50	96	11,226	424

Table B.20 *Fortune* 500 Corporations in Category 28, Motor Vehicles and Parts (Arranged in Order by Number of Libraries)

Corporations with Libraries	RAssets	Libraries	International Systems		Professional Librarians		Subscriptions	Employees	RSales
		No.	Yes	No	No.	Mean	No.	No.	
General Motors	2	22	X		44	2.00	5,204	734,000	2
Ford Motor	4	7	X		15	2.14	2,255	464,731	3
TRW	85	6		X	17	2.83	1,389	88,341	76
Chrysler	13	4	X		6	1.50	724	255,929	11
Borg-Warner	121	3		X	4	1.33	1,010	44,207	108
Signal Companies	100	2		X	2	1.00	825	33,500	121
Budd	250	1		X	1	1.00	180	22,000	230
Eaton	117	1		X	1	1.00	50	50,225	110
International Harvester	31	1		X	1	1.00	230	110,990	26
Smith (A. O.)	333	1		X	1	1.00	400	16,057	305
Corporations without Libraries									
American Motors	178							33,143	93
White Motor	181							17,877	147
Fruehauf	157							26,363	153
Dana	195							23,000	188
Paccar	310							9,977	221
Questor	350							10,446	422
Houdaille Industries	464							7,800	464
Sheller-Globe	424							14,173	499

Table B.21 *Fortune* 500 Corporations in Category 29, Musical Instruments, Toys, and Sporting Goods

Corporations with Libraries	RAssets	Libraries No.	International Systems Yes	International Systems No	Professional Librarians No.	Professional Librarians Mean	Subscriptions No.	Employees No.	RSales
AMF	185	1		X	2	2.00	195	33,573	197
Corporations without Libraries									
Brunswick	207							25,800	245
Mattel	446							12,500	434

Table B.22 *Fortune* 500 Corporations in Category 30, Office Machinery (Arranged in Order by Number of Libraries)

Corporations with Libraries	RAssets	Libraries No.	International Systems Yes	International Systems No	Professional Librarians No.	Professional Librarians Mean	Subscriptions No.	Employees No.	RSales
International Business Machines	6	25	X		46	1.84	10,220	292,350	9
Honeywell	46	14	X		14	1.00	2,208	92,173	68
Sperry Rand	60	12	X		13	1.08	2,199	98,777	70
Burroughs	63	4		X	4	1.00	774	51,586	134
Litton	57	3		X	3	1.00	520	106,500	53
National Cash Register	61	3	X		3	1.00	732	81,000	97
Addressograph Multigraph	281	2		X	2	1.00	225	23,300	321
Control Data	72	2	X		3	1.50	305	45,258	187
Pitney-Bowes	320	1		X	1	1.00	200	17,467	374
Corporations without Libraries									
Digital Equipment	289							6,300	388

Table B.23 *Fortune* 500 Corporations in Category 31, Paper and Wood Products (Arranged in Order by Number of Libraries)

Corporations with Libraries	RAssets	Libraries No.	International Systems Yes	International Systems No	Professional Librarians No.	Professional Librarians Mean	Subscriptions No.	Employees No.	RSales
Boise Cascade	98	4		X	4	1.00	490	28,000	137
International Paper	44	4	X		5	1.25	864	52,715	56
Weyerhaeuser	42	4		X	4	1.00	1,363	48,983	73
Crown Zellerbach	101	3	X		3	1.00	786	31,850	109
Mead	150	3		X	4	1.33	320	27,000	132
Scott Paper	142	3		X	5	1.67	560	20,400	178
St. Regis Paper	118	2		X	3	1.50	600	30,000	135
Walter (Jim)	103	2		X	2	1.00	250	39,043	155
Avery Products	433	1		X	1	1.00	70	6,572	485
Champion International	70	1		X	1	1.00	300	50,092	72
Georgia-Pacific	55	1		X	1	1.00	50	36,275	79
Hammermill Paper	307	1		X	1	1.00	85	10,700	292
Kimberly-Clark	129	1		X	2	2.00	450	28,847	138
Nashua	405	1		X	1	1.00	165	7,167	465
Potlatch	296	1		X	1	1.00	100	10,229	345
Southwest Forest Industries	336	1		X	0	0.00	16	9,000	352
Westvaco	218	1		X	2	2.00	150	16,260	235
Corporations without Libraries									
Evans Products	211							15,250	177
Union Camp	187							14,810	219

Table B.23 *Continued*

Corporations without Libraries	RAssets	Libraries	International Systems	Professional Librarians	Subscriptions	Employees	RSales
Diamond International	267					19,700	246
Container Corp. of America	212					20,863	247
Great Northern Nekoosa	237					10,100	268
Bemis	352					14,227	290
Hoerner Waldorf	353					9,400	357
Louisiana-Pacific	248					9,400	366
Saxon Industries	351					7,737	371
Williamette Industries	331					6,900	418
Masonite	366					8,354	438
Federal Paper Board	400					6,700	443
Inland Container	415					4,689	449
Fibreboard	416					6,300	489
Olinkraft	406					6,083	493

Table B.24 *Fortune* 500 Corporations in Category 32, Petroleum Refining (Arranged in Order by Number of Libraries)

Corporations with Libraries	RAssets	Libraries	International Systems		Professional Librarians		Subscriptions	Employees	RSales
		No.	Yes	No	No.	Mean	No.	No.	
Exxon	1	20	X		38	1.90	4,238	133,000	1
Shell Oil	16	17	X		27	1.59	19,763	32,287	14
Mobil Oil	5	11	X		19	1.73	2,704	73,100	5
Gulf Oil	7	9	X		18	2.00	3,893	52,700	7
Tenneco	14	7		X	12	1.71	1,642	81,016	24
Cities Service	41	6		X	7	1.17	961	17,400	61
Atlantic Richfield	15	5		X	12	2.40	2,990	28,771	18
Occidental Petroleum	32	5		X	8	1.60	685	34,400	20
Phillips Petroleum	28	5		X	19	3.80	837	30,802	25
Standard Oil of California	8	5	X		21	4.20	3,670	39,540	6
Standard Oil (Ind.)	11	5	X		14	2.80	1,693	47,217	13
Getty Oil	37	4		X	4	1.00	434	11,364	62
Sun Oil	27	4	X		15	3.75	1,416	27,707	37
Continental Oil	22	3.8		X	5.8	1.53	930	41,174	16
Marathon Oil	77	3		X	5	1.67	1,600	9,465	60
Murphy Oil	154	3		X	1	.33	150	3,838	231
Texaco	3	3		X	3	1.00	338	76,420	4
Ashland Oil	83	2		X	3	1.50	453	27,000	50
Union Oil of California	30	2		X	4	2.00	869	15,364	34
American Petrofina	244	1		X	0	1.00	-1	3,043	213
Farmland Industries	225	1		X	1	1.00	-1	6,400	162
Kerr-McGee	135	1		X	1	1.00	155	10,105	129
Oil Shale	450	1		X	1	1.00	60	1,264	431
Standard Oil (Ohio)	48	1		X	1	1.00	-1	20,300	87

Table B.24 *Continued*

Corporations without Libraries	RAssets	Libraries	International Systems	Professional Librarians	Subscriptions	Employees	RSales
Amerada Hess	54					5,779	38
Coastal States Gas	86					4,399	154
Charter	304					4,000	173
Commonwealth Oil	257					2,398	189
Clark Oil & Refining	377					4,296	299
Tesoro Petroleum	341					2,400	331
Crown Central Petroleum	465					1,111	399
Superior Oil	183					3,346	448
United Refining	490					1,589	497

Table B.25 *Fortune* 500 Corporations in Category 33, Pharmaceuticals (Arranged in Order by Number of Libraries)

Corporations with Libraries	RAssets	Libraries No.	International Systems Yes	International Systems No	Professional Librarians No.	Professional Librarians Mean	Subscriptions No.	Employees No.	RSales
Warner-Lambert	95	8	X		17	2.13	2,139	58,500	102
Merck	127	7	X		11	1.57	2,270	27,000	152
Bristol-Myers	155	6		X	16	2.70	2,491	29,700	125
Eli Lilly	125	6	X		14	2.33	2,400	24,700	176
Searle	204	6	X		6	1.00	1,419	18,700	288
Abbott Laboratories	184	5	X		18	3.60	1,638	22,829	249
American Home Products	128	5	X		5	1.00	1,657	45,703	92
Squibb	147	5	X		12	2.40	1,829	34,000	201
Sterling Drug	217	5		X	10	2.00	829	27,376	229
Morton-Norwich Products	290	4		X	22	5.50	1,735	12,800	346
Richardson-Merrell	273	4		X	8	2.00	1,042	14,600	300
Smithkline	265	4	X		7	1.75	1,490	13,225	326
Upjohn	208	4		X	8	2.00	1,377	16,550	242
Pfizer	88	3	X		9	3.00	1,700	39,800	130
Baxter Laboratories	239	2		X	6	3.00	715	19,700	361
Schering-Plough	221	2		X	24	12.00	1,117	15,600	266
Miles Laboratories	348	1		X	9	9.00	1,550	8,651	420

Corporations without Libraries

NONE

Table B.26 *Fortune* 500 Corporations in Category 34, Publishing and Printing (Arranged in Order by Number of Libraries)

Corporations with Libraries	RAssets	Libraries	International Systems		Professional Librarians		Subscriptions	Employees	RSales
		No.	Yes	No	No.	Mean	No.	No.	
Knight-Ridder Newspapers	276	8.7		X	7.7	.75	302	14,155	306
McGraw-Hill	285	7		X	18	2.57	1,807	12,314	332
Gannett	373	5		X	4	.80	27	13,879	454
New York Times	439	4		X	3	.75	525	6,700	414
Times Mirror	242	3		X	12	4.00	145	15,130	260
Times, Inc.	199	2	X		10	5.00	650	12,600	239
Washington Post	430	2		X	16	8.00	530	4,900	498
Donnelly (R.R.) & Sons	324	1		X	1	1.00	100	11,600	370
MacMillan	279	1		X	1	1.00	110	17,900	360

Corporations without Libraries

NONE

Table B.27 *Fortune* 500 Corporations in Category 35, Rubber (Arranged in Order by Number of Libraries)

Corporations with Libraries	RAssets	Libraries	International Systems		Professional Librarians		Subscriptions	Employees	RSales
			Yes	No	No.	Mean			
		No.					No.	No.	
Goodyear	25	4		X	13	3.25	1,110	154,166	23
Uniroyal	92	3.5		X	4	1.14	975	63,845	82
General Tire & Rubber	103	3	X		3	1.00	492	39,043	115
Goodrich	93	3		X	10	3.33	796	48,929	96
Firestone Tire & Rubber	38	2		X	4	2.00	200	120,000	40
Corporations without Libraries									
Dayco	395							14,100	382

Table B.28 *Fortune* 500 Corporations in Category 36, Shipbuilding, Railroad Equipment, Mobile Homes (Arranged in Order by Number of Libraries)

Corporations with Libraries	RAssets	Libraries No.	International Systems Yes	International Systems No	Professional Librarians No.	Professional Librarians Mean	Subscriptions No.	Employees No.	RSales
ACF Industries	215	2		X	2	1.00	163	12,200	323
Pullman	186	2	X		1	0.50	552	25,288	144
General Transportation	131	1		X	1	1.00	500	11,700	330
Corporations without Libraries									
Fuqua Industries	288							16,275	316
Bangar Punta	412							6,218	451
Skyline	491							4,000	480
Fleetwood Enterprises	488							6,300	483
Champion Home Builders	487							5,800	488

Table B.29 *Fortune* 500 Corporations in Category 37, Soaps, Cosmetics (Arranged in Order by Number of Libraries)

Corporations with Libraries	RAssets	Libraries	International Systems		Professional Librarians		Subscriptions	Employees	RSales
		No.	Yes	No	No.	Mean	No.	No.	
Lever Brothers	369	8	X		2	.25	2,410	6,900	269
Procter and Gamble	35	7	X		3	.43	714	50,000	28
Colgate Palmolive	111	3	X		8	2.67	731	43,600	69
Avon Products	198	2		X	2	1.00	420	26,900	159
Revlon	241	2		X	4	2.00	700	18,000	291
Chesebrough-Ponds	295	1		X	1	1.00	150	15,363	309
Purex	399	1		X	1	1.00	100	8,500	401

Corporations without Libraries

None

Table B.30 *Fortune* 500 Corporations in Category 38, Textiles (Arranged in Order by Number of Libraries)

Corporations with Libraries	RAssets	Libraries	International Systems		Professional Librarians		Subscriptions	Employees	RSales
		No.	Yes	No	No.	Mean	No.	No.	
Burlington Industries	94	1		X	1	1.00	292	81,000	81
Cone Mills	410	1		X	1	1.00	160	14,100	383
Dan Rivers	365	1		X	1	1.00	50	19,000	377
Lowenstein (M) & Sons	325	1		X	1	1.00	-1	16,000	307
Sperry and Hutchinson	233	1		X	3	3.00	60	17,000	296
Stevens (J.P.)	196	1		X	2	2.00	175	46,000	157
United Merchants & Manufacturers	149	1		X	1	1.00	44	36,000	212
West Point–Pepperell	334	1		X	1	1.00	210	23,220	297
Corporations without Libraries									
Spring Mills	293							19,700	293
Mohasco	328							16,379	315
Cannon Mills	384							20,000	410
Collins and Aikman	418							10,000	439
Fieldcrest Mills	458							11,700	481

Table B.31 *Fortune* 500 Corporations in Category 39, Tobacco (Arranged in Order by Number of Libraries)

Corporations with Libraries	RAssets	Libraries	International Systems		Professional Librarians		Subscriptions	Employees	RSales
		No.	Yes	No	No.	Mean	No.	No.	
Liggett & Myers	235	2		X	5	2.50	220	6,700	284
Philip Morris	47	2		X	3	1.50	806	38,000	57
American Brands	51	1		X	1	1.00	184	55,000	86
R. J. Reynolds Industries	34	1		X	6	6.00	560	32,464	48
Corporations without Libraries									
Universal Leaf	441							12,000	285
Loews	122							11,703	320

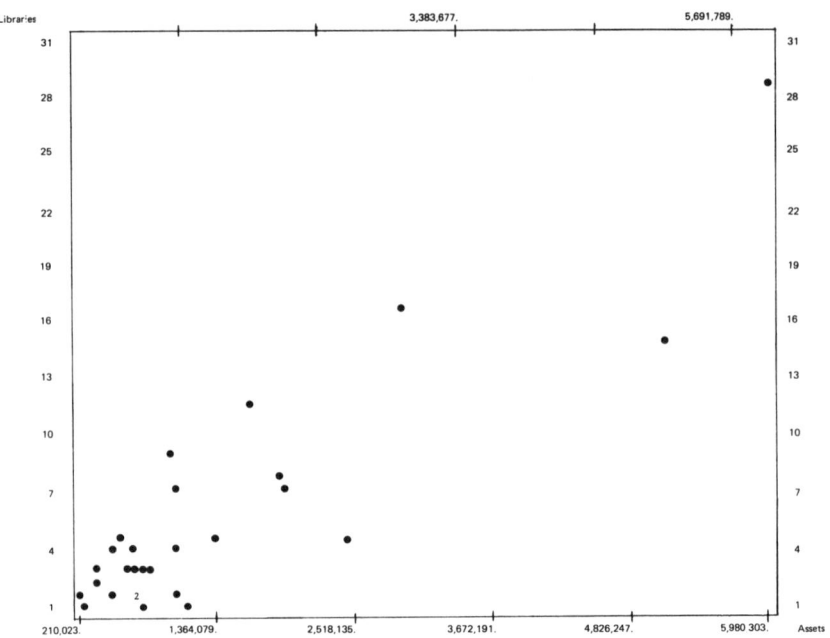

Figure B.1a "Scattergram" of CHEMICALS Industrial Classification-Number of Libraries vs Assets (in $ thousands)

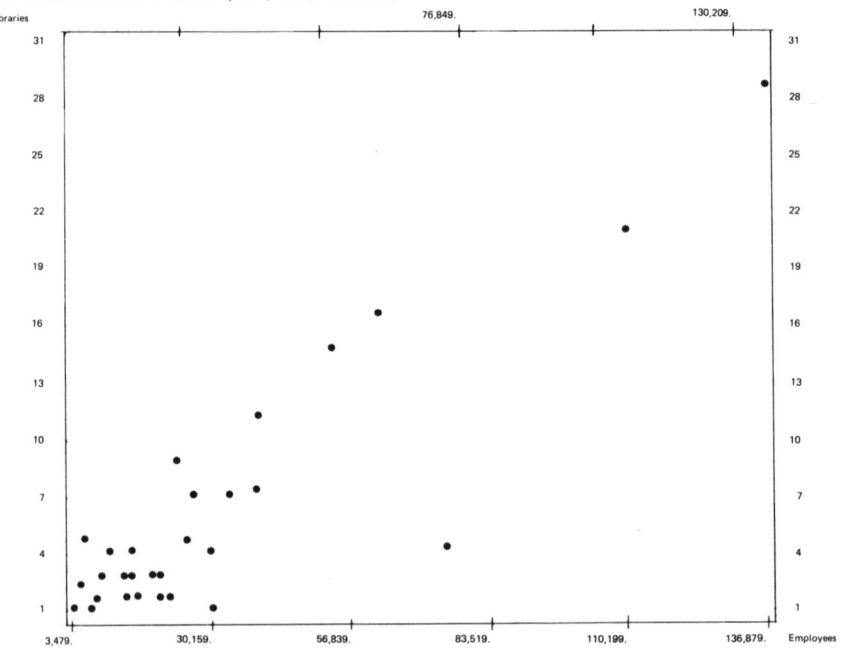

Figure B.1b "Scattergram" of CHEMICALS Industrial Classification—Number of Libraries vs Number of Company Employees

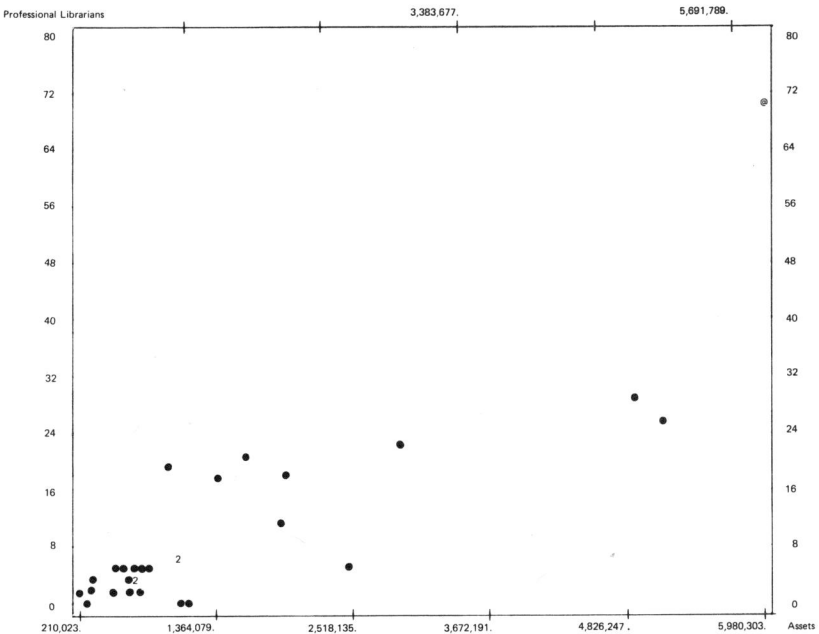

Figure B.1c "Scattergram" of CHEMICALS Industrial Classification—Number of Professional Libraries vs Assets (in $ thousands)

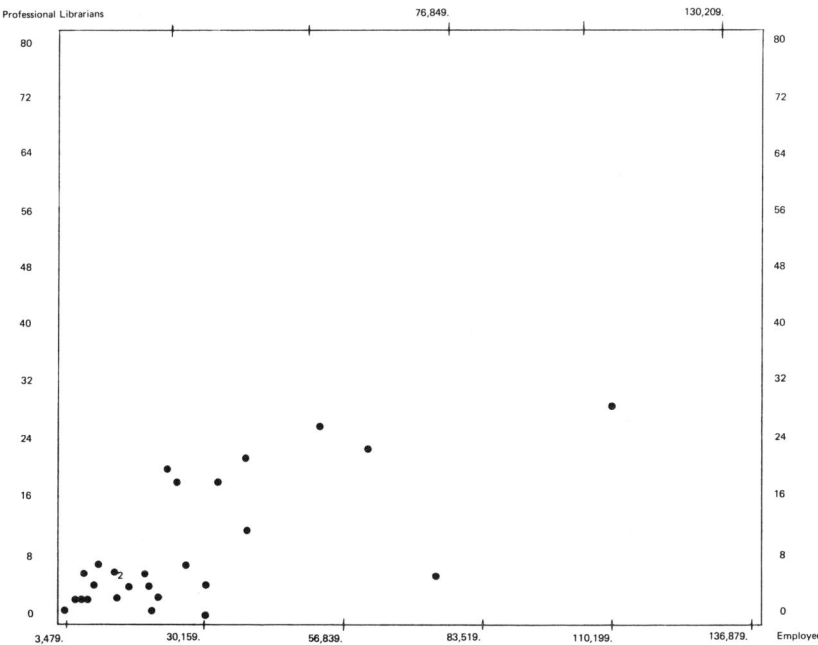

Figure B.1d "Scattergram" of CHEMICALS Industrial Classification—Number of Professional Libraries vs Number of Company Employees

273

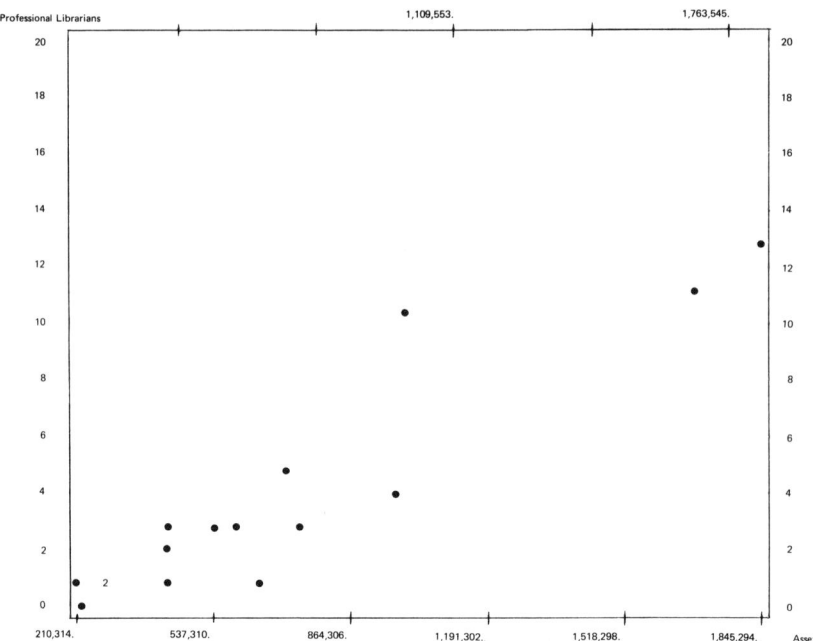

Figure B.2 "Scattergram" of GLASS, CEMENT, GYPSUM, CONCRETE, Industrial Classification—Number of Professional Libraries vs Assets (in $ thousands)

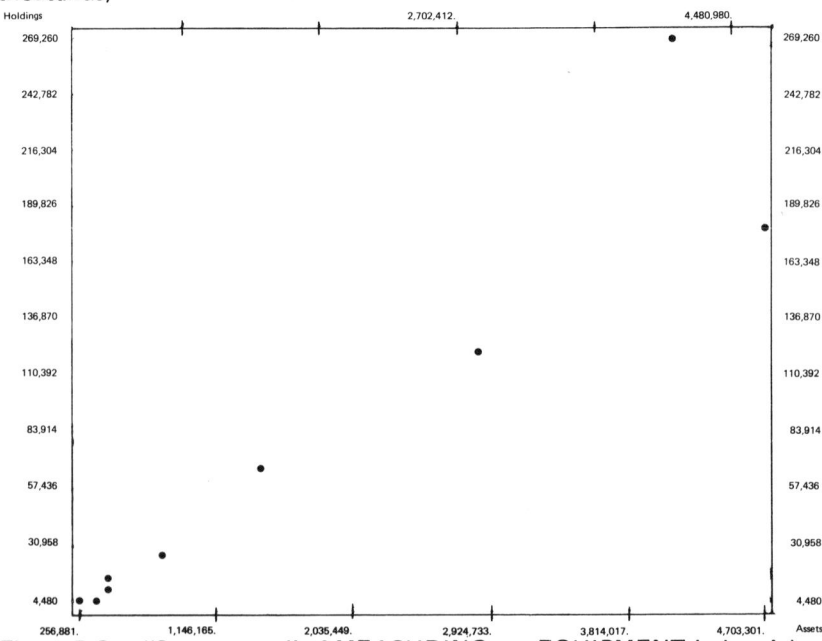

Figure B.3a "Scattergram" of MEASURING ... EQUIPMENT Industrial Classification—Number of Holdings vs Assets (in $ thousands)

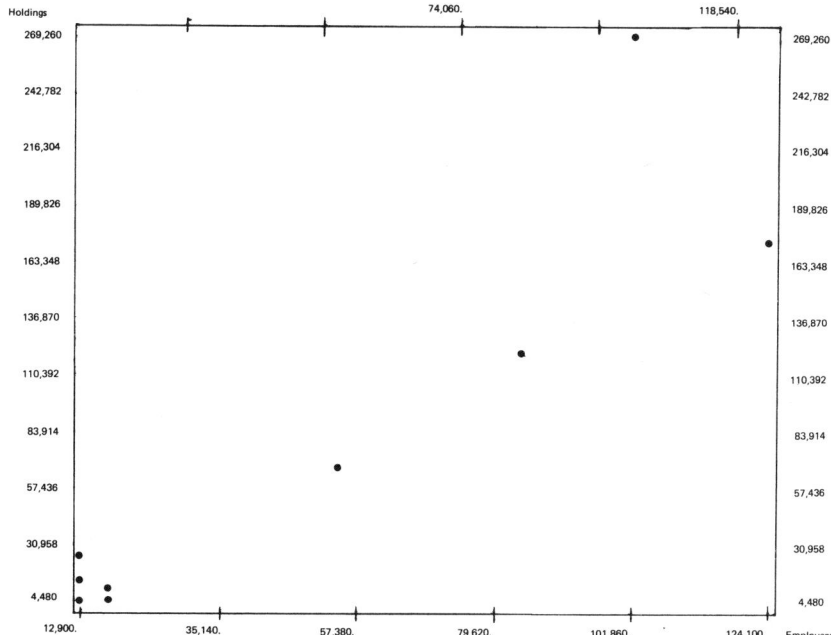

Figure B.3b "Scattergram" of MEASURING...EQUIPMENT Industrial Classification—Number of Holdings vs Number of Company Employees

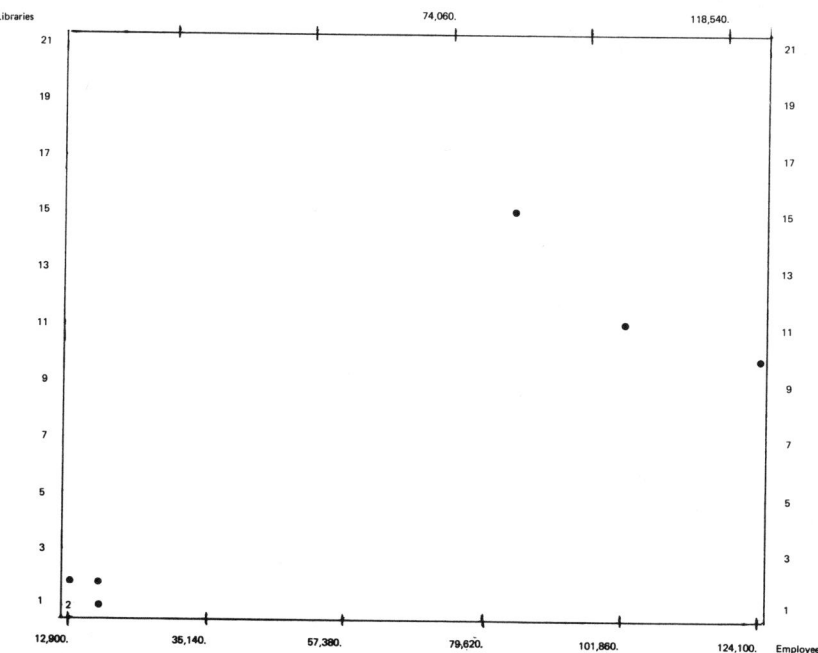

Figure B.3c "Scattergram" of MEASURING . . . EQUIPMENT Industrial Classification—Number of Libraries vs Number of Company Employees

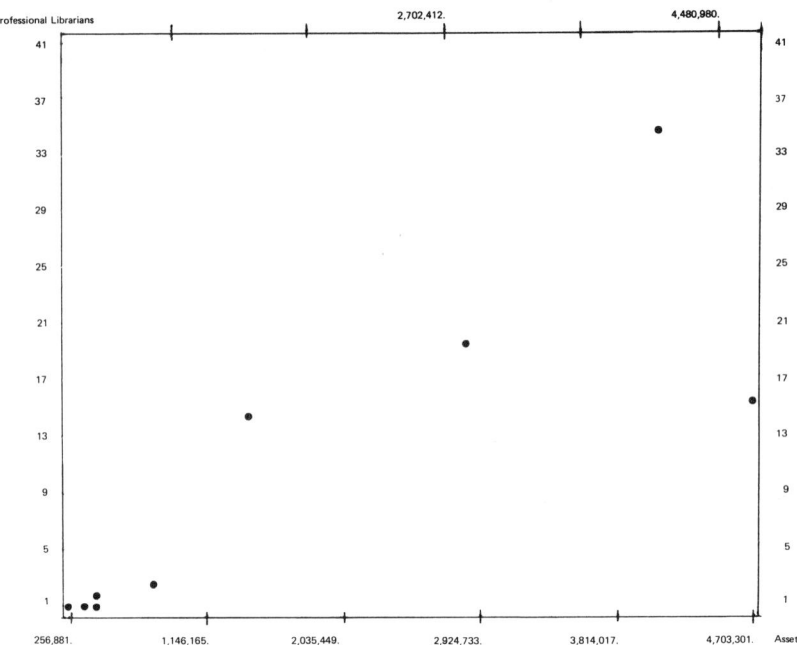

Figure B.3d "Scattergram" of MEASURING . . . EQUIPMENT Industrial Classification—Number of Professional Librarians vs Assets (in $ thousands)

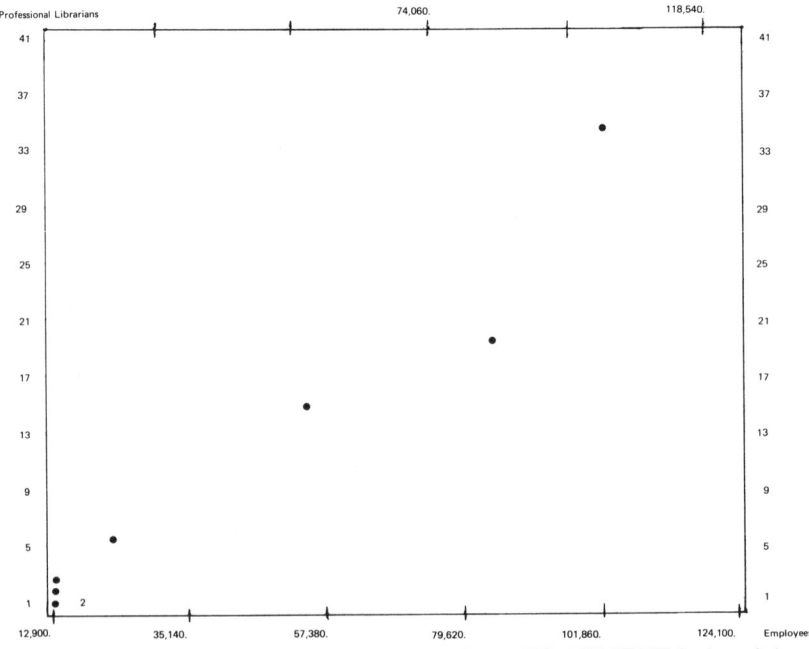

Figure B.3e "Scattergram" of MEASURING . . . EQUIPMENT Industrial Classification—Number of Professional Librarians vs Number of Company Employees

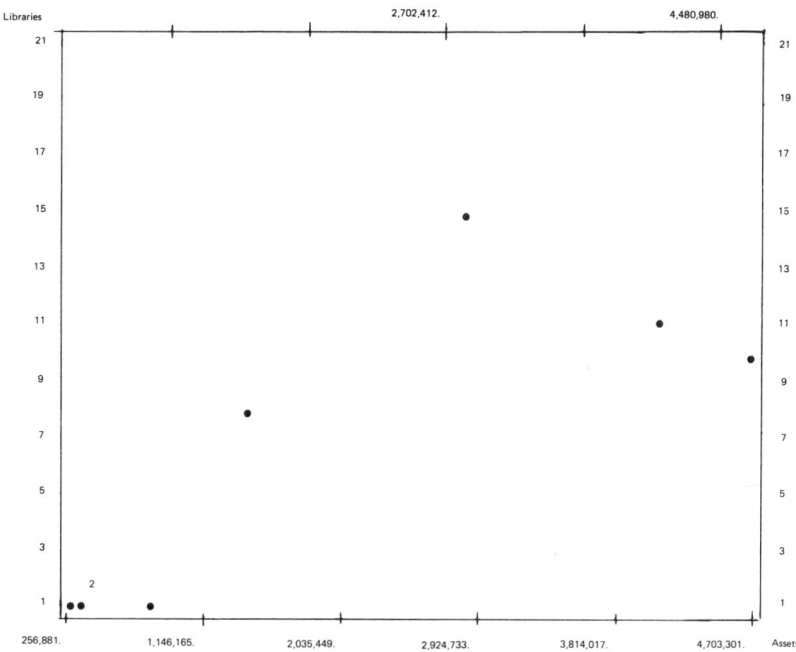

Figure B.3f "Scattergram" of MEASURING . . . EQUIPMENT Industrial Classification—Number of Libraries vs Assets (in $ thousands)

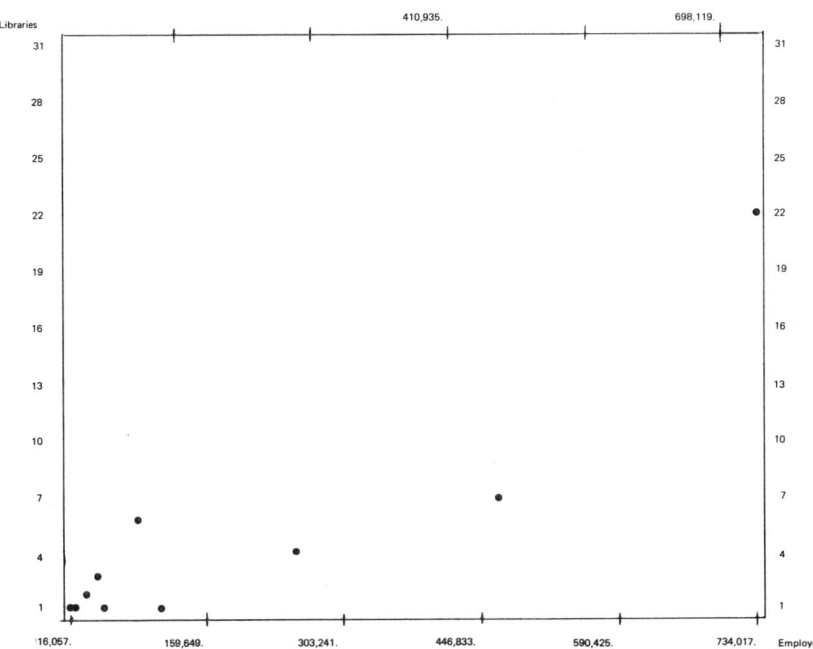

Figure B.4a "Scattergram" of MOTOR VEHICLES AND PARTS Industrial Classification—Number of Libraries vs Number of Company Employees

277

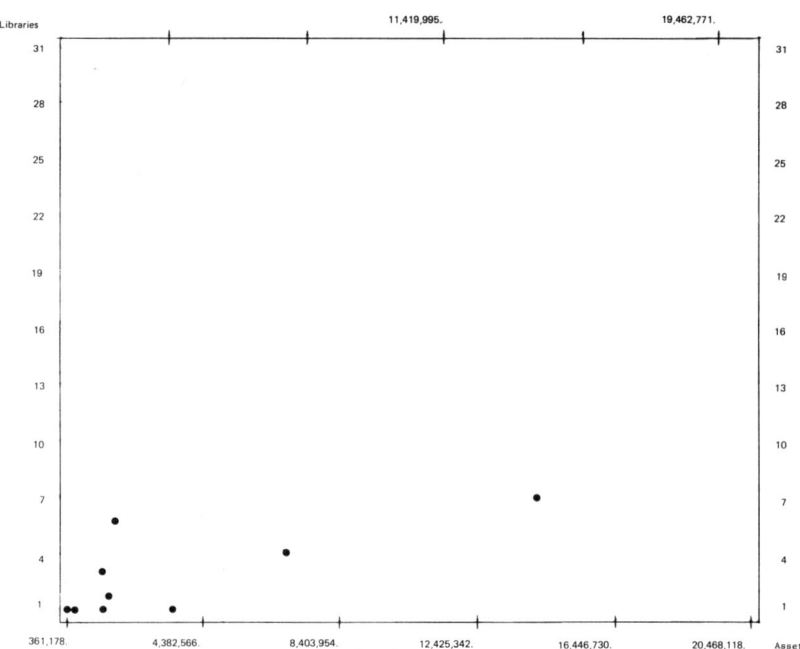

Figure B.4b "Scattergram" of MOTOR VEHICLES AND PARTS Industrial Classification—Number of Libraries vs Assets (in $ thousands)

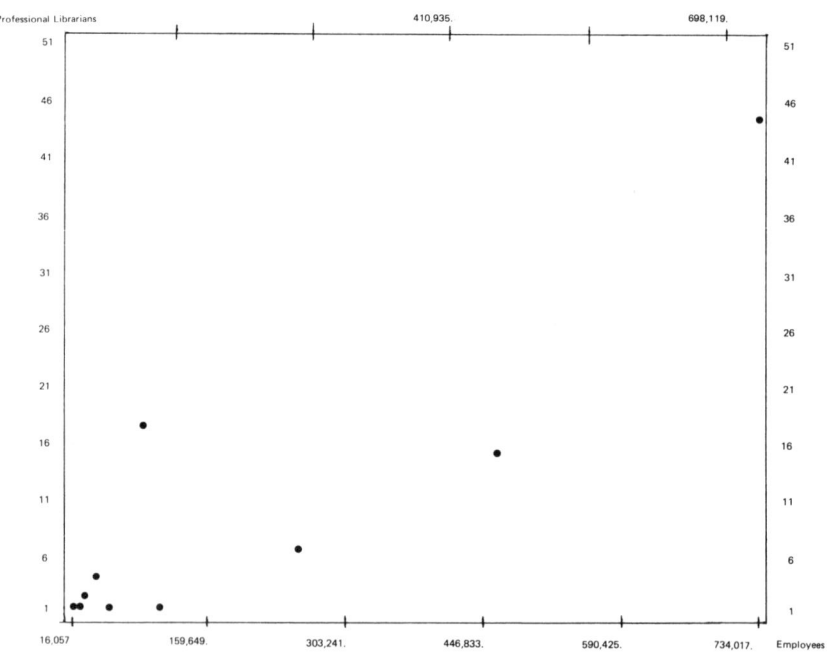

Figure B.4c "Scattergram" of MOTOR VEHICLES AND PARTS Industrial Classification—Number of Professional Librarians vs Number of Company Employees

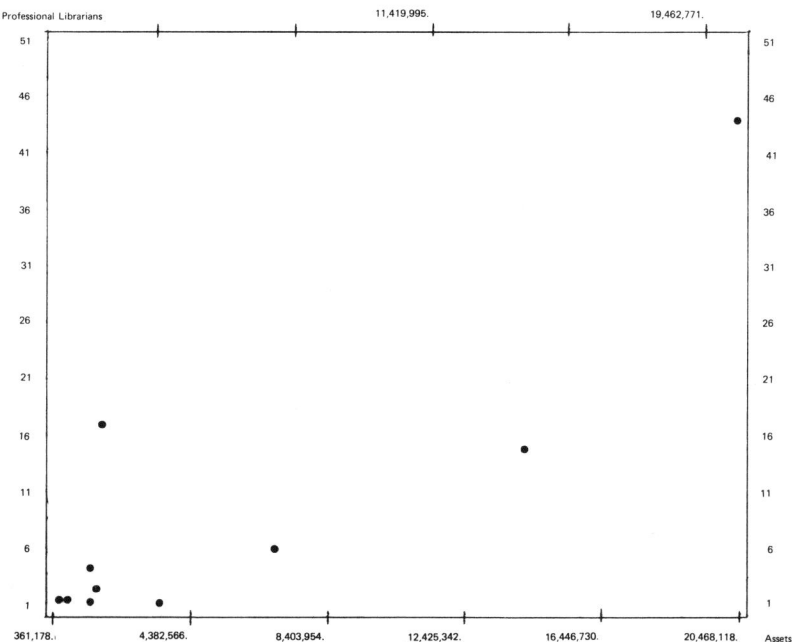

Figure B.4d "Scattergram" of MOTOR VEHICLES AND PARTS Industrial Classification—Number of Professional Librarians vs Assets (in $ thousands)

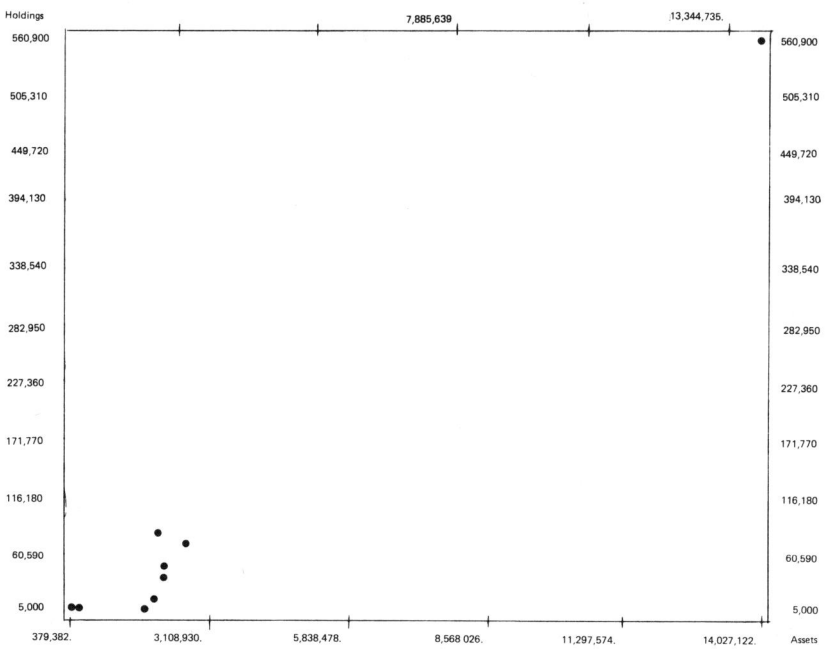

Figure B.5a "Scattergram" of OFFICE MACHINERY (INCL. COMPUTERS) Industrial Classification—Number of Holdings vs Assets (in $ thousands)

279

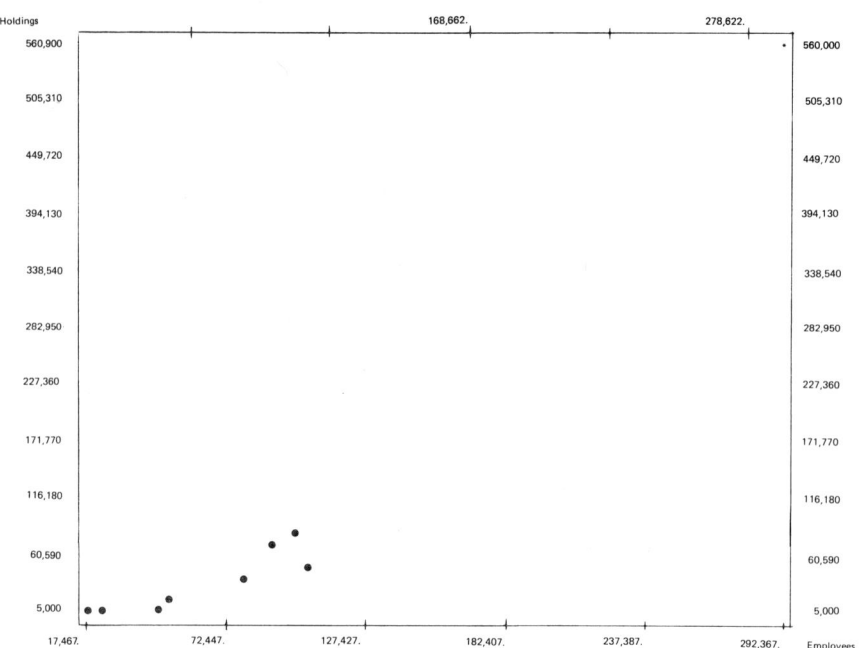

Figure B.5b "Scattergram" of OFFICE MACHINERY (INCL. COMPUTERS) Industrial Classification—Number of Holdings vs Number of Company Employees

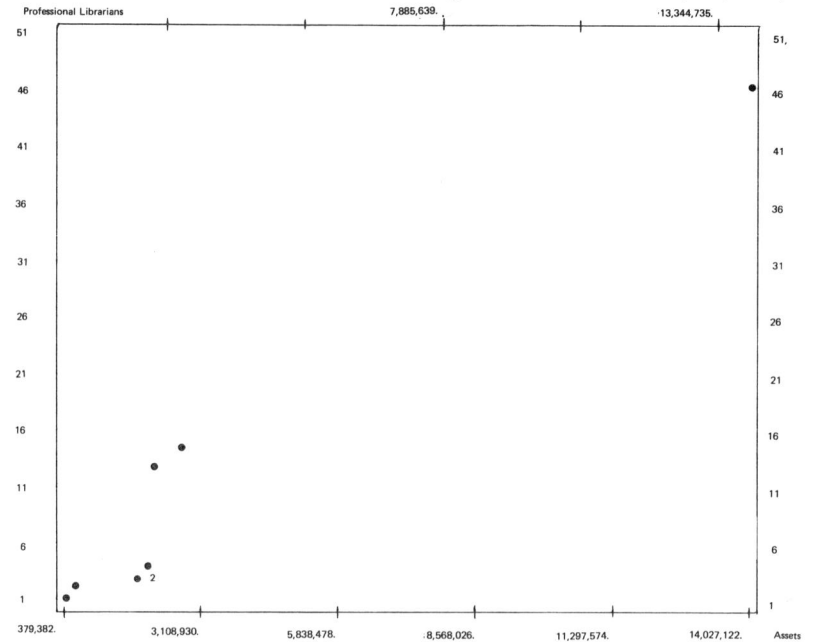

Figure B.5c "Scattergram" of OFFICE MACHINERY (INCL. COMPUTERS) Industrial Classification—Number of Professional Librarians vs Assets (in $ thousands)

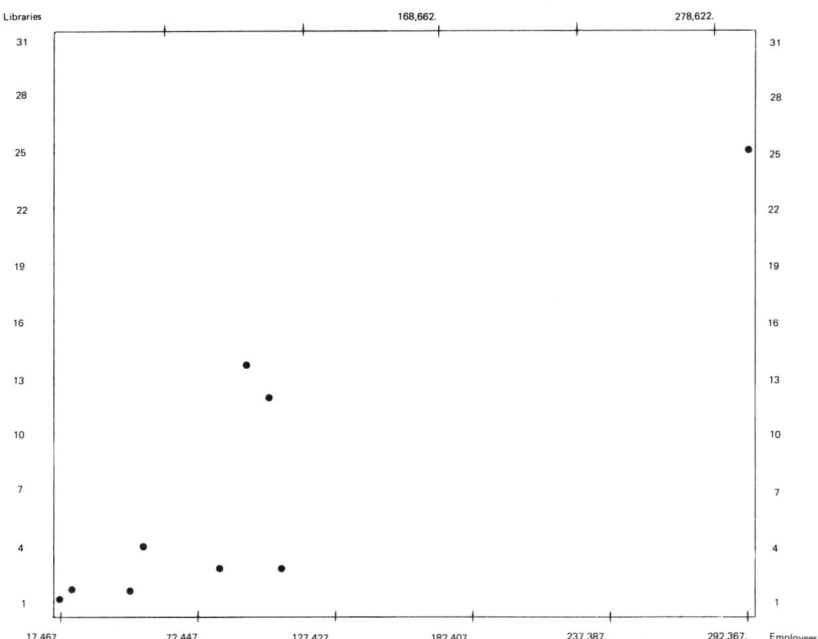

Figure B.5d "Scattergram" of OFFICE MACHINERY (INCL. COMPUTERS) Industrial Classification—Number of Professional Librarians vs Number of Company Employees

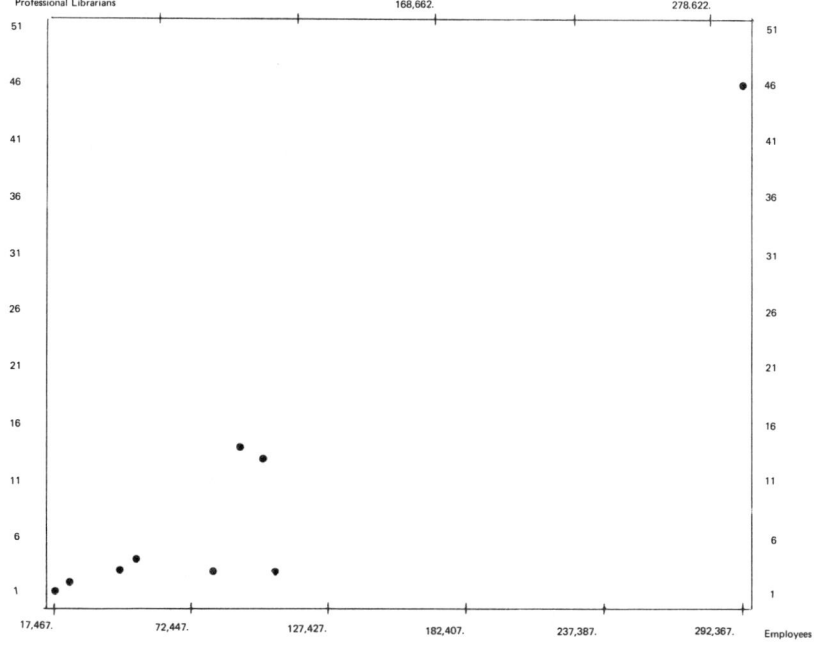

Figure B.5e "Scattergram" of OFFICE MACHINERY (INCL. COMPUTERS) Industrial Classification—Number of Libraries vs Number of Company Employees

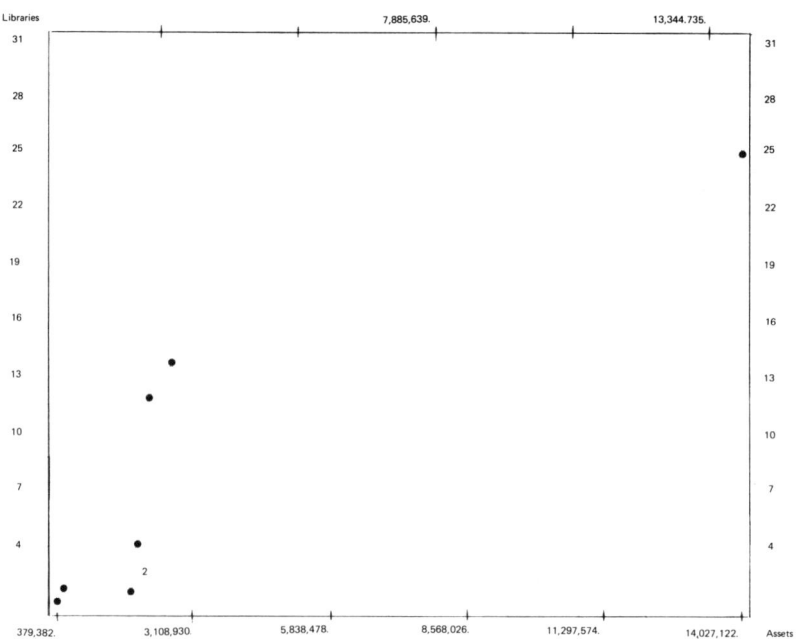

Figure B.5f "Scattergram" of OFFICE MACHINERY (INCL. COMPUTERS) Industrial Classification—Number of Libraries vs Assets (in $ thousands)

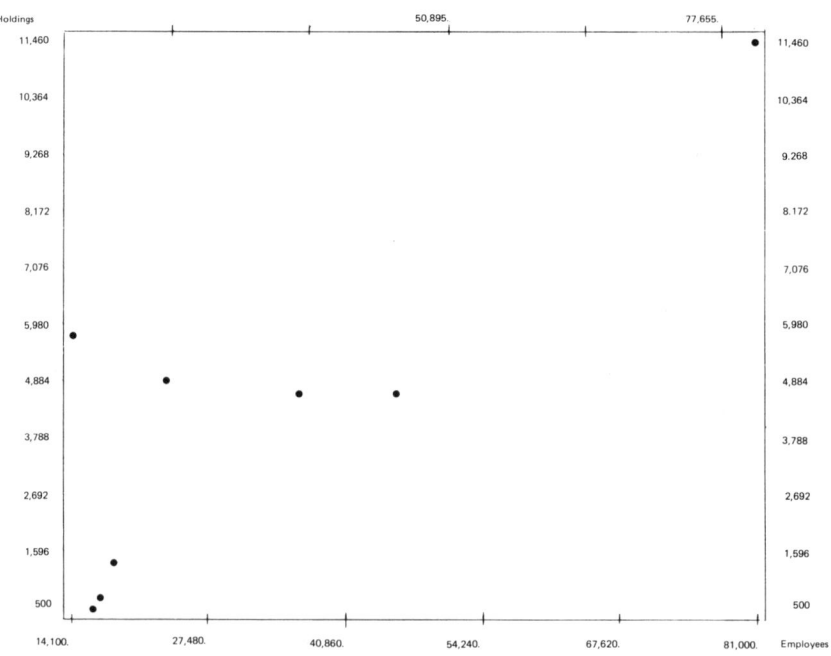

Figure B.6 "Scattergram" of TEXTILES Industrial Classification—Number of Holdings vs Number of Company Employees

Appendix C:

Alphabetic Listing of *Fortune* 500 Corporations, with Category Number and Industrial Classification

CORPORATIONS WITH LIBRARIES

Name	Category Number	Industrial Classification
Abbott Laboratories	33	Pharmaceuticals
ACF Industries	36	Shipbuilding . . .
Addressograph Multigraph	30	Office Machinery
Agway	18	Food
Air Products & Chemicals	16	Chemicals
Airco	16	Chemicals
Akzona	16	Chemicals
Allegheny Ludlum Industries	24	Metal Mfg.
Allied Chemical	16	Chemicals
Allis-Chalmers	17	Farm Machinery
Aluminum Co. of America	24	Metal Mfg.
American Metal Climax Inc.	24	Metal Mfg.
American Brands	39	Tobacco
American Broadcasting	15	Motion Pictures
American Can	25	Metal Products
American Cynamid	16	Chemicals
American Home Products	33	Pharmaceuticals
American Petrofina	32	Petroleum Refining
American Standard	25	Metal Products
AMF	29	Musical Instruments . . .
AMP	13	Appliances, Electronics
Amstar	18	Food

283

Name	Category Number	Industrial Classification
Anaconda	24	Metal Mfg.
Anchor Hocking	20	Glass, Cement ...
Anderson, Clayton	18	Food
Anheuser-Busch	14	Beverages
Archer-Daniels-Midland	18	Food
Armco Steel	24	Metal Mfg.
Armstrong Cork	27	Misc. Manufacture
ASARCO	24	Metal Mfg.
Ashland Oil	32	Petroleum Refining
Atlantic Richfield	32	Petroleum Refining
A-T-O	17	Farm Machinery
Avco	11	Aircraft
Avery Products	31	Paper and Wood
Avon Products	37	Soaps, Cosmetics
Babcock & Wilcox	17	Farm Machinery
Bath Industries	27	Misc. Manufacture
Bausch & Lomb	23	Measuring ... Equipment
Baxter Laboratories	33	Pharmaceuticals
Becton, Dickinson	23	Measuring ... Equipment
Bell & Howell	23	Measuring ... Equipment
Bendix	13	Appliances, Electronics
Bethlehem Steel	24	Metal Mfg.
Boeing	11	Aircraft
Boise Cascade	31	Paper and Wood
Borden	18	Food
Borg-Warner	28	Motor Vehicles/Parts
Bristol-Myers	33	Pharmaceuticals
Brockway Glass	20	Glass, Cement ...
Budd	28	Motor Vehicles/Parts
Bunker Ramo	13	Appliances, Electronics
Burlington Industries	38	Textiles
Burroughs	30	Office Machinery
Cabot	16	Chemicals
Campbell Soup	18	Food
Campbell Taggart	18	Food
Carborundum	20	Glass, Cement ...
Carnation	18	Food
Carrier	17	Farm Machinery
Castle & Cooke	18	Food
Carterpillar Tractor	17	Farm Machinery

Appendix C 285

Name	Category Number	Industrial Classification
Celanese	16	Chemicals
Central Soya	18	Food
Cessna Aircraft	11	Aircraft
Champion International	31	Paper and Wood
Chemetron	16	Chemicals
Chesebrough-Pond's	37	Soaps, Cosmetics
Chicago Bridge & Iron	25	Metal Proudcts
Chrysler	28	Motor Vehicles/Parts
Cincinnati Milacron	17	Farm Machinery
Cities Service	32	Petroleum Refining
Clark Equipment	17	Farm Machinery
Coca-Cola	14	Beverages
Colgate-Palmolive	37	Soaps, Cosmetics
Colt Industries	25	Metal Products
Columbia Broadcasting	15	Motion Pictures
Combustion Engineering	25	Metal Products
Cone Mills	38	Textiles
Continental Can	25	Metal Products
Continental Oil	32	Petroleum Refining
Control Data Corp.	30	Office Machinery
Corning Glass Works	20	Glass, Cement . . .
CPC International	18	Food
Crane	25	Metal Products
Crown Zellerbach	31	Paper and Wood
Cutler-Hammer	13	Appliances, Electronics
Cyclops	24	Metal Mfg.
Dan River	38	Textiles
Dart Industries	16	Chemicals
Deere	17	Farm Machinery
Diamond Shamrock	16	Chemicals
R. R. Donnelley & Sons	34	Publishing & Printing
Dow Chemical	16	Chemicals
Dresser Industries	17	Farm Machinery
DuPont	16	Chemicals
Eastman Kodak	23	Measuring . . . Equipment
Eaton	28	Motor Vehicles/Parts
Eli Lilly	33	Pharmaceuticals
Emhart	25	Metal Products
ESB	13	Appliances, Electronics
Esmark	18	Food

Name	Category Number	Industrial Classification
Ethyl	16	Chemicals
Exxon	32	Petroleum Refining
Fairchild Camera & Instrument	13	Appliances, Electronics
Farmland Industries	32	Petroleum Refining
Ferro	16	Chemicals
Firestone Tire & Rubber	35	Rubber
Flintkote	20	Glass, Cement . . .
FMC	17	Farm Machinery
Ford Motor	28	Motor Vehicles/Parts
Foster Wheeler	17	Farm Machinery
GAF	20	Glass, Cement . . .
Gannett	34	Publishing & Printing
General American Transportation	36	Shipbuilding . . .
General Cable	24	Metal Mfg.
General Dynamics	11	Aircraft
General Electric	13	Appliances, Electronics
General Foods	18	Food
General Mills	18	Food
General Motors	28	Motor Vehicles/Parts
General Refractories	20	Glass, Cement . . .
General Tire & Rubber	35	Rubber
Georgia-Pacific	31	Paper and Wood
Getty Oil	32	Petroleum Refining
Gillette	25	Metal Products
Goodrich (B.F.)	35	Rubber
Goodyear Tire & Rubber	35	Rubber
Gould	13	Appliances, Electronics
Grace (W.R.)	16	Chemicals
Green Giant	18	Food
Greyhound	18	Food
Grumman	11	Aircraft
Gulf & Western Ind.	25	Metal Products
Gulf Oil	32	Petroleum Refining
Hammermill Paper	31	Paper and Wood
Harris	13	Appliances, Electronics
Heinz (H.J.)	18	Food
Hercules	16	Chemicals
Hershey Foods	18	Food
Hewlett-Packard	13	Appliances, Electronics
Honeywell	30	Office Machinery

Appendix C 287

Name	Category Number	Industrial Classification
Hoover	13	Appliances, Electronics
Indian Head	25	Metal Products
Ingersoll-Rand	17	Farm Machinery
Inland Steel	24	Metal Mfg.
Insilco	21	Jewelry/Silverware
International Business Machines	30	Office Machinery
International Harvester	28	Motor Vehicles/Parts
International Minerals & Chemical	16	Chemicals
International Paper	31	Paper and Wood
International Tel. & Tel.	13	Appliances, Electronics
Jim Walter	31	Paper and Wood
Johns-Manville	20	Glass, Cement . . .
Johnson & Johnson	23	Measuring . . . Equipment
Kaiser Aluminum & Chemical	24	Metal Mfg.
Kaiser Industries	24	Megal Mfg.
Kennecott Copper	24	Metal Mfg.
Kerr-McGee	32	Petroleum Refining
Kimberly-Clark	31	Paper and Wood
Knight-Ridder Newpapers	34	Publishing & Printing
Koppers	16	Chemicals
Kraftco	18	Food
Lear Siegler	13	Appliances, Electronics
Lever Brothers	37	Soaps, Cosmetics
Libbey-Owens-Ford	20	Glass, Cement . . .
Libby, McNeill & Libby	18	Food
Liggett & Myers	39	Tobacco
Lipton (Thomas J.)	18	Food
Litton Industries	30	Office Machinery
Lockheed Aircraft	11	Aircraft
Lone Star Industries	20	Glass, Cement . . .
M. Lowenstein & Sons	38	Textiles
LTV Corporation	18	Food
Lubrizol	16	Chemicals
Lykes-Youngstown	24	Metal Mfg.
McDonnell Douglas	11	Aircraft
McGraw-Hill	34	Publishing & Printing
Macmillan	34	Publishing & Printing
Marathon Oil	32	Petroleum Refining
Martin Marietta	11	Aircraft
MCA	15	Motion Picture

Name	Category Number	Industrial Classification
Mead	31	Paper and Wood
Merck	33	Pharmaceuticals
Midland-Ross	17	Farm Machinery
Miles Laboratories	33	Pharmaceuticals
Minnesota Mining & Manufacturing	23	Measuring . . . Equipment
Mobil Oil	32	Petroleum Refining
Monsanto	16	Chemicals
Morton-Norwich Products	33	Pharmaceuticals
Motorola	13	Appliances, Electronics
Murphy Oil	32	Petroleum Refining
Nabisco	18	Food
Nashua	31	Paper and Wood
National Cash Register	30	Office Machinery
National Distillers & Chemical	25	Metal Products
National Steel	24	Metal Mfg.
New York Times	34	Publishing & Printing
NL Industries	16	Chemicals
North American Philips	13	Appliances, Electronics
Northrop	11	Aircraft
Northwest Industries	12	Apparel
Norton	20	Glass, Cement . . .
Norton Simon	18	Food
Occidental Petroleum	32	Petroleum Refining
Oilshale	32	Petroleum Refining
Olin	16	Chemicals
Oscar Mayer	18	Food
Outboard Marine	17	Farm Machinery
Owens-Corning Fiberglas	20	Glass, Cement . . .
Owens-Illinois	20	Glass, Cement . . .
Pabst Brewing	14	Beverages
Peavey	18	Food
Pennwalt	16	Chemicals
Pennzoil	26	Mining
PepsiCo	14	Beverages
Pet	18	Food
Pfizer	33	Pharmaceuticals
Philip Morris	39	Tobacco
Phillips Petroleum	32	Petroleum Refining
Pillsbury	18	Food
Pitney-Bowes	30	Office Machinery

Name	Category Number	Industrial Classification
Polaroid	23	Measuring . . . Equipment
Potlatch Forests	31	Paper and Wood
PPG Industries	20	Glass, Cement . . .
Procter & Gamble	37	Soaps, Cosmetics
Pullman	36	Shipbuilding . . .
Purex	37	Soaps, Cosmetics
Quaker Oats	18	Food
Ralston Purina	18	Food
Raytheon	13	Appliances, Electronics
RCA	13	Appliances, Electronics
Republic Steel	24	Metal Mfg.
Revlon	37	Soaps, Cosmetics
R. J. Reynolds Industries	39	Tobacco
Reynolds Metals	24	Metal Mfg.
Richardson-Merrell	33	Pharmaceuticals
Rockwell International	11	Aircraft
Rohm & Haas	16	Chemicals
Rohr Industries	11	Aircraft
St. Regis Paper	31	Paper and Wood
Schering-Plough	33	Pharmaceuticals
Schlitz (Jos.) Brewing	14	Beverages
SCM	16	Chemicals
Scott Paper	31	Paper and Wood
J. F. Seagram & Sons	14	Beverages
Searle (G. D.)	33	Pharmaceuticals
Shell Oil	32	Petroleum Refining
Sherwin-Williams	16	Chemicals
Signal Companies	28	Motor Vehicles/Parts
Singer	13	Appliances, Electronics
A. O. Smith	28	Motor Vehicles/Parts
Smithkline	33	Pharmaceuticals
Southwest Forest Industries	31	Paper and Wood
Sperry & Hutchinson	38	Textiles
Sperry Rand	30	Office Machinery
Square D	13	Appliances, Electronics
Squibb	33	Pharmaceuticals
A. E. Staley Mfg.	18	Food
Standard Brands	18	Food
Standard Oil of California	32	Petroleum Refining
Standard Oil of Indiana	32	Petroleum Refining

Name	Category Number	Industrial Classification
Standard Oil of Ohio	32	Petroleum Refining
Stauffer Chemical	16	Chemicals
Sterling Drug	33	Pharmaceuticals
J. P. Stevens	38	Textiles
Studebaker-Worthington	13	Appliances, Electronics
Sun Oil	32	Petroleum Refining
Sundstrand	17	Farm Machinery
Sybron	23	Measuring . . . Equipment
Teledyne	13	Appliances, Electronics
Tenneco	32	Petroleum Refining
Texaco	32	Petroleum Refining
Texas Instruments	13	Appliances, Electronics
Texasgulf	26	Mining
Textron	11	Aircraft
Thiokol Chemicals	11	Aircraft
Time, Inc.	34	Publishing & Printing
Times Mirror	34	Publishing & Printing
Timken	17	Farm Machinery
TRW	28	Motor Vehicles/Parts
Union Carbide	16	Chemicals
Union Oil of California	32	Petroleum Refining
Uniroyal	35	Rubber
United Aircraft	11	Aircraft
United Brands	18	Food
United Merchants & Manufacturers	38	Textiles
U.S. Gypsum	20	Glass, Cement . . .
U.S. Steel	24	Metal Mfg.
Universal Oil Products	25	Metal Products
Upjohn	33	Pharmaceuticals
USM	17	Farm Machinery
UV Industries	24	Metal Mfg.
Varian Associates	13	Appliances, Electronics
Vulcan Materials	20	Glass, Cement . . .
Warnaco	12	Apparel
Warner-Lambert	33	Pharmaceuticals
Washington Post	34	Publishing & Printing
West Point-Pepperell	38	Textiles
Western Electric	13	Appliances, Electronics
Westinghouse Electric	13	Appliances, Electronics
Westvaco	31	Paper and Wood

Appendix C 291

Name	Category Number	Industrial Classification
Weyerhaeuser	31	Paper and Wood
Wheelabrator-Frye	17	Farm Machinery
Wheeling-Pittsburgh Steel	24	Metal Mfg.
Whirlpool	13	Appliances, Electronics
White Consolidated Industries	13	Appliances, Electronics
Whittaker	25	Metal Products
Witco Chemical	16	Chemicals
Xerox	23	Measuring . . . Equipment
Zenith Radio	13	Appliances, Electronics

CORPORATIONS WITHOUT LIBRARIES

Name	Category Number	Industrial Classification
Alco Standard	17	Farm Machinery
Allied Products	25	Metal Products
Alumax	24	Metal Mfg.
Amerada Hess	32	Petroleum Refining
American Bakeries	18	Food
American Beef Packers	18	Food
American Chain & Cable	25	Metal Products
American Hoist & Derrick	17	Farm Machinery
American Motors	28	Motor Vehicles/Parts
Amsted Industries	24	Metal Mfg.
Amtel	17	Farm Machinery
Associated Milk Producers	18	Food
Avnet	13	Appliances, Electronics
Bangor Punta	36	Shipbuilding . . .
Beatrice Foods	18	Food
Belco Petroleum	26	Mining
Bemis	31	Paper and Wood
Black & Decker Mfg.	17	Farm Machinery
Blue Bell	12	Apparel
Bluebird	18	Food
Brewer (C.)	18	Food
Briggs & Stratton	17	Farm Machinery
Brown Group	22	Leather
Brunswick	29	Musical Instruments . . .

Name	Category Number	Industrial Classification
Butler Mfg.	25	Metal Products
Cannon Mills	38	Textiles
Ceco	25	Metal Products
Cenco	22	Leather
Cerro	24	Metal Mfg.
Certain-teed Products	20	Glass, Cement ...
Champion Home Builders	36	Shipbuilding ...
Champion Spark Plug	13	Appliances, Electronics
Charter	32	Petroleum Refining
Chromalloy American	24	Metal Mfg.
Clark Oil & Refining	32	Petroleum Refining
Clorox	16	Chemicals
Cluett, Peabody	12	Apparel
Coastal States Gas	32	Petroleum Refining
Collins & Aikman	38	Textiles
Commonwealth Oil Refining	32	Petroleum Refining
ConAgra	18	Food
Consolidated Foods	18	Food
Container Corp. of America	31	Paper and Wood
Cook Industries	18	Food
Cooper Industries	17	Farm Machinery
Copperweld	24	Metal Mfg.
Crown Central Petroleum	32	Petroleum Refining
Crown Cork & Seal	25	Metal Products
Cummins Engine	17	Farm Machinery
Cyprus Mines	26	Mining
Dairylea Cooperative	18	Food
Dana	28	Motor Vehicles/Parts
Dayco	35	Rubber
Del Monte	18	Food
Diamond International	31	Paper and Wood
Di Giorgio	18	Food
Digital Equipment	30	Office Machinery
Dover	17	Farm Machinery
Eagle-Picher Industries	25	Metal Products
Eastern Gas & Fuel Associates	26	Mining
Eltra	13	Appliances, Electronics
Emerson Electric	13	Appliances, Electronics
Evans Products	31	Paper and Wood
Ex-Cell-O	17	Farm Machinery

Name	Category Number	Industrial Classification
Fairmont Foods	18	Food
Fedders	13	Appliances, Electronics
Federal Co.	18	Food
Federal-Mogul	17	Farm Machinery
Federal Paper Board	31	Paper and Wood
Fibreboard	31	Paper and Wood
Fieldcrest Mills	38	Textiles
Flavorland Industries	18	Food
Fleetwood Enterprises	36	Shipbuilding . . .
Fruehauf	28	Motor Vehicles/Parts
Fuqua Industries	36	Shipbuilding . . .
Gardner-Denver	17	Farm Machinery
General Cinema	14	Beverages
General Host	18	Food
General Instrument	13	Appliances, Electronics
General Signal	13	Appliances, Electronics
Genesco	12	Apparel
Gold Kist	18	Food
Great Northern Nekoosa	31	Paper and Wood
Handy & Harman	24	Metal Mfg.
Hanes	12	Apparel
Harsco	25	Metal Products
Hart Schaffner & Marx	12	Apparel
Heublein	14	Beverages
Hobart	17	Farm Machinery
Hoerner Waldorf	31	Paper and Wood
Hormel (Geo. A.)	18	Food
Houdaille Industries	28	Motor Vehicles/Parts
Howmet	24	Metal Mfg.
Hygrade Food Products	18	Food
Idle Wild Foods	18	Food
Illinois Central Industries	24	Metal Mfg.
Inland Container	31	Paper and Wood
Inmont	16	Chemicals
Interco	22	Leather
Interlake	24	Metal Mfg.
International MultiFoods	18	Food
Interstate Brands	18	Food
Iowa Beef Processors	18	Food
I-T-E Imperial	13	Appliances, Electronics

Name	Category Number	Industrial Classification
Jonathan Logan	12	Apparel
Joy Manufacturing	17	Farm Machinery
Kane-Miller	18	Food
Kayser-Roth	12	Apparel
Kellogg	18	Food
Kellwood	12	Apparel
Keystone Consolidated Industries	24	Metal Mfg.
Kidde (Walter)	17	Farm Machinery
Koehring	17	Farm Machinery
Land O'Lakes	18	Food
Levi Strauss	12	Apparel
Loews	39	Tobacco
Louisiana-Pacific	31	Paper and Wood
Masonite	31	Paper and Wood
Mattel	29	Musical Instruments ...
MBPXL	18	Food
McGraw-Edison	13	Appliances, Electronics
McLouth Steel	24	Metal Mfg.
Microdot	25	Metal Products
Mohasco	38	Textiles
Monfort of Colorado	18	Food
National Can	25	Metal Products
National Gypsum	20	Glass, Cement ...
National Service Ind.	19	Furniture
Newmont Mining	26	Mining
Norris Industries	25	Metal Products
Northwestern Steel & Wire	24	Metal Mfg.
NVF	24	Metal Mfg.
Ogden	24	Metal Mfg.
Olinkraft	31	Paper and Wood
Otis Elevator	17	Farm Machinery
Paccar	28	Motor Vehicles/Parts
Parker-Hannifin	25	Metal Products
Penn-Dixie Industries	24	Metal Mfg.
Phelps Dodge	24	Metal Mfg.
Phillips-Van Heusen	12	Apparel
Pittston	26	Mining
Porter (H. K.)	24	Metal Mfg.
Questor	28	Motor Vehicles/Parts
Rath Packing	18	Food

Name	Category Number	Industrial Classification
Reichhold Chemicals	16	Chemicals
Reliance Electric	13	Appliances, Electronics
Revere Copper & Brass	24	Metal Mfg.
Rexnord	17	Farm Machinery
Riviana Foods	18	Food
Robertson (H. H.)	25	Metal Products
Roper	13	Appliances, Electronics
St. Joe Minerals	24	Metal Mfg.
Savannah Foods & Industries	18	Food
Saxon Industries	31	Paper and Wood
Scott & Fetzer	13	Appliances, Electronics
Scovill Mfg.	13	Appliances, Electronics
Seaboard Allied Milling	18	Food
Sheller-Globe	28	Motor Vehicles/Parts
Signode	24	Metal Mfg.
Simmons	19	Furniture
Skyline	36	Shipbuilding . . .
Southdown	14	Beverages
Southern Industries	18	Food
Spencer Foods	18	Food
Springs Mills	38	Textiles
Stanley Works	25	Metal Products
Stokely-Van Camp	18	Food
Sunbeam	13	Appliances, Electronics
Superior Oil	32	Petroleum Refining
Talley Industries	23	Measuring . . . Equipment
Tecumseh Products	17	Farm Machinery
Tesoro Petroleum	32	Petroleum Refining
Trane	17	Farm Machinery
Trans Union	17	Farm Machinery
Tyler	25	Metal Products
Union Camp	31	Paper and Wood
United Refining	32	Petroleum Refining
U.S. Industries	12	Apparel
U.S. Shoe	22	Leather
Universal Leaf Tobacco	39	Tobacco
Utah International	26	Mining
VF	12	Apparel
Wallace-Murray	25	Metal Products
Ward Foods	18	Food

Name	Category Number	Industrial Classification
Warner Communications	15	Motion Pictures
Westmoreland Coal	26	Mining
White Motor	28	Motor Vehicles/Parts
Willamette Industries	31	Paper and Wood
Williams Companies	16	Chemicals

Bibliography

Note: Items marked with * are in a *class of material*. Readers should look for other current items by the same types of publishers or organizations on similar subjects.

ASIS Handbook and Directory [Latest Edition]. Washington, D.C.: American Society for Information Science, issued annually.

ASLIB Directory. London: ASLIB, 1970, 1971, 2 vols.

ASLIB Membership List, 1971/72. London, 1971, 83 pp.

American Library Directory [Latest Edition]. New York: Bowker, issued annually.

*American Management Association. Fundamentals of Records Management [Announcement Brochure]. Royal Coach Motor Hotel, Atlanta, October 6-10, 1975 (Course #12535-48).

Anderson, B. L. *Special Libraries and Information Centers in Canada: A Directory.* Ottawa: Canadian Library Association, 1970, 169 pp.

Annals of the IEEE [Brochure with Subject List]. A New Computer-based Service that Provides Quick and Inexpensive Access to the Entire IEEE Periodical Literature. New York, January 1975.

Arthur D. Little, Inc. *The 3R's Program: Meeting Industry's Informational Needs.* Report to Division of Library Development, New York State Library. Cambridge, Mass., September 1967, 71 pp.

*Aspen Systems Corp. Information Management Services; Health Information Services [Brochure]. Gaithersburg, Md., 1976.

Bahn, Catherine. "Administration and Management of Scientific and Technical Libraries." *Sci-Tech News* 30, no. 3 (July 1976): 55-57.

Baker, W. O., et al. "Computers and Research." *Science* 195, no. 4283 (March 18, 1977): 1134-39.

Bearman, Toni Carbo, and William A. Kunberger. *A Study of Coverage Overlap Among Fourteen Major Science and Technology Abstracting and Indexing Services.* Philadelphia: National Federation of Abstracting and Indexing Services, February 1977, 75 pp. (NFAIS-77/1). Packet of microfiche included.

Bell Laboratories, Inc. *Technical Information Libraries.* Murray Hill, N.J., 197-?, 20 pp.

*Biller, Alexander S. "Much More Than Hardware" [Suggested parallel career paths through Document Production or Secretarial Administration]. *Word Processing Magazine* (IBM Office Products Division), 1972, 3 pp. Reprint.

Branscomb, Lewis W. "Promising Research in the Computer Industry." *Physics Today* 29, no. 1 (January 1976): 54-61.

Burchinal, Lee. "Recent Trends in Communication of Scientific and Technical Information." *Notes and Comments* (Engineering Index, Inc.) 2, no. 4 (December 1975): 1-2.

Burns, J. Christopher. "Evolution of Office Information Systems." *Datamation* 73, no. 4 (April 1977): 60-64.

Carlson, Walter M. *The Economics of Information Transfer.* Prepared for presentation March 12, 1969, to the Division of Engineering, New York Academy of Sciences, in New York. Armonk, N.Y., 1969, 30 pp.

Cushman, Helen M. Baker. "The Modern Business Archivist." *The American Archivist* 33, no. 1 (January 1970): 19-24.

Danish Library Association. Work Simplification Committee. *Work Simplification in Danish Public Libraries* [Abridged Version]. Trans. from the Danish by Rudolph C. Ellsworth. Chicago: Library Technology Project, American Library Association, 1969, 256 pp. (LTP Publication No. 15).

English, Eileen W. "Hits and Misses." *Special Libraries* 66, no. 5-6 (May-June 1975): 237-40.

Epstein, A. H., et al. *Bibliographic Automation of Large Library Operations Using a Time-Sharing System: Phase 1.* Final Report, Project No. 7-1145, Grant No. OEG-1-7-071145-4428, Office of Education, U.S. Department of Health, Education and Welfare. Stanford, Calif.: Stanford University Libraries, April 1971, 101 pp.

"Executive Briefing . . . The Office of the Future, an In-depth Analysis of How Word-processing Will Reshape the Corporate Office." *Business Week,* no. 2387 (June 30, 1975): 48-84.

Ferber, Robert, Comp., et al. A Basic Bibliography on Marketing Research [1974 Revision]. New York: American Marketing Association, 1974, 299 pp.

Fiore, Michael V. "The Secretarial Role in Transition." *Supervisory Management* 16, no. 11 (November 1971): 22-27.

Fortune. Fortune's 1975 Directory of the 500 Largest U.S. Industrial Corporations [By Industry Classification]. New York: *Fortune,* 1975, 11 pp.

"Fortune's 500 Largest Industrials in U.S., 1975." *Fortune,* 91, no. 5 (May 1975): 208-35. Also note later May issues.

Fry, Bernard M., and Herbert S. White. *Publishers and Libraries: A Study of Scholarly and Research Journals.* Lexington, Mass.: Lexington Books, D. C. Heath and Co., 1977, 166 pp.

Galbraith, Jay. *Designing Complex Organizations.* Reading, Mass.: Addison-Wesley, 1973, 150 pp.

Grattidge, Walter, and M. King. Information for Industrial R and D—Prices, Cost, Choices and Responses. Preprint for JANUS Seminar, New York, January 12, 1977, 34 pp.

Hamburg, Morris, et al. *Library Planning and Decision-making Systems.* Cambridge, Mass.: MIT Press, 1974, 274 pp.

Hammer, Donald P., ed. *The Information Age: Its Development, Its Impact.* Metuchen, N.J.: The Scarecrow Press, 1976, 275 pp.

Harmon, E. Glynn. "Information Science Education and Training." *Annual Review of Information Science and Technology* 11 (1976): 347-80.

Hawkins, Donald T. "Impact of On-Line Systems on a Literature Searching Service." *Special Libraries* 67, no. 12 (December 1976): 559-67.

_____. "Semiconductor Journals." *Journal of Chemical Information and Computer Science* 16, no. 1 (February 1976): 21-23.

_____. "Unconventional Uses of On-Line Information Retrieval Systems, or, On-Line Bibliometric Studies." *Journal of the American Society for Information Science* 28, no. 1 (1977).

Heiliger, Edward M., and Paul B. Henderson, Jr. *Library Automation: Experience, Methodology, and Technology of the Library as an Information System.* New York: McGraw-Hill, c1971, 333 pp.

Hewlett, William. "Profit, People, and Contributions." *Perspective* (Purdue University), (July-August 1976): 12.

Hodge, Bartow, and Robert N. Hodgson. *Management and the Computer in Information and Control Systems.* New York: McGraw-Hill, c1969, 297 pp.

Industrial Research Laboratories of the United States, 14th ed. New York: Bowker, 1975, 585 pp.

International Conference on Training for Information Work (Rome, November 15-19, 1971). *Conference Edition of the Papers.* Rome: Italian National Information Institute, 1971, 369 pp.

Jackson, Eugene B. *An Empirical Basis for Establishing Budget Levels for Industrial Special Libraries.* Contributed Paper No. 106, for presentation at the 64th Annual Special Libraries Association Conference, Pittsburgh, June 10-14, 1973. Austin, Tex., 1973, 5 pp.

_____ "Enter at Your Own Risk [The GM Research Laboratories Library]." *Library Journal* 82, no. 9 (May 1, 1975): 1146-51.

_____. "International Industrial Special Library Systems—A Neglected Nucleator for International Information Transfer." Paper 9 in Contributed Papers to the American Society for Information Science, Annual Meeting, October 23-26, 1972, Washington, D.C., 6 pp.

_____. "Portrait of a Special Library System." *Library Journal* 87, no. 19 (November 1, 1962): 3963-65.

_____, and Donald D. Hendricks. *Feasibility of Centralized Processing for Five Medical Library Components of the University of Texas System.* NIH Grant LM 01207 to the University of Texas Health Science Center. Austin and Dallas, 1973, 162 pp.

_____, and Ruth L. Jackson. "The Industrial Special Library Universe—A 'Base Line' Study of Its Extent and Characteristics." *Journal of the American Society for Information Science* 28, no. 3 (May 1977): 135-52.

___, and Ruth L. Jackson. "The Personnel, Material and Financial Resources of the Library Systems of 311 Industrial Corporations." Submitted to ERIC Clearinghouse, October 1977, 30 pp. (ERIC #IR005-222)

___, and Ronald E. Wyllys. "Professional Education in Information Science— Its Recent Past and Probable Future." In Donald P. Hammer, ed., *The Information Age: Its Development, Its Impact.* Metuchen, N.J.: The Scarecrow Press, 1976, pp. 166-209.

Jennings, E. R. "Advances in Technical Information Services—Some Implications for Engineering Managers." In Joint Engineering Management Conference (Washington, D.C., September 26-27, 1966), *Creating Second Sources of Engineering Manpower.* New York: The Institute of Electrical and Electronics Engineers, 1966, pp. 101-12. Commentary by Eugene B. Jackson, p. 117-18.

Kennedy, R. A. "Bell Laboratories' Library Real-Time Loan System (BELLREL)." *Journal of Library Automation* 1, no. 2 (June 1968): 128-46.

___. "Bell Laboratories On-Line Circulation Control System: One Year's Experience." *Proceedings, 1969 Clinic on Library Applications of Data Processing, University of Illinois, Urbana, April 27-30, 1969.* 1970, p. 14-30.

___, and W. K. Sipfle. "MERCURY—A Computer-Aided System for Distributing Documents." (To be published).

Kilgour, Frederick G. "Historical Development of Library Computerization." In Donald P. Hammer, ed., *The Information Age.* Metuchen, N.J.: The Scarecrow Press, 1976, p. 241-57.

King, Donald W., and Edward C. Bryant. *The Evaluation of Information Services and Products.* Washington, D.C.: Information Resources Press, 1971, 306 pp.

___, et al. *Statistical Indicators of Scientific and Technical Communication, 1960-1980.* Vol. 1: A Summary Report for National Science Foundation, Division of Science Information. Rockville, Md.: King Research, Inc., Center for Quantitative Sciences, 1976, 99 pp. Sold by the Superintendent of Documents, Washington, D.C.

Kruzas, Anthony Thomas. *Business and Industrial Libraries in the United States, 1820-1940.* New York: SLA, 1965, 133 pp.

___. *Directory of Special Libraries and Information Centers,* 1st ed. Detroit: Gale Research Co., c1968-69, 2 vols.

___, et al., eds. *Encyclopedia of Information Systems and Services,* 2d International ed. Ann Arbor, Mich.: Edwards Bros., 1974, 1277 pp.

Lancaster, F. W. "Assessment of the Technical Information Requirements of Users." In *Contemporary Problems in Technical Library and Information Center Management: A State-of-the-Art.* Washington, D.C.: American Society for Information Science, 1974, pp. 59-85.

———, and Jeanne M. Owen. "Information Retrieval by Computer," In Donald P. Hammer, ed., *The Information Age.* Metuchen, N.J.: The Scarecrow Press, 1976, pp. 1-33.

———, and E. G. Fayen. *Information Retrieval On-Line.* Los Angeles: Melville Publishing, 1973, 597 pp.

———, and M. J. Joncich. *The Measurement and Evaluation of Library Services.* Washington, D.C.: Information Resources Press, 1977, 470 pp.

Leonard, Lawrence E., et al. *Centralized Book Processing; a Feasibility Study Based on Colorado Academic Libraries.* Metuchen, N.J.: The Scarecrow Press, 1969, 401 pp.

Leonard, R. S. "Objectives and Standards for Special Libraries." *Special Libraries* 55, no. 10 (December 1964): 672-80.

Licklider, J. C. R. "An On-Line Information Network," In Carl F. J. Overhage and R. Joyce Harman, eds., *Intrex; Report of a Planning Conference on Information Transfer Experiments, September 3, 1965.* Cambridge, Mass.: MIT Press, 1965, pp. 147-55.

Locke, W. N. "Library Requirements." Preprint for SJCC Panel, Computers in Service to Libraries of the Future, Boston, May 15, 1969.

Lowry, W. Kenneth. "Use of Computers in Information Systems." *Science* 175, no. 4024 (February 25, 1972): 841-46.

McCarn, Davis B., and Joseph Leiter. "On-Line Services in Medicine and Beyond." *Science* 181, no. 4097 (July 27, 1973): 318, 324.

McConkey, Dale D. *Management by Objectives for Staff Managers.* N.Y.: Vantage Press, 1972, 210 pp.

Mackenzie, R. Alec. "Are Executives' Secretaries Obsolete?" *Personnel* 48, no. 5 (September/October 1971): 60-64.

Management Information Systems and the Information Specialist. Proceedings of a Symposium Held at Purdue University, July 12-13, 1965. Sponsored by the Krannert Graduate School of Industrial Administration and the University Libraries. Lafayette, Ind., 1966, 138 pp.

National Academy of Sciences, Committee on Scientific and Technical Communication. *Scientific and Technical Communication; a Pressing National Problem and Recommendations for its Solution.* A Synopsis of the Report. Washington, D.C.: National Academy of Sciences, 1969, 30 pp.

*National Microfilm Association [Announcement Brochure]. Module 1—Fundamentals of Micrographics; Module 2—Retrieval and Systems Design; Module 3—Inspection and Quality Control; Module 4—Computer Output Microfilm (COM). Airport Marina Hotel, San Francisco, September 9-11, and Barbizon Plaza Hotel, New York City, October 7-9, 1975.

New York (State) Education Department, Division of Library Development. *Profiles of the NYSILL Subject Referral Libraries in New York State.* Reprinted from *The Bookmark,* 1969-70. Albany, 1970, 32 pp.

_____. *Profiles of the Reference and Research Library Resources Systems in New York State.* Reprinted from *The Bookmark,* 1969-70. Albany, 1970, 41 pp.

*New York Metropolitan Reference and Research Library Agency (METRO). *When Two Heads are Better . . . Call Metro's Consultant Service.* New York: METRO, 1975, 2 pp. (fanfold).

North, J., et al. *Libraries and Industry.* Final Report, Project #88-21, Contract No. OEC2-7-010105-1523, U.S. Department of Health, Education and Welfare, Office of Education, Bureau of Research. Palo Alto, Calif.: Programming Services, 31 August 1967, 1 vol.

"The On-Line Intellectual Community." In Carl F. J. Overhage and R. Joyce Harman, eds., *INTREX; Report of a Planning Conference on Information Transfer Experiments, September 3, 1965.* Cambridge, Mass.: MIT Press, 1965, pp. 25-41.

Overhage, Carl F. J., and R. Joyce Harman, eds., *INTREX; Report of a Planning Conference on Information Transfer Experiments, September 3, 1965.* Cambridge, Mass.: MIT Press, 1965, 276 pp.

Palmer, Richard P. *Case Studies in Library Computer Systems.* New York: Bowker, 1973, 214 pp.

"Profiles of Special Libraries . . . ABC Manufacturing Corporation; . . . DEF Industrial Corporation." *Special Libraries* 57, no. 3 (March 1966): 179-84; " . . . GHI Public Utilities Firm; . . . JKL Bank." *Special Libraries* 57, no. 4 (April 1966): 227-31; " . . . MNOP Advertising Agency Library; . . . Research and Development Division of the QRS Chemical Manufacturing Company." *Special Libraries* 57, no. 5 (May/June 1966): 327-31.

Pyhrr, Peter A. *Zero-Base Budgeting, a Practical Management Tool for Evaluating Expenses.* New York: Wiley, 1973, 213 pp.

Randall, Gordon E. "Budgeting for Libraries." *Special Libraries* 67, no. 1 (January 1976): 8-12.

_____. "Randall's Rationalized Ratios." *Special Libraries* 66, no. 1 (January 1975): 6-11.

Rees, Alan, ed. *Contemporary Problems in Technical Library and Information Center Management: A State-of-the-Art.* Washington, D.C.; American Society for Information Science, 1974, 211 pp.

**Review of Available Literature on Applications and Properties of Nickel-Containing Materials* [Brochure]. New York: The International Nickel Co., June 1975, 24 pp.

Roberts, Ammarette. "Starting a Records Management Program." Texas Chapter, Special Libraries Association, *Bulletin* 26, no. 3 (April 1975): 82-96.

Rosenbloom, Richard S., and Francis W. Wolek. *Technology and Information Transfer; A Survey of Practice in Industrial Organizations.* Cambridge, Mass.: Division of Research, Graduate School of Business Administration, Harvard University, 1970, 174 pp.

_____, and Francis W. Wolek. *Technology, Information and Organization; Information Transfer in Industrial R&D.* Cambridge, Mass.: Graduate School of Business Administration, Harvard University, June 1967, 255 pp.

Ross, I. C. "A Cataloger's Authority List Maintenance System." *Journal of the American Society for Information Science* 27, no 4 (July-August 1976): 224-29.

"SLA Salary Survey, 1976" *Special Libraries* 67, no. 12 (December 1976): 597-624.

*Schade, Otto H. *Image Quality; A Comparison of Photographic and Television Systems.* Princeton, N.J.: RCA Laboratories, 1975, 84 pp.

Schur, Herbert. *Education and Training of Information Specialists for the 1970's.* Sheffield, Eng.: Postgraduate School of Librarianship and Information Science, University of Sheffield, January 1972, 114 pp. (DAS/STINFO/72:9).

Self-Study Report Presented to the Committee on Accreditation of the American Library Association. Austin: Graduate School of Library Science, University of Texas at Austin, 1975, 332 pp.

Sipfle, W. K. "Bell Laboratories Book Acquisition, Accounting and Cataloging System (BELLTIP)." (To be published).

Southwest Educational Development Corp. *ERIC Clearinghouse on Information Resources* [Proposed]. NE-R-00-4-0001, submitted to National Institute of Education, in cooperation with Graduate School of Library Science, University of Texas at Austin. Austin, October 10, 1973, 192 pp.

Spaulding, F. H. and R. O. Stanton. "Computer-Aided Selection in a Library Network." *Journal of American Society for Information Science* 27, no. 5-6 (September-October 1976): 269-80.

"Special Interest Groups (SIGS)." In *ASIS Handbook & Directory,* 1975 Edition. *Bulletin* of the American Society for Information Science 2, no. 2 (August 1975): vii.

Special Libraries Association. *Directory of Members as of July 15, 1964.* New York: SLA, 1964 (now also issued annually in October), 113 pp. Also, European Subscribers to SLA Publications [Lay-up of Mailing List Cards as of August 1965]. 21 pp. Photocopy.

_____. Institutions where SLA Members are Employed: An SLA Directory. New York: SLA, 1977. 173 pp.

_____, Special Committee on the Pilot Education Project. *Equal Pay for Equal Work; Women in Special Libraries.* New York, SLA, 1976, 24 pp.

Stevens, Charles H. "Design Predictions: Information—1988 Style." *EDN* 13, no. 15 (December 1968): 47-50.

Strauss, Lucille J., et al. *Scientific and Technical Libraries; Their Organization and Administration.* New York: Interscience Publishers, 1964, 398 pp.

Systems Development Corporation, Technology Staff. *Technology in Libraries.* Technical Memorandum 3602. Santa Monica, Calif., 15 August 1967, 1 vol.

Tagliacozzo, Renata, and Manfred Kochen. *Information-Seeking Behavior of Catalog Users.* Ann Arbor: Mental Health Research Institute, University of Michigan, 1970, 38 pp. (Communication 272).

UNISIST. *Study Report on the Feasibility of a World Science Information System.* Prepared by the United Nations Educational, Scientific and Cultural Organization and the International Council of Scientific Unions. Paris: UNESCO, 1971, 161 pp.

UNISIST, Intergovernmental Conference for the Establishment of a World Science Information System (Paris, October 4-8, 1971). *Final Report.* Paris: UNESCO, 1971, 60 pp.

"Uncle Sam Still the Records Management Champ." *Information and Records Management* 9, no. 12 (December 1975): 6.

Weil, Ben H. *Benefits From Researcher Use of the Published Literature at the EXXON Research Center.* Preprint for the Information Industry's Association, National Information Conference and Exposition, Washington, D.C., April 20, 1977, 4 + 7 pp.

Weiss, Irvin. "Evaluation of ORBIT and DIALOG Using Six Data Bases." *Special Libraries* 67, no. 12 (December 1976): 574-81.

Wessel, C. J., et al. *Criteria for Evaluating the Effectiveness of Library Operations and Services.* Phase II: Data Gathering and Evaluation. Final Report on Phase II, Contract DA-28017-AMC-3483(A) for Picatinny Arsenal, Dover, N.J. Washington, D.C.: John I. Thompson & Co., August 1968, 109 pp. (ATLIS Report no. 19).

White, Herbert S. "Library Management in the Tight Budget Seventies; Problems, Challenges and Opportunities." *Bulletin of the Medical Library Association* 65, no. 1 (January 1977): 6-12.

_____, and Bernard M. Fry. "Economic Interaction Between Special Libraries and Publishers of Scholarly and Research Journals; Results of an NSF Study." *Special Libraries* 68, no. 3 (March 1977): 109-14.

Wolek, Francis W. *The Complexity of Messages in Science and Engineering: An Influence on Patterns of Communications.* Working Paper No. 110. Philadelphia: Department of Industry, Wharton School of Finance and Commerce, University of Pennsylvania, February 1970, 52 pp.

_____, and Belver C. Griffith. *Policy and Informal Communications in Applied Science and Technology.* Working Paper No. 133. Philadelphia: Department of Management, The Wharton School, University of Pennsylvania, 197-?, 24 pp.

World Trade Institute. International Records and Information Processing Conference [Announcement Brochure]. World Trade Center, PONY/NJ, New York City, November 17-19, 1975.

Young, M. L., H. C. Young, and A. T. Kruzas, eds. *Directory of Special Libraries and Information Centers,* 3d ed. Detroit: Gale Research Co., 1974, 3 vols. Vol. 1: Special Libraries and Information Centers in the U.S. and Canada; Vol. 2: Geographic-Personnel Index; Vol. 3: New Special Libraries. A Periodic Supplement. . . .

Index

We believe that indexes are most important as quality indicators for books and as specific aids to both the principal intended audience and others who hope to make effective use of them. As a consequence, we have given preference in the index's compilation to terminology and topics that should be of greatest interest and usefulness to higher industrial managers. At the same time, we trust our library/information science colleagues and students are able to use it to find topics and opinions of interest and assistance to them.

Acronyms are listed either under the acronym or under the fully spelled-out form, depending upon which is judged to be the most familiar. Cross-references are given to the alternative form; for example, COM stands for Computer Output Microfilm, which is the term used in the index. In a few cases there is no spelled-out form of the acronym, either because there never was one or the original meaning is no longer valid.

The index is arranged on a word-by-word basis, with entries alphabetized letter by letter. Subject indexing is by concepts rather than words. Cross-references (from a heading *not* used to one that is used) are very freely employed and are indicated by *See* . . . . On the other hand, a *See also* reference indicates that the present term is used and that the other term(s) listed are closely related and should be consulted as well.

This index *does* include references to the Tables and the Appendices in view of the special data they contain for purposes of comparison by management.

The first version of this index was prepared in December 1977 from the book's manuscript by the graduate students in the senior author's class in Abstracting and Indexing, L. S. 385T.4. Students participating were Susan Lynn Cochran, Suzy Giannoble, Babette Hiestand, Lisa Harms Holmes, Joe R. Moreno, Jr., with Jeanne C. Reynolds serving as leader. The present version was prepared by the junior author.

306 Index

AACR. *See* Anglo-American Cataloging Rules
Acquisitions, 23-31. *See also* Mechanization; Weeding
 administration of, 63-64
 at Bell Labs, 173-175
 centralization/decentralization, 74-75 (tables)
 definition, 23
 pilot systems and studies, 64
 through international operations, 188-189
Active/Passive Service
 approaches, 19
 characteristics, 71-72
 costs, 72
Administration
 of acquisitions, 63-64
 at Bell Labs, 173
 centralization/decentralization, 88-91 (tables)
 of dissemination and utilization of information, 67
 of generation and production of information, 66-67
 of international operations, 188-194
 of processing of information, 64-66
Administrative Specialist. *See* Director/Manager of the IIS
AIP. *See* American Institute of Physics
ALA. *See* American Library Association
Alerting Services. *See* Selective Dissemination of Information (SDI)
Alexander, R. W., an on-line, real-time, integrated library system, 201-206 (table)
Allocation of Funds. *See* Budget of the IIS
AMA. *See* American Management Association
American Chemical Society, economics of chemical information, 6
American Documentation Institute (ADI). *See* ASIS
American Institute of Physics (AIP), classification scheme, 38
American Library Association (ALA)
 cataloging rules, 31-33
 interlibrary loan code, 95
American Management Association (AMA), seminars, 7, 107, 156-162
American National Standards Institute (ANSI), standards available from its Committee Z39, on library work, documentation and related publishing practices, 33 (table)
American Records Management Association (ARMA), seminars, 156
American Society for Information Science. *See* ASIS
Anglo-American Cataloging Rules (AACR), 31-33
Announcement Services, 50-53
ANSI. *See* American National Standards Institute (ANSI)
ARMA. *See* American Records Management Association (ARMA)
ASIS. (American Society for Information Science), 19
 Special Interest Groups (SIGS), 101, 130
Automation. *See* Mechanization

BELDEX Indexing System, 169-170
Bell Laboratories Library Network
 acquisitions and processing (BELLTIP), 172, 174-175
 book catalog of, 172
 centralization/decentralization, 74-91 (tables), 166-167
 circulation control (BELLREL), 171-172, 174
 collection development, 173-174
 computer systems, 169-173
 indexing system (BELLDEX), 169-170
 on-line searching, 171
 personnel, 168
 publications, 168
 scope, 165-166
 selective dissemination of information
  BELLPAR/BELLTAB, 170-171
  MERCURY, 170
 telecommunication services, 169
 users, 165, 175
BELLPAR/BELLTAB SDI System, 170-171
BELLREL Circulation Control System, 171-172, 174
BELLTIP Acquisitions and Processing System, 172, 174-175
Bibliometric User Studies, 126
Book Trade Literature
 acquisition of, 23-24
 cost for *Fortune* 500 corporations, 187
 descriptive cataloging of, 31-32

subject cataloging/classification of, 37-39
Budget of the IIS, 129-139. See also Planning, Programming and Budgeting System (PPBS); Zero-based Budgeting
  calculations based on borrowers, 133-134
  calculations based on Most Probable Users (MPU), 131-133
  calculations based on "Useful Life Principle," 132
  current expenditures, 129-130
  establishment of, 129
  potential saving areas, 130

Career Upgrading Program, 68. See also Continuing Education
Cataloging. See Processing of Information; type of material to be cataloged, i.e., Book Trade Literature, Periodicals, etc.
Centralization/Decentralization of Functions, 72-92
  at Bell Labs, 74-91 (tables), 166-167
  at DuPont, GE, GM and IBM, 74-91 (tables)
  by specific functions, 74-91 (tables)
Circulation System at Bell Labs (BELLREL), 171-172, 174
Citation Counts. See Bibliometric User Studies
Classification of Materials. See Processing of Information; type of material to be classified, i.e., Book Trade Literature, Periodicals, etc.
Classification Schemes, 37-38
Closed Information. See Open/Closed Information
Collection Development. See Bell Laboratories Library Network
COM. See Computer Output Microfilm
Company Goals. See Goals, Corporate
Company Publications. See Dissemination and Utilization of Information; "Make" or "Buy" Decisions; Reports, Internal
Company Specifications. See Specifications, Company
Computer Output Microfilm (COM), 46, 161
Computers. See Mechanization

Consultants, 110-116
  agreement or contract with, 111-112
  case study, 113-116
  company definition of the problem, 111
  compensation of, 112
  conduct user studies, 128
  findings of, 112
  implementation of recommendations, 112
  selection of, 111
Continuing Education, 107-108
Corporate Goals. See Goals, Corporate
Correspondence
  acquisition of, 28
  as information source, 15
  definition, 146
  descriptive cataloging of, 35
  subject cataloging/classification of, 41
Correspondence Control, 145-155. See also Mechanization
  automated system of, 149-151
    data elements, 152 (table)
  case study, 146-154
  control numbering system, 148
  correspondence control point, 148-149
  definitions of vital record, loss or destruction and historical record, 146
  problems, 147-148
  security, 147-148
  systems specialist job description, 154 (table)
"Cosmopolitans." See "Gatekeepers"
Cost Benefits, 210-211, 212 (table)
Cost Effectiveness, 210, 213 (table)
Cost Reporting, 210, 212 (table)
Cost of Scientific and Technical Communications, 10-11
Current Awareness. See Selective Dissemination of Information (SDI)

Data Bases, On-line. See On-line Data Bases
Dayton Engineering Laboratories (DELCO), 18
DDC. See Defense Documentation Center (DDC)
Deacquisitions. See Weeding
Decentralization of the IIS. See Centralization/Decentralization of Functions

308 Index

Defense Documentation Center (DDC), 34, 37
DELCO. *See* Dayton Engineering Laboratories (DELCO)
Deposit Accounts for Government Documents, 25
Dewey Decimal Classification, 37-38
Director/Manager of the IIS, 92-102. *See also* Personnel
  administrative specialist as, 96
  information scientist as
    advantages and disadvantages, 95
    professional preparation, 101-102
  librarian as
    advantages and disadvantages, 95
    professional preparation, 96-101
  management position guide for, 93-94
  rating of background potential by function, 97 (table)
  subject specialist as
    advantages and disadvantages, 96
    professional preparation, 102
Discounts to Professional/Technical Society Member for Publications, 24
Dissemination and Utilization of Information, 50-61. *See also* Announcement Services; Mechanization; Selective Dissemination of Information (SDI)
  administration of, 67
  at Bell Labs, 167-171
  centralization/decentralization, 84-87 (tables)
  cost benefits, 6
  in international operations, 194
  pilot systems and studies, 67
Distribution of Information. *See* Dissemination and Utilization of Information
Documents, Government. *See* Government Documents
DuPont de Nemours & Co., Inc., E. I., centralization/decentralization of IIS functions, 74-91 (tables)

Economics of Information, 211, 213 (tables)
Employees. *See* Personnel
Engineering Index, Inc., 6
Engineers Joint Council (EJC), 6, 37

Evaluation. *See Fortune* 500 Corporations with IISs; Industrial Information Systems (IIS)
Exchange of Information. *See* Information Exchange (Formal and Informal)
External Reports. *See* Reports, External

Facilities and Construction Information, distribution of, 59-60
Fiscal/Comptroller Information, distribution of, 58
Ford Motor Company Engineering Library, 18
Foreign Government Documents. *See* Government Documents
Foreign Operations. *See* International Operations of the IIS
Formal Information Exchange. *See* Information Exchange (Formal and Informal)
Fortune 500 Corporations
  functional units, rank order, 195-196
  international industrial library systems, 8, 188-195
  study of, 177-178
Fortune 500 Corporations Alphabetical Listing with Category Number and Industrial Classification, 283-296
Fortune 500 Corporations by Industrial Category. *See also* 33 Microfiche in Pocket
  alphabetical listing
    Aircraft (#11), 234 (table B.3)
    Apparel (#12), 235 (table B.4)
    Appliances, Electronics (#13), 236-237 (table B.5)
    Beverages (#14), 238 (table B.6)
    Broadcasting and Motion Picture Production and Distribution (#15), 239 (table B.7)
    Chemicals (#16), 240-241 (table B.8)
    Farm and Industrial Machinery (#17), 242-243 (table B.9)
    Food (#18), 244-246 (table B.10)
    Furniture (#19), 247 (table B.11)
    Glass, Cement, Gypsum, Concrete (#20), 248 (table B.12)
    Jewelry and Silverware (#21), 249 (table B.13)
    Leather and Leather Products (#22),

Index 309

250 (table B.14)
Measuring, Scientific and Photographic Equipment (#23), 251 (table B.15)
Metal Manufacturing (#24), 252-253 (table B.16)
Metal Products (#25), 254-255 (table B.17)
Mining (#26), 256 (table B.18)
Miscellaneous Manufacturing (#27), 257 (table B.19)
Motor Vehicles and Parts (#28), 258 (table B.20)
Musical Instruments, Toys, and Sporting Goods (#29), 259 (table B.21)
Office Machinery (#30), 260 (table B.22)
Paper and Wood Products (#31), 261-262 (table B.23)
Petroleum Refining (#32), 263-264 (table B.24)
Pharmaceuticals (#33), 265 (table B.25)
Publishing and Printing (#34), 266 (table B.26)
Rubber (#35), 267 (table B.27)
Shipbuilding, Railroad Equipment, Mobile Homes (#36), 268 (table B.28)
Soaps, Cosmetics (#37), 269 (table B.29)
Textiles (#38), 270 (table B.30)
Tobacco (#39), 271 (table B.31)
scattergrams of statistically significant cross correlations
Chemicals, 272-273 (figs. B.1a-B.1d)
Glass, Cement . . ., 274 (fig. B.2)
Measuring . . . Equipment, 274-277 (figs. B.3a-B.3f)
Motor Vehicles and Parts, 277-279 (figs. B.4a-B.4d)
Office Machinery (incl. Computers), 279-282 (figs. B.5a-B.5f)
Textiles, 282 (fig. B.6)
statistics on
employees, column 9, tables B.3-B.31
international systems, column 4-5, tables B.3-B.31
libraries, column 3, tables B.3-B.31
professional librarians, column 6-7, tables B.3-B.31
rank in assets, column 2, tables B.3-B.31
rank in sales, column 10, tables B.3-B.31
subscriptions, column 8, tables B.3-B.31
Fortune 500 Corporations with IISs
evaluation of
by industrial classification, 178-180
by internationally operated systems, 181
by materials-periodical subscriptions, 183
by number of libraries, 181
by number of professional librarians/ information officers employed, 182
financial implications of IIS, 187
relationships between measures, 184-186
summary data, 230-231 (table B.1)
Fortune 500 Corporations without IISs, summary data, 232-233 (table B.2)
Free Materials
acquisitions of, 27-28
descriptive cataloging of, 35
subject cataloging/classification of, 40

"Gatekeepers," 53, 102, 121-122, 127
General Electric Corporation, centralization/ decentralization of IIS functions, 74-91 (tables)
General Motors Corporation, centralization/ decentralization of IIS functions, 74-91 (tables)
GM Research Laboratories Library, 4, 18, Appendix A
Generation of Information. *See also* Graphics; Production of Information
administration of, 66-67
at Bell Labs, 167-168
centralization/decentralization, 80-81 (tables)
content development, 43
definition of, 43-44
editorial policy, 44
form of material, 44-45
in international operations, 193-194
pilot systems and studies, 66-67
Goals, Corporate, 68-69

Index

Government Documents
    acquisition of, 25-26
    centralization/decentralization, 74, 76
    deposit accounts, 25
    descriptive cataloging of, 33-34
    subject cataloging/classification of, 39
Government Patents. *See* Patents, Government
Government Specifications. *See* Specifications, Government
Graphics, 45, 80-81 (tables)

Hawthorne Effect in User Studies, 125

IBM (International Business Machines Corporation)
    centralization/decentralization of IIS functions, 74-91 (tables)
    word processing concept, 141-143
IBM Technical Information Retrieval Center (ITIRC), 194
"Iceberg Effect," 3
IIS. *See* Industrial Information Systems
Indexes
    acquisition of, 28-29
    as sources of subject headings, 37-38
    descriptive cataloging of, 36
    subject cataloging/classification of, 41
Indexing of Materials. *See* Mechanization; Processing of Information; Selective Dissemination of Information (SDI); type of material to be indexed, i.e., Book Trade Literature, Government Documents, etc.
Industrial Information Systems (IIS) (includes concepts not evident in Table of Contents). *See also* Bell Laboratories Library Network; Budget of the IIS; Director/Manager of the IIS; *Fortune* 500 Corporations; International Operations of the IIS; Mechanization; Personnel and specific functions, i.e., Acquisitions, Administration, etc.
    accessibility of, 127
    cost benefit analysis, 209-215
    definition of, 13
    dichotomies, 18-21
    effects on industry, 8
    effects of management, 8
    establishment of, 9-10, 13-16
    future direction of, 9, 214
    history of, 17-18
    inventory of existing information collections, 13-16
    public relations for, 126-127
    rules for management, 8
    variations within, 195-197
Informal Information Exchange. *See* Information Exchange (Formal and Informal)
Information. *See also* Open/Closed Information and specific functions, i.e., Processing of Information, etc.
    economics of, 10-11
Information Centers. *See* Industrial Information Systems (IIS)
Information Exchange (Formal and Informal), 29-30
    centralization/decentralization of, 74
    descriptive cataloging of, 36
    subject cataloging/classification of, 41
Information Needs, 2-3
Information Scientist. *See* Director/Manager of the IIS
Information Sources, 3-5, 14-16
In-House Materials. *See* Dissemination and Utilization of Information; "Make or Buy" Decisions; Reports, Internal
Interlibrary Loan, ALA Code for, 95
Internal Reports. *See* Reports, Internal
International Business Machines Corporation. *See* IBM
International Operations of the IIS. *See also Fortune* 500 Corporations
    acquisitions, 188-189
    administration, 194
    comparison with domestic operations, 190-193 (tables)
    dissemination and utilization of information, 194
    generation and production of information, 193-194
    processing of information, 189
    translations, acquisition of, 189
International Standards Organization (ISO), 32
Interviews in User Studies, 124-125

Index   311

ISO. *See* International Standards Organization (ISO)
ITIRC. *See* IBM Technical Information Retrieval Center

Japan Broadcasting Company (NKH), 7
Jobber as Source for Purchasing Books and Periodicals, 24
Journals. *See* Periodicals

Kettering, Charles F., 18

Laboratory Notebooks
    acquisition of, 27
    as information source, 15
    descriptive cataloging of, 35
    subject cataloging/classification of, 40
Legal Materials, distribution of, 58
Librarians. *See* Director/Manager of the IIS; Personnel
Libraries. *See* Industrial Information Systems (IIS)
Library Manager. *See* Personnel
Library of Congress
    classification scheme, 37-38
    subject heading list, 37
"Library Penetration" Ratio, 177
Literature. *See* Book Trade Literature; Open/Closed Information
Lutz, Caroline W., 18

MacDonald, Rachel M., 18
Magazines. *See* Periodicals
"Make or Buy" Decisions, 29, 36, 41, 43
Management
    implications of information systems for, 7-10
    information services to, 173-174
    rules for considering information systems, 8
Management by Objectives (MBO), 135
Management Information Systems (MIS), 7
Management of the IIS. *See* Director/Manager of the IIS
Marketing Information, distribution of, 60-61
Marketing the IIS, 211, 213 (table)
MBO. *See* Management by Objectives (MBO)
Mechanization
    Alexander's on-line, real-time, integrated library system, 201-206 (table)
    at Bell Labs, 169-173
    hardware/software considerations, 201
    implementation procedures, 200-208
    in-house computer expertise, 207
    networks, 199
MEDLARS, 6
MEDLINE, 6
MERCURY SDI System, 170
Microcopy
    as replacement for printed materials, 28
    descriptive cataloging of, 35
    subject cataloging/classification of, 40
Miller, R. B., human problem-solving tasks, 20
MIS. *See* Management Information System (MIS)
Monographs. *See* Book Trade Literature
Monsanto Chemical Company, mechanized processing of laboratory notebooks and reports, 19
Most Probable User (MPU), 131-135
MPU. *See* Most Probable User (MPU)

National Cash Register Company (NCR), 18
National Industrial Conference Board (NICB), seminar, 7
National Library of Medicine (NLM), 6
National Micrographics Association (NMA), seminars, 156-172
National Scientific and Technical Information System (NSTIS), 6
National Technical Information Service (NTIS), 34
    report on costs of information service, 10
NCR. *See* National Cash Register Company (NCR)
"Negative Cost Benefit," 210-211
Networks
    Bell Laboratories Library Network, 165-176
    international operations of the IIS, 188-195
    Singer Company network, 199
NICB. *See* National Industrial Conference Board (NICB)
NKH. *See* Japan Broadcasting Company (NKH)
NLM. *See* National Library of Medicine (NLM)

NMA. *See* National Micrographics Association (NMA)
No-cost Materials. *See* Free Materials
Non-Users of the IIS, 122. *See also* User Studies; Users of the IIS
NTIS. *See* National Technical Information Service (NTIS)

OCLC, Use at Bell Labs, 172
Ohio College Library Center. *See* OCLC
On-line Data Bases. *See also* names of specific data bases, i.e., MEDLARS, TOXLINE
  acquisition of, 29
  Alexander's on-line, real-time, integrated library system, 201-206 (table)
  at Bell Labs, 171-173
  centralization/decentralization, 78-79
  descriptive cataloging of, 36
  subject cataloging/classification of, 41
Open/Closed Information, 3-5, 207-208
Ordering. *See* Acquisitions

Pamphlets, descriptive cataloging of, 32
Passive Service. *See* Active/Passive Service
Patent Office, U.S., 26-27
  subject headings of, 40
Patents, Government
  acquisition of, 27
  as information source, 15
  centralization/decentralization, 74, 76
  descriptive cataloging of, 34
  subject cataloging/classification of, 40
Periodicals
  acquisition of, 24-25
  cost for *Fortune* 500 Corporations, 187
  descriptive cataloging of, 32
Personnel, 105-110. *See also* Director/Manager of the IIS
  at Bell Labs, 168
  career upgrading program, 68
  company vs professional loyalty, 108
  continuing education, 107
  cost accounting, 209
  cost for *Fortune* 500 Corporations, 187
  fringe benefits, 107
  library manager job description, 106-107
  overall cost, 105
  performance evaluation, 108
  promotion and/or separation, 109
  salaries, 107
  unions, 109-110
  women professionals, 105-106
Personnel Information, distribution of, 58
Pilot Systems and Studies
  for acquisitions, 64
  for dissemination and utilization of information, 67
  for generation and production of information, 66-67
  for mechanization, 207
  for processing of information, 65
Planning, Programming and Budgeting System (PPBS), 135-136, 210, 213 (table)
Processing of Information (This heading includes the traditional library functions of cataloging, subject classification, and subject indexing), 30-42. *See also* Mechanization and type of material to be processed, i.e., Book Trade Literature, Periodicals, etc.
  administration of, 64-66
  at Bell Labs, 172-173
  centralization/decentralization, 76-79
  definition of, 30-31
  descriptive cataloging, 31-37
  in international operations of the IIS, 189-190
  pilot systems and studies, 65
  subject cataloging/classification, 37-42
Production Information, distribution of, 60
Production of Information. *See also* Generation of Information
  administration of, 66-67
  at Bell Labs, 167-168
  centralization/decentralization, 80-83
  commercial analysis, 48
  definition of, 43
  form of material, 46-47
  in international operations, 193-194
  pilot systems and studies, 66-67
  public relations analysis, 47-48
  reproduction costs, 46
  technical analysis, 48-49
Professional Societies, 38. *See also* names of specific societies, i.e., American Management Association, Special Libraries Association, etc.
  as acquisitions source for purchasing

Index   313

books and periodicals, 24
Professionals. *See* Director/Manager of the IIS; Personnel
Project LEX (Engineers Joint Council (EJC)/Defense Documentation Center (DDC), 37
Proprietary Information. *See* Open/Closed Information
Public Relations Information, distribution of, 58
Publishers as Source for Purchasing Books and Periodicals, 23-24
Purchasing. *See* Acquisitions

Questionnaires in User Studies, 122-124

R&D (Research and Development), expenditures for, 10-11
Records Management, 155-163. *See also* Mechanization
   Air Force Documentation Management Program, 155-156
   costs of, 155
   definition of, 156-157
   seminars on, 156-162
Referral and Switching. *See* Switching and Referral
Reports, External
   acquisition of, 27
   descriptive cataloging of, 34
   subject cataloging/classification of, 40
Reports, Internal
   acquisition of, 27
   as information source, 14-15
   descriptive cataloging of, 35
   security of, 27
   subject cataloging/classification of, 40
Research and Development. *See* R&D
Research Information, distribution of, 59

Salaries, 107. *See also* Budget of the IIS
SDI. *See* Selective Dissemination of Information (SDI)
Selection of Materials. *See* Acquisitions
Selective Dissemination of Information (SDI), 5-6, 52-53
   at Bell Labs (using BELLPAR/BELLTAB and MERCURY), 170-171
Seminars
   as information source, 15-16
   on records management, 157-162

Serials. *See* Periodicals
"Sideslipping," 170
SLA. *See* Special Libraries Association
Social Concerns Information, distribution of, 59
Societies, Professional/Technical. *See* Professional Societies
Sources of Information. *See* Information Sources
Special Libraries Association
   loan collection of special subject heading lists and classification schemes, 38
   "Profiles" and "Objectives and Standards," 130
   salary surveys, 107
Specifications
   company
      acquisition of, 26
      descriptive cataloging of, 34
      subject cataloging/classification of, 40
   government
      acquisition of, 26
      descriptive cataloging of, 34
      subject cataloging/classification of, 39
   trade associations
      acquisition of, 26
      descriptive cataloging of, 34
      subject cataloging/classification of, 39
Specifications as Information Source, 15
Staff. *See* Personnel
Standard Expense Classification (SEC) Codes, 209
Standards as Information Source, 15. *See also* American National Standards Institute (ANSI); International Standards Organization (ISO)
"Stars." *See* "Gatekeepers"
"State-of-Art" Requests and Compilations, 56-57
Storage of Records. *See* Correspondence Control; Records Management
Subject Specialist. *See* Director/Manager of the IIS
Superintendent of Documents Classification Scheme, 33-34
Surveys in User Studies, 122-124

Switching and Referral, definition of, 6

Technical Reports. *See* Reports, External; Reports, Internal
Technical Societies. *See* Professional Societies
Technology Information, distribution of, 59
Telecommunication Services, at Bell Labs, 169
Thesaurus of Engineering Terms (Project LEX of Engineers Joint Council/ Defense Documentation Center), 37
"Tickler Files," 19
TOXLINE, 6
Trade Association Specifications. *See* Specifications, Trade Association
Translations
  acquisition from international operations, 189
  production of, 49-50

UDC. *See* Universal Decimal Classification (UDC)
United Engineering Trustees, 6
U. S. Patent Office. *See* Patent Office, U.S.
Universal Decimal Classification (UDC), 38-39
Useful Life Principle, 132
User Needs. *See* Information Needs
User Studies, 122-124
  bibliometric studies, 126
  Hawthorne effect in, 125
  interviews, 124-125
  observation, 125
  other techniques, 125-126
  panel of subject experts technique, 126
  questionnaires, 122-124
  results, 126-128
  written surveys, 122-124

Users of the IIS, 119-124. *See also* Most Probable User (MPU)
  analysis of problem solving tasks, 20 (fig.)
  at Bell Labs, 165, 175
  information needs, 2-3
  types of, 119-122
  user training, 68
Utilization of Information. *See* Dissemination and Utilization of Information

Variations within IISs, 195-197
Vendors Catalogs, as information source, 15
Visual Aids. *See* Graphics

Wedenbine, Emma E., 18
Weeding
  at Bell Labs, 173-174
  centralization/decentralization, 78-79
  cost reporting of, 210
  descriptive cataloging of, 36
  recommendations for, 30
  subject cataloging/classification of, 41
Western Company, example of MBO, 135
Withdrawal of Materials. *See* Weeding
Women Professionals, in library and information science, 105-106
Word Processing, 141-145
  at IBM, 141-143
  definition of, 141
Word Processing System, 143-145
  case study, 144-145
  organization, 143-144
World Trade Center, seminars, 7, 156
World Trade Institute (WTI), seminars, 157-162
WTI. *See* World Trade Institute (WTI)

Zero-based Budgeting, definition of, 138